R
001.942
R

Columbia County Library

3 0759 10098148 4

Y0-BQD-135

DISCARD

UFO! DANGER IN THE AIR

Jenny Randles

Magale
Trust

Randles, Jenny.
UFO! : danger in the air

STERLING PUBLISHING CO., INC.
New York

CLOC Library
220 E. Main, Box 668
Magnolia, AR 71753

This book is dedicated to the memory of Ralph Noyes, who died just as it was finalized. For fifteen years he was a tremendous source of encouragement and assistance in my work, being open and honest in all of his dealings with me.

He was also a true gentleman.

Special thanks to Roy Sandbach for the line illustrations.

Library of Congress Cataloging-in-Publication Data

Randles, Jenny.
   [Something in the air]
   UFO! : danger in the sky / Jenny Randles.
     p. cm.
   Originally published: Something in the air. Great Britain : Robert Hale, Ltd., c1996.
   Includes index.
   ISBN 0-8069-8713-8
   1. Unidentified flying objects—Sightings and encounters. 2. Aircraft accidents. I. Title.
TL789.3.R355   1999
001.942—dc21   98-50987
                                                    CIP

10 9 8 7 6 5 4 3 2 1

Published by Sterling Publishing Company, Inc.
387 Park Avenue South, New York, N.Y. 10016
Originally published in Great Britain by Robert Hale Ltd. under the title
Something in the Air
© 1998 by Jenny Randles
American edition © 1999 Sterling Publishing Co., Inc.
Distributed in Canada by Sterling Publishing
c/o Canadian Manda Group, One Atlantic Avenue, Suite 105
Toronto, Ontario, Canada M6K 3E7
Distributed in Great Britain and Europe by Cassell PLC
Wellington House, 125 Strand, London WC2R 0BB, England
Distributed in Australia by Capricorn Link (Australia) Pty Ltd.
P.O. Box 6651, Baulkham Hills, Business Centre, NSW 2153, Australia
Manufactured in the United States of America
All rights reserved

Sterling ISBN 0-8069-8713-8

CONTENTS

ILLUSTRATIONS

Between pages 128 and 129

Credits

Italian Air Force: 2. NASA: 4. *New UFOlogist* and Wim van Utrecht: 5. Belgian Air Force: 6. Roy Sandbach: 7–12. MoD: 14.

INTRODUCTION

It came out of the dark night like a dagger. There was no way to avoid it. One moment the skies over the Derbyshire hills were empty, save the twinkling of evening lights in the cottages and farmhouses below. Then the huge wedge shape was heading straight for the cockpit of the loaded passenger jetliner without any time for the pilot and his first officer to respond.

The copilot ducked. It was an instinctive reaction and one easy to forgive. The captain endeavored to protect his British Airways Boeing 737 and its passengers, but there was really nothing that he could do. Thankfully, the object was not on a collision course. It rushed past his right wing at speed and was gone within a few seconds—5 at the most, he was later to estimate.

Thousands of feet below the now deeply shocked crew, the small Peak District town of Whaley Bridge, sheathed by a blanket of cloud from the ensuing drama, saw and heard nothing. Nor did any of Captain Wills's passengers know of the hand fate had just dealt them. They continued their final 10 minutes of preparation before landing as if nothing had happened, then disembarked and continued their onward journey. Many were not to learn the truth until a "near-miss" investigation by the Civil Aviation Authority was concluded. This event stunned the nation some 12 months later.

The British Airways Boeing 737 was on a 2-hour flight from Milan to Manchester. It was a journey repeated most days of the week. Never before in their careers had either of the senior aircrew witnessed something as astonishing as this. But now they were aware of a fact that many of their colleagues have had to face at some point. There is something in the air and its identity is unknown.

When you come as close as these men did to colliding at a closing speed of 1000 mph then you can be sure that the question of identification is not academic. It is not an issue to be debated on TV talk shows or at conferences staged by wide-eyed UFO buffs who proclaim that aliens are invading the earth. It is a matter of supreme importance that deserves proper and immediate investigation. For, of course, next time such an event occurs the outcome might prove much less fortunate. Indeed, there are good grounds to ask whether such a situation has already had more terrible consequences.

We certainly know that the experience of British Airways Flight 5061 is not unique. Very far from it, in fact. This case, which we will discuss in more detail later in this book, occurred on January 6, 1995, at 6:48 p.m. But in the period from 1991–1997, it was only one of over thirty similar events to occur above the skies of Britain alone.

And this phenomenon is not confined to the United Kingdom. It represents a global threat.

Over Brazil, in May 1986, strange balls of light were chased in daring flight by military aircraft. The confrontation was almost deadly.

Above New Zealand's South Island, lights cavorted at will beside a cargo plane ferrying newspapers. This whole experience was captured on film. As an awestruck passenger, who had hitched a ride and chanced to film the event, said "live" into his microphone, "Let's hope they're friendly."

A holiday jet over Spain found itself in a death-defying midair encounter with a strange object. It was forced to make an emergency landing. Other flights crossing this densely trafficked part of Europe saw strange things too, before they shot away to be pursued by military jets.

Over the mainland of the U.S., an Eastern Airlines passenger plane was buzzed by a rocket-like object that possibly sent a wake of turbulence rocking them in the sky. It was, said the pilot, "a darned close thing."

As this book will make abundantly clear, there is no country on earth where events of this magnitude do not seem to have taken place. This is of considerable concern to anyone who ever trusts his life to an aircraft and the rules of aeronautics.

Has catastrophe ever followed these many "near misses?" It seems that it may well have done.

Over a quiet East Anglian forest in England in August 1984, a cargo flight from Stansted to Amsterdam was struck in midair by something falling through the sky from above. The Trislander lost an engine but managed to fly on with the remaining two and touched down safely. Inspection immediately revealed a gaping hole in the side of the fuselage. There could be no doubt that something large and heavy had struck the plane and punched its way right through the surface. But what on earth could do such a thing? Despite a year of investigation, the Civil Aviation Authority failed to come up with an answer.

Then there are the cases where there was no salvation for those on board. In March 1968, an Aer Lingus plane on a passenger run from Cork to London was hit without warning in midair and plunged towards the Irish Sea with only the poignant words of the pilot echoing in the ears of air traffic control advising that they were spiraling out of control. Nobody survived to tell what it was that struck Viscount Oscar Mike. But, according to the official investigation, there was no other aircraft up there to account for the collision. No other *identified* aircraft, that is. The accident that befell this Aer Lingus aircraft is only one of several where all obvious causes have been eliminated and still the truth remains unknown. Something in the air struck the aircraft with terrible consequences and huge loss of life. That something is at present unexplained.

There are also mysteries such as that of Frederick Valentich, flying his

Cessna across the Bass Strait from Melbourne, Australia, in October 1978. He was going to buy some shellfish from King Island. Instead, he reported strange lights above him that caused his engine to fail. Then there was silence. He had utterly vanished. Despite years of investigation, the cause of his presumed death remains as inexplicable as ever. He had become one more victim of this truly frightening phenomenon.

I have talked repeatedly in this introduction about strange lights or mysterious objects seen in close proximity to aircraft during what are usually non-catastrophic events. But I must stress immediately that this book is not a treatise about UFOs in the sense that you may understand that term. You will read no frantic allegations that aliens are taking over the earth.

Certainly, it is a book about "unidentified flying objects" and their close encounters with aircrafts in mid-flight. It is packed with cases that frankly should be of great concern to many who have no idea that these things are taking place. But it should most definitely not be assumed that by "UFO" I mean a spacecraft coming here from another planet.

While I have an open mind as to whether such things may exist, the evidence is far from overwhelming that they do. Nor is this book the appropriate place to debate that argument. My work here concerns physically real phenomena that are not open to speculation as to whether they exist or not. The objects that come into close confrontation with aircrafts day after day indisputably do exist. The only question outstanding is how we should interpret them. By definition, these objects are UFOs because they are flying and unidentified. But that is as far as we can go at this stage. "UFO" and "alien spaceship" are emphatically not synonymous terms.

It is my contention that the cases which fill this book prove that there is truly something in the air and, on occasion, it comes into close proximity with our commercial air traffic. But that something, in my view, most probably has a terrestrial—not an extraterrestrial—interpretation. Its solution will be found within the province of science and the forces of nature—not light-years beyond this planet.

If we are to understand this mystery and find ways to prevent these situations from recurring, then we must get away from the sensationalism and the nonsense that pervade all mention of the term UFO. I urge you to forget little green men and starships locked up in secret government hangars, and focus on the hard facts that these case histories inescapably represent.

The data in this book results from official investigations by trained aviation experts and does not depend upon the pie-eyed speculation of UFOlogists. Much of it has been adopted by UFO buffs as proof of their own beliefs. But facts remain facts whatever someone later chooses to do with them. Only when we work from the hard evidence can we lay bare the true extent of the problem that we face and attempt to set our leading experts in physics, meteorology, and aviation into finding out what is going on amidst this most disturbing phenomenon. This book merely takes the first step in leading us towards asking the right questions, instead of ignoring them as we have done for far too long. I hope that in a short while you will come to realize that this matter is too important to ridicule or run away from.

If you regard UFOs in either manner and plan a trip aboard an aircraft in the not too distant future, then I strongly suggest that you suspend your judgment for the duration of this book. After reading the evidence, you may well come to a rather different conclusion about such things. You may also realize that there is very good reason to be concerned.

Jenny Randles, Derbyshire, England, 1998

1 STRANGE LIGHTS IN THE NIGHT

Since time began, strange lights have been seen in the nighttime sky and mankind has had a passion for imposing supernatural interpretations upon them. We can see this easily through the naming of the stars and constellations. Ancient man drew patterns around these far distant points of light—he connected the dots, in effect, just as children still do in puzzles of that type.

Orion the Hunter or the Great Bear are not really up there even in outline. Indeed, it takes rather a vivid imagination to begin to see them. However, to our ancestors, it was important to create some meaning behind these great lights in the sky, and ascribing to them such godly attributes was a good way of doing that. As a species, we like to name and deify all things that we do not readily understand. Both those rules apply today to UFOs, and although I do not wish to dwell on the problems of the UFO phenomenon, we must appreciate why the case histories in this book are (in my view) so often wrongly interpreted as out of this world.

In many respects, this process from past millennia continues exactly the same way now when someone sees a strange object in the sky. Although the term "object" or "craft" is frequently used to sharpen the idea that these things are structured devices, the truth is that the witness often sees little more than a glow or a light. When you strip many UFO reports down to their essence, you find that the portholes and propulsion systems of an alien spaceship are little more than an illusion read into a quite basic light phenomenon.

We can illustrate this by a number of well-documented cases. One of my favorite examples concerns an encounter over Lincolnshire, England, in February 1975. A terrified man and woman in a car observed a glowing object in the sky. It had two bright lights. Convinced that these were on the side of a structured craft that was following them in some nightmare pursuit, they drove away at top speed across the landscape. Eventually, they escaped the clutches of the "spaceship" and reported their frightening adventure to the police. When the constable arrived to take down the statements of the still shocked young couple, he amazed them by revealing a sketch made for him by another witness who had seen something very similar.

The drawings made in the police constable's notebook from all these witnesses had close comparisons. They depicted a curved structure with two brilliant lights. But they were not exactly the same. One, for instance, described it as being more like a face. Another envisaged it as a squatter's house craft. The only things that were exactly the same in each of the witness descriptions of the UFO that zipped across Lincolnshire that night were the two bright lights (see Illustration #7).

There is a very good reason for that. The lights were all that was really there!

In this case, there had been an unusual stellar occurrence in which a brilliant planet, then close to the earth, had wandered across the heavens and, by chance, for just a few days was in apparent proximity to an extremely bright star. Stars do not move relative to one another, whereas planets do so from day to day. Stars and planets appear to move relative to the earth each night (although, in fact, it is the rotation of the earth and its passage around the sun that creates this illusion). The outcome of these various, predictable scientific phenomena was the spectacle of two bright lights next to one another in the sky where no such combination had occurred before, or would occur again for some years to come. Most people were completely unfamiliar with such events.

What happened next was precisely what had been happening since mankind first named the constellations. The unusual sight in the sky was considered "godly" in nature and, in the late 20th century, our gods come in the form of little green men. So these witnesses envisaged the lights as being "on" an alien craft, and their mind filled in the nonexistent shape of a craft around them.

The origin of the UFO, investigated very effectively at the time by Nigel Watson, is indisputable when the positions of the star and planet in the sky are compared with the sighting that followed. It may seem as if I am demeaning the witnesses by stating this with such assurance, but I am doing no such thing. This is how human perception operates. It has absolutely nothing to do with a person's ability to judge things or with his intelligence. Nor does their occupation matter. Pilots and aircrews are just as susceptible to this phenomenon as are terrified young couples in a car on a lonely country road. We should remember this during the remainder of this book.

We see it exemplified in many ways through optical illusions. Psychologists study these with fascination because they teach us a good deal about the way that our ability to perceive is far from straightforward. Look at the example in Illustration #8 and gauge for yourself just how easy it is to "see" things that are not there, or be fooled into seeing shapes and patterns that logic dictates are incorrect. Even when you know and tell yourself repeatedly that what you are seeing is not what you really ought to be seeing, it does not affect the outcome. The brightest minds on the planet are just as fooled by an optical illusion as anybody else, because it is a product of the way our senses function.

Very often UFO researchers choose to ignore the consequences. Several times a year there are situations where emergency services are called out to investigate reports of an air crash. This occurred most famously on New Year's Eve 1978, when hundreds of witnesses across Northern Europe called the police and fire departments to describe a blazing rocket-shaped device with a line of windows along the edge. This was said to be plunging from the sky in obvious distress. But when the accident and emergency procedures were put in motion, there was nothing to be found.

Why was this? Very simply because the object seen in the sky was not a rocket-shaped craft or blazing aircraft, and it did not plunge to the ground as most witnesses assumed it did. This was the spectacular burn-up of some chunks of metal from a Soviet military satellite, Cosmos 1068. It entered the earth's atmosphere many miles up, was consumed by the heat of friction, and vaporized in a pyrotechnical death throe long before it came close to the surface.

Fortunately, in this case, the event was caught on camera. Films show that the stimulus for the countless reports of a strange UFO was in fact merely a series of unconnected lights caused by the fires igniting the trail of debris. This blazed across the heavens and it was our old friend, the vagary of human perception, that once more connected the dots. Because the witnesses were certain that they were seeing an aircraft-sized object at an aircraft-like height, they constructed in their minds a long cigar shape and perceived the disconnected glows as being illuminated windows along its edge.

Everybody did this. We had reports from pilots, air traffic control officers, policemen, garbage collectors, and housewives. The extremely powerful illusion has often been repeated. In March 1997, a very similar phenomenon occurred over the wild moors of the Derbyshire Peak District in northern England—very close to the location where the British Airways crew encountered their UFO in midair 2 years earlier. Once again, police and mountain rescue teams were told that a blazing aircraft was falling from the sky, and a massive hunt was put in motion that lasted 24 hours and cost tens of thousands of dollars. (See Illustration #9.)

In this case, there was no easy answer in the sense that no reentry of debris from outer space was scheduled that night. However, natural rocks and pieces of matter in space enter our atmosphere and burn up in very similar fashion almost every night. Most are fairly feeble and impossible to see unless you happen to be looking in the right place at the right moment. But some can be so big that they create a great spectacle that lasts for up to a minute. These are called bolides, and, while rare, they happen somewhere on earth every few weeks; if the sky is clear (as it was over Derbyshire that March 1997 night) or many people are looking out (as they were observing the then very impressive Hale-Bopp comet), there are going to be many sightings. By now, you should have no trouble estimating what most witnesses will conclude that they have seen.

As we saw from the previous cases, it is utterly predictable that people will perceive the glows of light as being illuminations on the side of structured objects. These objects will be regarded either as alien spacecrafts (if the witnesses are particularly drawn to that conclusion) or as a falling air-craft that requires the aid of emergency services (if they are rather more down-to-earth in their interpretation). Both perceptions are wrong but completely understandable given what we know about the workings of the human mind in the face of unusual light stimuli.

We can even experience this effect made to order thanks to an intriguing set of photographs taken in a remote Scandinavian valley known as Hessdalen during the mid 1980s. These pictures were snapped by a team of scientists who went out there to try to figure out what local villagers in this frozen location near the Arctic Circle were seeing night after night. They had been reporting drifting glows of light across the mountains since 1981. Speculation was that some kind of natural earth energy, or plasma, was to blame. But the team operating what came to be called "Project Hessdalen" had to go out there, brave incredibly low temperatures for weeks on end, and use radar, spectrographs, and special cameras to film the phenomenon during its sporadic appearances.

They were remarkably successful and some amazing photographs were obtained. These prove very instructive because some of them appear to show solid objects, even bell-shaped crafts. In fact, analysis clearly proves that the phenomena are gaseous plasmas and not actual crafts. Often separate "blobs" of energy are seen by the eye as if they are parts of a unified craft and this is simply because the human mind prefers order and pattern to jumble and chaos. We do the same thing when "seeing" people and animals in the random shapes of clouds.

The lesson all this teaches is clear. Just because a UFO seen by a witness, however credible, appears to that person to be a structured object, this does not mean that a structured object was actually present. All too often alien spacecrafts are built by the shipyards of the mind.

I am certain from my 25 years of investigating UFO reports in the field that this process goes on all of the time. However this might upset some of my peers, I must say that a great deal of the apparent structure and solidity you see reported behind UFOs comes from the inner space dimension of the human mind and not from any outer space reality that such objects allegedly possess. Of course, expectation plays a huge part as well. Living in the space age and brought up on stories of aliens and abductions by little green beings, we are already primed to interpret unexplained lights in the sky in such an exotic fashion. Nobody is immune to this pressure.

In 1993, a fascinating piece of camcorder footage was submitted to the local TV station in Cornwall, England. I studied it afterwards and it is beautifully instructive. It was taken by a family who was going on a day trip to London. Being such a long drive, they set off before dawn and after a while noticed a brilliant glow in the sky. The camera and associated microphone recorded what happened next.

As you watch the footage, you can see the excitement mounting. These witnesses have no idea what the light really is but soon come to believe that it is probably a UFO, with all the connotations this suggests within today's space-age society. Before long, they are heard debating the consequences of staying too close, and one woman, evidently worried, says that she has heard how the aliens in these ships kidnap people and perform terrible medical experiments upon them.

The fear of the UFO and its probable evaluation led here to the tension of a close encounter. But the truth is very mundane. I have no doubt whatsoever that the big white light seen by these witnesses and filmed by their camcorder was the planet Venus. It was spectacularly brilliant in the early morning sky at just the spot where they were pointing their lens. They had not seen it during recent days because they were not normally out at that early hour.

The suggestion of a shape and structure to the craft that the witnesses perceived was a result of two things—the natural tendency to connect the dots that I have already discussed and the inability of the camera lens to focus on what was just a point of light. As such, it failed, like all camcorders fail, to create a meaningful image, and a fuzzy blob resulted. Endless UFOs on film emerge in precisely this way.

How often have I heard witnesses tell me that the UFO "changed shape" when, in fact, this is because their camera, or their eyes, are not able to focus properly and their struggles produce the effect of a changing shape. Similarly, I have often heard witnesses tell me, when I try to explain away a sighting, that it "cannot be Venus because the UFO moved in a jerky motion or zigzag fashion and stars don't move." Unfortunately, ignoring the fact that Venus is a planet (not a star) and it does move (although too slowly to be readily seen by the naked eye), the effect of motion in this case results from something called autokinesis. It is yet another factor we have to take into account.

Autokinesis occurs when the eyes see a bright light. Not only do they try to focus on it, causing it to change shape, but the motion of the eye itself, as it is "locked on" to this static target, translates through our senses into the object moving. The jerky motion of the UFO is, in truth, the result of the eyes in motion, not the object. But the illusion is so powerful we take some persuading.

Similarly, all of us see the moon as bigger when it is near the horizon than when it is high in the sky. Look again during the next full moon and you will see what I mean. We see it this way because, near ground level, it is judged alongside other objects, such as trees and houses. High in the sky, there is nothing for comparison so that the eyes and senses make different judgments and greatly reduce the moon's apparent size. This is further proof that human beings are easily fooled into seeing things that simply are not there. Pilots judging UFOs with only dark sky for comparison may not appreciate this.

Thus, there are countless ways in which human senses and our reactions to strange lights in the sky can interfere with the accurate reporting of something in the air. We cannot ignore such matters when we continue our investigation into aerial encounters throughout this book. But all too often people do ignore them and think that by suggesting such things I am debunking their stories. Not so. We are merely facing up to the realities of how people see UFOs.

Our cultural expectations of what is being seen complicate matters further. These ensure that strange lights in the sky are always perceived in ways that are relevant to the time in which they occur. Remember how ancient man deified the stars. That was extended to any sudden or unusual lights that appeared in the heavens. You can see this often in ancient stories where Chinese reports speak of "fiery dragons" and Roman texts tell how "blazing swords" filled the air. These, and many other colorful accounts, were probably descriptions of what we would regard today as an alien UFO but which were probably (then as now) just a natural, but not yet understood, phenomenon, such as a bolide burning up in the atmosphere. There have always been phenomena created by the earth, or its atmosphere, or the wonders of the universe that our knowledge has not yet managed to unravel. In the thousands of years before science evaluated these things, they were seen by mankind as supernatural events. We named them and were in awe of them—exactly as we have seen already.

Today, we live in the space age and, thus, we apply space-age names like "spaceships" and "aliens" to these events and attribute out-of-this-world consequences to them. But just because a witness tells us that he sees no alien craft, and we cannot accept that such a thing exists, does not mean that they did not see something interesting in the first place. Indeed, perhaps it was something unusual, something that would be new to science. It is this decision to cast out the baby with the bathwater—or, rather, the real UFOs with the illusionary starships—which has caused us for so long to miss out on making valuable progress. All of the reasoning in this chapter decrees that this occurs. Regardless of the fact that people see things that are often not as they seem, all the phenomena reported here result from a genuine stimulus of some kind. Something really was in the sky and we should never forget that.

During waves of activity in 1896, 1909, and 1913, witnesses to strange lights in the sky in what were still very much pre-space-age days reported what they saw in different terms. They saw exotic flying machines of terrestrial origin—fantastic airships, in fact. This should not be surprising. It was, after all, the dawn of the era when mankind first learned to fly, so it was a theme that was culturally topical, and the obvious hook for the human mind in the face of strange lights was an amazing airship piloted by an eccentric but brilliant inventor.

During 1913, when such airships were seen over Britain, the then Admiralty Minister Winston Churchill led protests in Parliament on the supposition (false as it turned out) that lights seen from East Anglia to Kent were German spies planning an invasion. This is interestingly akin to the War of the Worlds images that were to accompany sightings of the same sort of lights 50 years later when they were interpreted as alien spaceships instead of secret airships.

By the 1930s, aircrafts were flying occasional trips and it was the age of the pioneer aviator, setting off on daring missions and pitting his wits against the elements. Strange lights were still being seen in the sky. They were almost exactly the same as the ones over the Midwest in the United States (1896) or Europe (1909 and 1913), but now they were accepted into popular culture as what came to be called "ghost airplanes."

A typical case occurred on December 24, 1933, over Kalix, in Sweden, when an object was seen by many heading westwards. It had beams of light sweeping the ground below as it passed silently overhead. The phantom airships of decades earlier often had a similar searchlight beam attached, according to witnesses. But just as no actual airships were ever traced to account for such sightings at the turn of the century, and it is most unlikely that there were any in the area capable of producing the reports, these encounters with ghost airplanes provide a similar lack of resolution. The Scandinavian authorities got together to investigate the matter and were determined to find out who was foolishly flying through often frozen, wintry skies at a time when night flying in perfect condi-tions was still a major risk. They failed. On March 10, 1934, the Norwegian general Henriek Johannessen explained that reports were still coming in and added, "We cannot reject all of these observations as illusions."

Before long, the military, in Churchill mode, was convinced that an enemy of some sort was to blame. On April 30, 1934, Major General Reuterswald, who had commanded the region of Upper Norrland where there had been many reports, commented, "There can be no doubt about illegal air traffic over our secret military areas. There are many reports from reliable people which describe close observations of the enigmatic flier...the question is: Who or whom are they, and why have they been invading our air territory?"

Sometimes witnesses saw the shape of an aircraft when there was appar-ently no real aircraft there. This should come as no surprise given this chapter's argument that the forms taken by anomalous lights depend upon cultural expectation of their shape. In 1934, that was very evidently of ghost airplanes.

During World War II, flying was much more practiced and routine. But the strange lights were still in the sky and, this time, they were fre-quently seen in close proximity to the aircraft. It was the first era in which mass flying was common and hundreds of aircraft were in the sky at the same time. The circumstances in which something strange could be seen were thus greatly expanded.

By November 1944, so many American bombing crews returning from Germany and occupied territories had seen these glowing lights that an intelligence gathering mission began. I recall entertainer Michael Bentine (then an intelligence officer working with free Polish troops in Britain) explaining to me that he had the task of getting the stories of these strange lights from his crews. Time after time, they were coming home talking about these objects that buzzed their planes. Then, the American intelligence agencies came to take over.

The Americans told Bentine that they assumed these lights were some kind of secret Nazi weapon. The problem was that this weapon was not apparently doing anything! Now declassified files show the extent to which these lights were being seen during the winter of 1944–45. They were known by the Americans as "Foo Fighters" (a corruption of the French word feu, or fire). However, nobody ever figured out what the Nazis were doing with these lights and the war was quickly over. Only then was it discovered that the Germans had reports from their aircrews of the same lights and they thought they were a secret Yankee weapon!

All we can say with certainty is that the same strange lights that have always been up there in the sky were perceived in great numbers by this sudden flood of aircrews who were roaming the skies on predatory and bombing missions during the 1940s. They did so in yet another culturally topical fashion—imagining that they saw a secret military weapon.

Immediately after World War II, it happened all over again. Between January and November 1946, almost one thousand reports were made across Scandinavia of cylinderlike lights that shot across the sky. Once more a reconnaissance of military areas by some enemy power was feared. Several times there were reports of crashes, and a Swedish lake was thoroughly searched by military forces after one "ghost rocket" (as these things were now being cutely named) seemingly fell into the water. But, just like the airships, airplanes, and Foo Fighters beforehand, all attempts to explain the lights in rational terms failed. The authorities suspected that the Soviet Union may have been using captured Nazi V weapons to try to develop intercontinental ballistic missiles and were covertly launching them over neutral countries regardless of the dangers. This was emphatically denied, but it brought high-powered American and British aviation authorities to Scandinavia to investigate for themselves.

Once again, the sightings stopped, and there is absolutely no evidence that there really were any secret Soviet missile launches. If there were, the USSR gained no advantage in rocketry as a consequence. A major Scandinavian defense report concluded that some sightings were natural phenomena, like meteors, but others were unexplained. Yet again, the conclusion, imperfect as it was, has to be that there was something in the air and this was evaluated according to the topical expectation of both the era and the place in question.

The progression from phantom airships to ghost airplanes to Foo Fighters to ghost rockets in the 50 years from 1896 to 1946 is fascinating and has been studied in great detail by some researchers. (The bibliography offers resources for you to study further, if you desire.) This strange light stimulus in the sky has been rediscovered and reinvented as if it were a new mystery with a new relevance periodically attached to give it a name and status as the years have gone by. The way in which the transmutations of the explanations occurred so rapidly is likely to mirror the way in which many aspects of our lives have seen rapid progress, evolution, and development during this same half century.

Certainly, it should be easy to deduce that when a private pilot flew over the Cascade Mountains in Washington on June 24, 1947, and spotted strange lights in the sky, the stage was set for yet another chapter in the continuing transformation of this phenomenon. We could almost have predicted the likely form that the new phase would take, since the thoughts of society then turned to space and our quest to get a human into orbit within the next 15 years. The new "enemy" behind these age-old lights was almost bound to be perceived as coming from another planet.

Movies, TV, and radio were full of space stories as the 1940s became the 1950s. It was inevitable that the creation of a new name by a reporter ("flying saucer") and the widespread promotion by the media of the idea that these lights were alien spacecrafts from another world would become popular.

Of course, much else was different in this postwar environment; science and technology were about to take off rapidly and the quick-fire successes of the orbital missions, moon landings, and beyond ensured that the image of space stayed strongly in the human consciousness for decades. This probably contributed to the stability of the new interpretation of these lights in the sky.

The idea of alien invaders was a remarkably successful evaluation. Unlike the transient nature of German weapons, which did not outlast the end of the war, it fitted neatly with the growing desire for the human race not to be alone. There simply was no need to change horses again. The alien spacecraft motif was just the job for the foreseeable future and became the new topical hook on which the sightings of these strange lights in the sky were attached.

The amazing spread of the media is a further reason why this phenomenon has had far more endurance than any of its predecessors. When phantom airships were seen, there was not even radio to convey the news. It carried slowly by word of mouth and local newspapers. But when the alien UFOs took over the mantle of interpretation, radio was at its zenith, TV was growing rapidly, and other media were set to boom expansively. Under these conditions, the alien contact scenario was widely disseminated and has proved a godsend to the mass media. It sells papers, brings in TV viewers, and has been transformed into countless movies.

This latest interpretation of "something in the air" became a lucrative source of income for those very forces that were shaping public thinking during the second part of the 20th century. This includes the burgeoning UFO community who came to fight for truth and proclaim cover-ups by the authorities in such a way that they ensured the continuation of the new paradigm. To many UFOlogists, evidence is not what counts. Getting publicity can be a drug.

It was all so inescapable if you think it through. Today's UFOs are a product of our media and free market economies, but like the airships, airplanes, Foo Fighters, and ghost rockets before them—not to mention fiery dragons and blazing swords—they may not be the true answer. Nonetheless, the things that are seen do result from a genuine phenomenon triggering each false impression. The literal reality of a mother ship from afar may be very much in doubt, but there is no doubt that there is something in the air, something that has led people to believe they have seen such a craft.

Our quest now is to review the evidence of these midair encounters as they appear in abundance throughout the coming chapters. But we must do so in understanding of these facts and mindful of their implications. Then, later on, we can try to figure out what is really causing all of these incredible false perceptions.

2 THE FIRST MARTYR

On January 7, 1948, one event affected matters hugely. It was just 6 months after the name "flying saucer" was created by news-hungry media and precisely as the official U.S. government military investigation of the phenomenon was getting under way. It obviously gave enormous impetus to what came to be called "Project Blue Book." This top secret study was known to the general public far more poetically as "Project Saucer."

The events that unfolded on that winter's day in midwestern America shaped many things for years to come. They fundamentally altered the public view and directed the official interpretation of this mystery. For on that otherwise uneventful afternoon, a pilot became the first known martyr to this strange phenomenon. Many saw him as a victim of an interplanetary war, and there was nothing better to ensure that the battle will continue, regardless of the odds, than the loss of one's own.

In retrospect, free from the pressures put upon the new military machine to get answers immediately or to appease the public baying for the truth, it is less difficult to sort this case out. Having the ability to take several steps back from the need to view these strange things in the sky as alien spacecraft, we can see this case very differently from how it was judged at the time. That in itself is invaluable, because it provides a perfect test bed for honing the skills of investigation that we must adopt with more recent cases that we shall study in this book.

At approximately 1:15 p.m. that day, the local military airport at Godman Field, Kentucky, received a call from the Maysville highway patrol some 80 miles east. They had reports from motorists of a silvery light high in the sky and wanted to know whether Godman had any aircraft in flight. The base did not and checks with Wright Patterson AFB (Air Force Base) in Dayton, Ohio—the home of the barely operational UFO project—revealed that they knew of no activity that could explain this light either.

However, by the time Godman had made these inquiries, the police were back on the phone. This time a report had been logged from witnesses at Owensboro, some 140 miles west of the first sighting location. The object seemed identical, but if this light had moved that distance in just 20 minutes, it was traveling at several hundred miles per hour. Seemingly unconsidered, but equally feasible, is that the object was very high in the sky—miles high, in fact—which would allow it to be seen over a very wide area down on the ground and explain the closely timed sightings from two far distant points. High-speed motion would not then be necessary at all.

The staff at Godman was nonetheless concerned, because the track of any moving object took it right through their own backyard, and both they and Wright Patterson AFB were still convinced no aircraft should be up there. Very quickly, this had become a security issue.

At 1:45 p.m., Sergeant Quinton Blackwell, who was the control tower operator, scanned the skies to the south of the field looking for the object that had moved from Maysville to Owensboro. He picked out a dim, fuzzy white light that was stationary and very high, and alerted his superior officer; eventually, the operations officer came to take a look. By 2:20 p.m.—more than an hour after the first sighting—Colonel Guy Hix, base commander, was viewing the object through binoculars. It still seemed to be barely moving.

The descriptions offered by these four base officers are very significant. They provide the first real clue as to the identity of this object. They referred to an "ice cream cone" and "umbrella" and a "parachute canopy" as the closest resemblance to what they were seeing. Experienced UFOlogists will tell you that these are classic witness accounts of a high-altitude weather balloon.

Such balloons are today routinely released from many points around the world. They carry instruments to check upper level wind speeds and are ferried aloft to great heights (10 miles or more is not uncommon). The silvery canopy of the balloon opens out by expansion at the reduced atmospheric pressure levels and can become of enormous size. Drifting at speed (typically 30–50 mph at that height), they can be visible from one spot on the ground for several hours, moving so slowly that it is not immediately obvious to the naked eye that they have any motion at all. Catching high-level sunlight, they reflect as silvery or metallic in appearance.

Of course, in 1948 such events were less common than today and often the result of military operations. Civilian observers would probably not be familiar with what they were seeing. Indeed, UFOlogists will tell you that even today many people still do not always recognize such objects.

However, the staff at Godman and the operations room at Wright Patterson were far more knowledgeable on aviation matters. They had been aware of the possible identification of this object as a balloon. Unfortunately, records indicated to them that no such balloon should have been up there. As a result, it was fairly easy under the circumstances to put two and two together and make a spaceship.

As the ground staff at Godman wrestled with the identification of the light, fate intervened. Four F-51 Mustangs of the National Guard flew through the traffic zone. They were on a routine supply trip from Georgia to Standiford Field, further north in Kentucky. None of the aircraft, headed by Captain Thomas Mantell, had seen the UFO until they were alerted by Godman, and even then they still did not immediately see it. It was so high, distant, and faint that they had to be looking very carefully to spot it.

Godman requested that the flight investigate. One of the F-51 pilots reported he was low on fuel and continued his track to Standiford. The other three agreed to climb to try to see the object.

There is some dispute as to what happened next; most of it centered on the question of whether oxygen equipment was fitted to any of the planes. Pilots in those days were taught not to fly much over 15,000 feet without oxygen. At that height, oxygen is so thin that the brain becomes starved and loss of consciousness can follow extremely quickly. In an aircraft, the result of the pilot blacking out was already known to be catastrophic.

The two less-experienced pilots (lieutenants Clements and Hammond) did not have full, working oxygen equipment. One also lost his bearings. Consequently, they pulled out of the climb and tried to contact Captain Mantell to tell him to break off pursuit as well. But he ignored them.

Mantell's aircraft was not from the same unit as the other three and the debate as to whether he would have climbed well above 20,000 feet to at least 22,500 feet (his last estimated altitude) without oxygen has raged ever since. Either he did so recklessly (or bravely, if you choose to call it that) or he continued his pursuit of the silvery object believing he had protection from oxygen starvation. Nobody can be sure.

By 2:45 p.m., Mantell advised that he was going to try to level off at 25,000 feet. His two colleagues had now returned to lower altitude and were scanning the skies looking not just for the UFO but also their captain, as he was now lost somewhere amidst the blue sky.

One of the two wingmen did catch a brief glimpse of the UFO. His description that it was "shaped like a teardrop" and "seemed fluid" is a further strong suggestion that he was looking at a balloon.

Between this sighting and approximately 3:10 p.m., there were several garbled messages from Mantell in which ground control heard him say that the object was ahead and above him, had a metallic sheen, and seemed tremendous in size—none of which is inconsistent with a balloon. Moreover, he added that he did not seem to be getting any closer, which was assumed to mean that the object was traveling faster than he was and so was of fantastic origin. Of course, if the balloon were at 60,000 feet, as it could easily have been, then it was still far above Mantell at any height he could possibly have achieved in his Mustang. So the mystery of this failure to close the gap between aircraft and UFO could have a simple explanation.

One of the F-51 planes landed and refueled at Godman. It then joined in what had become a search-and-rescue mission for the now missing Captain Thomas Mantell. Meanwhile, at around 3:45 p.m., the "ice cream cone in the sky" finally faded into the distance and was no longer visible from Godman, although there were isolated reports from towns to the west. An interesting report at Madisonville, some 120 miles west of Godman, came about 10 minutes later and described how the witness had been puzzled by the light until he studied it through a telescope. Then he recognized that it was just a balloon.

Just before 5 p.m., Mantell's aircraft was found 5 miles from the town of Franklin. An eyewitness had seen it crash and reported it was flying vertically into the ground. He saw it break up close to ground level. Mantell was killed and his watch stopped at 3:18 p.m., the presumed time of impact. The eyewitness knew nothing about the light in the sky and saw no object other than the Mustang.

The crash was witnessed, as was the recovery of the wreckage. Countless people had reported the light in the sky. Both events were quickly linked in the public mind and the U.S. military could not dispute the fact that Mantell had apparently died chasing a UFO.

The media speculated on alien death rays destroying the plane (a reference to the way it had fallen apart in midair, although this was probably simply as a result of a near vertical fall from 5 miles up). The story that Mantell was a victim of a "war of the worlds" has persisted ever since. I recall a children's comic in the late 1950s in which a spaceship was illustrated shooting the Mustang from the skies.

Meanwhile, the official investigation was under way, and the problem for the U.S. Air Force at Wright Patterson was that they were not convinced that this comic book scenario was untrue!

As recently as 1995, retired Yorkshire police officer Tony Dodd reported on his interviews with Captain James Duesler. Living in retirement himself in England, Duesler had in 1948 been a member of the air accident board at Godman Field as well as a Mustang pilot like Mantell. He had seen the object from the control tower that day and said a piece of paper was stuck to the window to mark its exceedingly slow passage. Duesler described the object as "an inverted ice cream cone."

He further claimed that he was called to Franklin in the early hours to view the crash site and the distribution of the wreckage was hard to understand. It did not match the F-51 having nosedived, as the eyewitness described. Instead, it seemed to have "belly flopped" into a small clearing without damaging trees that encircled it.

Duesler seemed happy to accept that Mantell may have died as a result of losing control through oxygen starvation, suggesting that he did not have such equipment fitted. But he could not to this day understand the distribution of the wreckage, or the fact that the aircraft fuselage stayed completely intact despite what would have been a high-speed impact. He added that the day after the accident, an aero-engineer (called Loading) from the UFO project at Wright Patterson arrived and intimated that they suspected the object involved in the pursuit was an alien spaceship. He reputedly told the captain, "Thank God they are not hostile or we wouldn't stand a chance!"

If this really was the mode of thinking at Wright Patterson in the immediate aftermath of this accident, it may well explain the seemingly desperate attempts made to find an answer to silence the media. Dr. J. Allen Hynek, an astronomer from Dayton, had been drafted in as "science consultant" to the UFO project and was charged with finding an acceptable cause. Dr. Hynek worked for the military for the next 22 years until he was freed from his contract in 1969. During this time, he became deeply interested in UFOs and was convinced that something really was happening. He became Professor Emeritus at Northwestern University in Chicago and founded the first scientific UFO group (Center for UFO Studies), which since 1973 has established itself as a world leader. Until his death in 1986, he championed serious research without ever being convinced that alien spaceships were the answer.

I came to know Dr. Hynek quite well in his later years, and he told me of the pressures that he was put under by his mentors at Wright Patterson to solve the Mantell case. He had calculated that the planet Venus was in the same part of the southwestern sky and this was seized upon as the answer.

Even as the media were being fed this line, Dr. Hynek was trying to explain to his desperate bosses that it was almost impossible to see this planet in daylight—and it certainly would not have the appearance of a large metallic ice cream cone or canopy. It was just a point of light swamped by the illumination of the daytime sky.

This explanation was used to try to silence the media, but it was so feeble that it probably had the opposite effect. It created a groundswell of opinion that the powers that be were trying to hide the truth of an alien invasion. Cries of government cover-up have continued ever since. In fact, there was some element of truth in that idea, because the UFO project apparently did suspect this answer might be correct during its early days, although as the hard evidence failed to materialize, they quickly turned away from that possibility.

It is easy to see why mistakes were made in the public relations minefield that the death of Captain Thomas Mantell had become. The desire not to admit that aliens might be here and yet the inability to provide an effective alternative left the investigators floundering.

No doubt it would have been much easier if this case could have been solved as a balloon. The U.S. Air Force knew this was the possibility that best fitted all the facts. Unfortunately, try as they might, they could not find any trace of a balloon that might be up there. As such, they penned a masterpiece of sheer gobbledegook in their official report on the matter that went to the Pentagon some weeks later. This remained top secret until it was released by the U.S. Freedom of Information Bill in 1976. The report explained the object in the sky over Godman, Kentucky, as follows: "...it might have been Venus or it could have been a balloon. Maybe two balloons. It probably was Venus except that this is doubtful because Venus was too dim to be seen in the afternoon." Or, to translate—"Help!"

In 1953, when a new, benevolent air force captain, Ed Ruppelt, took over the reins at Project Blue Book, he recognized the importance of this case. Ruppelt became persuaded, just like Dr. Hynek, that there really was an unexplained phenomenon behind some of the UFO sightings and it was a potential aerial threat, as cases such as this clearly proved. Of course, sometimes, as here, the threat was indirect and resulted more from our response to the mystery than from any direct consequence it may have had upon air traffic.

Sadly, Ruppelt was to report that he had hit a brick wall in his attempts to find a balloon launch that might have been to blame. There was now reference to a project known as Skyhook, which, in 1948, had been top secret. As this was a naval experiment, the USAF (as a rival service) was not told about it and so would have not known if one of the project's balloons had flown across Godman Field.

Skyhook used high-altitude balloons of great size and, the files in 1953 alleged, these were launched from Clinton County Airport in Ohio. By studying wind speeds and directions, one of these balloons could have passed over Kentucky. The files (without evidence) just concluded that it did. The official explanation for Mantell's death was changed from a crash due to oxygen starvation (anoxia) while chasing a possible balloon to death while chasing a definite balloon. The only problem was that Ruppelt could trace absolutely no record of any such balloon launch from Clinton County.

So was this wishful thinking yet again? Were the authorities so desperate to solve the case that they were clutching at the straw offered by Skyhook?

In fact, the truth was revealed only in 1993 when Professor Charles Moore was traced in retirement and interviewed by the excellent (and refreshingly hard-headed) UFOlogist Barry Greenwood in Connecticut. Moore had been in charge of the military balloon project and had his own records of the Skyhook flights. He confirmed Ruppelt's diagnosis. There was no launch from Clinton County that could have caused the sighting. The official conclusion blaming this source was invented to get rid of a bothersome case. No balloons were launched from here prior to 1951.

However, on January 6, 1948, at 8 a.m., a Skyhook did go up from a site near Little Falls, Minnesota. Its remit was to investigate cosmic rays from space by floating high above the ground. Its progress was followed by way of reports of sightings. Indeed, knowing to look out for UFO reports helped scientists track the secret project. Moving at about 25 mph, it would have covered 750 miles during the 30 hours leading up to 2 p.m. on January 7. Its drift took it towards Kentucky. Godman Field was just under 750 miles from Little Falls. This has to be the culprit.

There seems almost no doubt that the object in the sky that prompted Captain Mantell to be sent in pursuit of a UFO was a covert naval experiment using a balloon. Moore argued that the navy may even have been unusually circumspect in revealing the truth for many years afterwards as they did not wish to be blamed for the death of this pilot.

Of course, the real cause of Thomas Mantell's death was neither the balloon nor the secrecy—although the latter was not unimportant, as Wright Patterson could have ended this mystery before it had begun if they had been aware of the Skyhook option. The true danger arose here from our all-too-human desire to seek mystery and to speculate freely about the wonders of the universe. The lure of the alien nature behind these strange phenomena, coupled with mankind's inherent determination to investigate come what may, were the major reasons why a brave pilot died that day.

From our point of view, we can see that when trying to identify something in the air a great deal of research and lateral thinking is required. We must look beyond the obvious and take many factors into account. These include the hard evidence as well as the soft evidence, such as the psychology and sociology of the time and place that are involved in the encounter.

As you will see, most cases will not resolve themselves quite as satisfactorily or as readily as this one has done, even though it took more than 40 years to do so. But it is reassuring to know that sometimes, when you try hard enough, an answer will appear, even if this solution came far too late to help Thomas Mantell from what proved a fatal pursuit.

3 JUST THE FACTS

Our efforts to unravel the truth about strange things in the sky are limited by the inability to obtain the best evidence or even any reasonable assurance of the regularity of such events. Without that evidence, scientific research is all too sparse—with the field left open to the media and the UFO buffs to speculate endlessly and sometimes quite absurdly. Science says it will not get involved because of the lack of the very evidence that its failure to investigate is suppressing. It is a vicious circle out of which we simply have to find a way.

Any serious scientific efforts to understand this mystery are hampered not only by the public obsession with believing it has a supernatural origin, but also by the attendant dilemma this creates for commercial operations. We are denied access to large amounts of evidence simply because the people who could make this evidence publicly available are afraid to do so. They fear the repercussions that they imagine this will bring.

However, a number of individuals have helped my cause. One man who is really qualified to study midair encounters between aircraft and strange lights in the sky is Dr. Richard Haines. From his base in Los Altos, California, he has for 30 years carefully documented hundreds of reports. He has been a valuable ally in my research.

The reason why Dr. Haines is uniquely placed to investigate this matter is his background. A psychologist who specializes in human visual perception, his work at the Ames Research Center has involved him in many related experiments. Moreover, he is a member of the Aerospace Medical Association and has worked with airlines and even NASA, helping to resolve problems regarding the perceptual capabilities of their pilots and crew. He also works for the International Society of Air Safety Investigators and so has direct association with near-miss situations.

It is indeed important that Dr. Haines has not only devoted so much time to this problem, but that he also profoundly believes there is something in the air which is currently unexplained and which has triggered numerous midair encounters. Notice the careful choice of words there. I did not say that he believes in UFOs; although I doubt he would mind if I had!

In October 1997, when we met most recently in Copenhagen, he expressed his reasons for his years of research very cogently. He said that the aviation authorities "must take these reports more seriously than they do. Lives are at stake if we continue to ignore them. At Denver, they installed millions of dollars' worth of equipment to detect wind shears after a one-in-a-million event caused a tragic air crash at this airport. Yet for mid-air encounters that threaten lives happen almost every week, very little time or money is being spent because of that word, UFO."

In a paper presented at a Pasadena conference to the American UFO community, Dr. Haines provided a massive statistical analysis of cases involving aircrew observations during the period from January 1, 1942, to December 31, 1952. He found no fewer than 283 cases on his database, which had been compiled thanks to his numerous contacts within both the civilian and military aviation industries. By 1997, he had over 2000 cases on file and 150 of them were so serious that the aircraft was at risk.

The figures are startling. Only thirty cases predated the Mantell affair, but from 1948 onward, the number grew rapidly each year. This trend has continued ever since, although pressures are now put on aircrews not to make sighting reports because of the stigma attached to any airline that is linked with a UFO and the little green men headlines that this is sure to generate.

Indeed, Dr. Haines has told me that it really is not possible to estimate exactly how many midair encounters are taking place today. Far too many pilots and copilots feel it inappropriate to make their sightings official, perhaps going no further than discussing them amongst fellow aircrew members. Dr. Haines's valiant efforts to legitimize this area of study have been compromised by the supernatural and sensationalistic way in which these phenomena are perceived by humanity as a whole.

I also talked with a Delta Airlines pilot, Kent Jeffery, who, like Dr. Haines, has come to believe that there is a genuine phenomenon, but who has a very objective approach to what it might be. He has been one of the UFO field's most effective critics, arguing from strength by analyzing the data and doing firsthand study. He, like me, believes that its most famous case, an alleged crash of an alien craft at Roswell, New Mexico, in 1947, is probably the result of an accident involving a covert scientific experiment that used high-altitude balloons. He reached this opinion after years of studying all the evidence. It is an honest belief, forged not because we are skeptics (we both believe there are real UFOs), but because that is what the facts seem to dictate. This kind of thinking does exist within UFOlogy and is not as rare as you might imagine.

As a pilot who regularly flies the transatlantic route, Jeffrey has become aware that there are genuine anomalies in the sky. He has talked with many fellow pilots who have seen things, but estimated to me that only a small fraction of them ever go public with their story. As he put it, "They, perhaps quite rightly, see this as essential to keeping their job. If you talk openly, then you are considered as not helping the cause of the airline. Most pilots understandably play it safe."

A similar problem came my way when I was called by a member of the ground staff for Dan Air, a British airline. He was aware of my interest in this subject but told me that he was literally placing his job in jeopardy by talking to me anonymously. However, he felt that I should be aware of a sighting that had occurred over the Dee Estuary, between the Wirral Peninsula and North Wales. This I could then try to investigate. The sighting itself was not unusual. The aircraft was on a cargo flight from Belfast to Liverpool, and the crew had seen a brilliant yellow flare-like object above them as they made their final approach. This was at 2:30 a.m. on July 12, 1981. The object had been recorded on radar at Liverpool Airport, which had picked up both this plane and the UFO in close proximity, but never near enough to initiate an official air miss incident. However, it was the decision of the airline not to take the matter further as it was "not policy to do so."

My informant told me I would never get confirmation because the aircrew involved had been told in no uncertain terms that "Dan Air has no intention of being known as the UFO airline." He was correct. I never did get any confirmation of the sighting—at least not from Dan Air. Yet, quite remarkably, I did obtain it several years later from two men who had been camping at Thurstaston on the Wirral—thus, having a clear view across the Dee Estuary. The men were completely unaware of the Dan Air aspect to this case, and had not seen, or at least noticed that there was an aircraft flying overhead at the time. But there is no doubt that the yellow ball of light reported above a factory chimney on the coast near Flint was the same thing that the Dan aircrew had seen that same night. It disappeared out to sea, hugging the tops of the Welsh mountains at first.

As with so many cases in this book, the object was merely an odd light phenomenon. It would be a wild leap of logic to assume that it was an alien spacecraft. However, it was undoubtedly something interesting, but its investigation was hampered by silence and fear.

Consider not being able to make any meaningful judgments about thunderstorms—enabling us to predict their next occurrence and warn air traffic to steer clear—all because it was realized that if a thunderstorm was reported by one of your personnel, it would end up in a tabloid newspaper under the headline: PILOT TELLS HOW THUNDERBOLTS FROM MOUNT OLYMPUS RAINED DOWN ON EARTH. Absurd as this sounds, it is exactly the problem we face.

Because of these latter day complications, it is quite useful to study cases between 1948 and 1952, as Richard Haines has done, for there were no external pressures on airlines in those early days, and the reports of what was being seen consequently flowed in more openly. I suspect that the picture we trace for those 5 years is not at all different from what is taking place today. Unfortunately, until attitudes change we may never be able to establish that for certain.

A highly influential case occurred on July 25, 1948, at 2:45 a.m. Captain Clarence Chiles and copilot John Whitted were in charge of an Eastern Airlines DC-3 while traversing a cloud-free moonlit sky at around 5000 feet. They were in the vicinity of Montgomery, Alabama, at the time.

Suddenly, both men spotted an object rushing straight towards them and reacted instinctively to take the aircraft out of danger of a collision. They partially "ducked," as anyone would have done under the circumstances. The encounter that followed lasted only a few seconds and just one passenger later reported seeing something rush past the right-hand window. He saw it as a "rocket-like streak of fire."

To the two experienced pilots, there was never any mincing of words. "It was like a Flash Gordon rocket ship," Chiles insisted. Both men later independently sketched what they saw for the official USAF-led investigation at Wright Patterson AFB. Their drawings were similar, but not identical. They show a cigar or oval craft with either a line of windows on the side or various lights, depending on which image you accept. Both say a blue spray or trail of light was coming from the rear of the object.

There was significant conflict over whether the object created any wake turbulence. The pilots believed that they had a very narrow squeak as this object flew past their cockpit and right wing, but they were uncertain whether this created a blast effect that rocked the DC-3 in its course. Later investigation suggested this was most likely a psychological feeling caused by the sudden motion of the crew as they "got out of the way." Certainly, none of the passengers reported turbulence from the passage of a UFO. Dr. J. Allen Hynek was again the scientist who researched the case for the Pentagon and he assured me that he did not think the aircraft was struck by any actual shock waves from the object, although he conceded that it was not impossible.

This point is very important. If a material object of any kind—be it an alien rocket ship or something less dramatic—flew within feet of the DC-3, as the Eastern Airlines crew believes it did, then it surely would create a shock wave and rock the aircraft in its path. If this turbulence did not occur, then it means either that the UFO was not physically present or, perhaps rather more likely, that it was considerably further away from the DC-3 than the pilots had judged it to be. As Dr. Haines explains, "Judging distance at night when only lights and a dark sky are involved is one of the most difficult things for a human being to do."

You will notice that there are significant similarities between the 1948 encounter and the case discussed in the introduction where a British Airways jet was heading into Manchester Airport in 1995. Indeed, I am convinced that both crews saw the same thing. If we can satisfactorily explain the Eastern Airlines episode, then the celebrated British Airways case may also be solved. But that is to get ahead of ourselves. I suggest you refer back to these pages later when you come to study my investigation of the British Airways close encounter.

Dr. Hynek told me that his main theory for the Eastern Airlines case was a fireball meteor, or bolide. He did find it hard to consider how two experienced observers could view such a trail of debris and come away convinced that they had seen a constructed craft. The insistence of the pilots that they had seen meteors before, and that this was definitely not one of them, caused Dr. Hynek to draw back from certainty.

However, there was an important rider in this case. A witness from the ground had seen something that sounded remarkably like what the aircrew reported. He was an engineer at a military base in nearby Georgia and he told of a cigarlike shape that was giving off a trail of phosphorous gas. This moved silently and at great speed across the sky. Unfortunately, he claimed to have seen the UFO at a time that was exactly one hour different from the Eastern Airlines pilot.

In conclusion, Dr. Hynek told the U.S. government it had a choice. If the timing on the ground or the reporting of it was wrong by an hour, then the engineer clearly saw the same object as the aircrew. From the descriptions, plus the speed and distances apart from which these two sightings were made, the object was clearly very high in the atmosphere and was probably a spectacular and highly unusual type of meteor, which was giving off blue gases as it burned up in the atmosphere.

Dr. Hynek felt it would be no surprise that the Eastern Airlines crew saw no similarity with the meteors they had witnessed before from the cockpit. Incandescent bolides such as these were far bigger, more extraordinary, and longer lasting than the brief flickers that were normally seen as meteors. It would be a once-in-a-lifetime experience for any aircrew. Indeed, most astronomers would probably never be lucky enough to see such a thing. On the other hand, if these were two separate reports and if the crew's conviction that they had seen a structured craft, "built by an intelligence" (as they put it), was real, then Dr. Hynek could offer no scientific explanation for what that was.

It would appear that the insistence of Chiles and Whitted that it was definitely no meteor persuaded the U.S. government that they may well have encountered an alien rocket ship. Within weeks of Dr. Hynek submitting his findings, the UFO project at Wright Patterson sent an "estimate of situation" report to the Pentagon. This used the Eastern Airlines case as a major plank in its argument that there were interplanetary visitors coming to earth!

The report went all the way to the USAF Chief of Staff, General Hoyt Vandenburg. But he rejected it on the quite reasonable grounds that it was supposition based only on interpretation of eyewitness testimony. This, he rightly argued, was not sufficient and was known to be open to misinterpretation.

Vandenburg demanded some kind of physical support for the theory, which the team at Wright Patterson soon realized was simply not forthcoming. Within months, most of the team who had been flushed with conviction after the Montgomery, Alabama, affair gave up in despair. The U.S. government brought in a far more skeptical team to take their place. Never again were "alien believers" put in charge of the U.S. government UFO project.

But what was the explanation for the Eastern Airlines encounter? I talked to Dr. Hynek 35 years later, when he had had the opportunity to compare it with thousands of other UFO sightings. By 1983, astronomers were fully aware, as they were not in 1948, that incandescent bolides were rare but real and that blue/green trails of gas and sparks were sometimes emitted due to plasma being vented. Wearing his UFOlogist's hat, Dr. Hynek also knew that witnesses tended to see bolides as constructed craft of cigar shape and to perceive the trail of illuminated debris as lights or windows along the side. This knowledge was good support for his original idea as to what had flown by the DC-3.

Dr. Hynek explained that it was a "judgment call." Most of the facts fitted the incandescent bolide theory, but his view depended upon key evidence, such as whether there really was a wake turbulence effect on the aircraft. His best guess was that the aircraft had encountered a very rare type of natural space phenomenon, and that it was probably miles high in the atmosphere and never came close to colliding with the DC-3. The perception that it did do so and that the glowing mass of rock and gas was a craft with windows or lights on its side was a perfectly understandable misperception caused by the way in which human beings tend to see such very short-lived and spectacular events when they are suddenly thrust into confrontation with them.

I have to say that Dr. Hynek was a highly praised astronomer and so much better equipped to judge than me, yet all of my experiences as a UFOlogist fully supports his evaluation. I have seen phenomena that I am absolutely certain were bolides or space junk burning up in the atmosphere, which were reported in very similar terms to the phenomenon seen by the Eastern Airlines crew. The object over Montgomery was, as Dr. Hynek himself agreed, of rare beauty and nature. That Clarence Chiles and John Whitted should describe it as they did does not surprise me at all.

Yet there are early cases that are not so easy to identify as this one. These clearly show that while hard evidence for an alien invasion might not be forthcoming, there is solid support for a real phenomenon of unknown origin in some episodes.

In June 1949, the crew of a USAF transport aircraft were flying over Mexico near the Yucatan Peninsula. At a height of approximately 8000 feet, a strange object of irregular shape and surrounded by a band of white smoke or mist appeared in their path. The pilot, copilot, and navigator saw it and watched with puzzlement as it appeared to vibrate and then rotate on a vertical axis. Suddenly the object left its stationary position and flew at speed towards the aircraft, passing by the right wing at an estimated distance of just a few feet. It then appeared to circle the fuselage in a tight arc. The pilot attempted to evade these close attentions and went into a steep dive, but the object continued to flash like a mirror reflecting sunlight.

At this point, all four engines on the aircraft began to malfunction. Taking no chances, the crew immediately bailed out of the plane, which moments later crashed into a swamp. As they parachuted to safety, they observed the object, which was only 1 or 2 feet in diameter, climb vertically upwards and disappear.

The only speculation that was ever offered officially about this incident was that some rare atmospheric electrical event, such as St. Elmo's fire, or ball lightning (see p. 157), might have been involved. Whatever the case, this intriguing example appears to be the result of some unknown phenomenon.

Another typical case was collated by Dr. Richard Haines via the crew of another Eastern Airlines plane—this time a Martin 404. The date was approximately October 1952 and they were traveling at 10 p.m. on a commercial flight above Trenton, New Jersey, at a height of about 8000 feet.

Suddenly, a yellow glow appeared ahead and the crew watched it approach them at an angle. They called ground control and were advised of the situation. Long Island radar confirmed that they had both the aircraft and the unidentified object on screen. They tracked it passing the Martin 404 at about a mile distant and then climbing steeply and accelerating upwards. Visually, the Eastern crew saw the light become elliptical in shape and turn blue in color as it disappeared.

It must have been quite disturbing to those in the government who were in possession of such evidence to know that these unidentified lights often seen in close proximity to aircraft were all too real. Their frequent presence on radar, such as here over the Eastern seaboard of the U.S., prove that point. But perhaps more worrying still was the fear expressed from thankfully rare incidents, such as the one over the Yucatan Peninsula, that suggested some kind of electrical field could be generated. If the field was so powerful that it could create mechanical problems in the air, then there really was something to be concerned about—regardless of whether alien spaceships were nothing more than figments of overactive imaginations. Natural phenomena are not merely pretty lights of no significance. They can still cause planes to crash. Dr. Richard Haines has over one hundred cases on his computer database where critical systems on board aircraft were affected by some energy generated by a UFO. There are too many for this not to be a real consequence of some strange phenomenon.

That some rare, potentially dangerous and as yet unidentified natural phenomenon might be coming into close contact with air traffic was given serious consideration prior to the mid-1950s. It was, I believe, a perfectly valid option. Evidence from more recent cases serves to intensify this prospect, as will be seen later in this book. Unfortunately, it was too often dismissed from discussion because of the erroneous assumption that such objects were UFOs—and UFOs had been shown to be no more than mistakenly identified balloons and bolides. Since UFOs were unlikely to be spacecraft from another world, then there were no real UFOs at all.

But there are real UFOs. They may not be alien craft, but as unidentified natural phenomena they are no less of a threat. Indeed, they may well be more deadly because of our apathetic response towards them. Extraterrestrials may not really be here, but the lure of the belief in them could be lulling us into dangerous complacency about whatever is truly flying through our skies.

4 A BREACH IN OUR DEFENSES

So far the majority of the cases discussed here have revolved around incidents in the U.S. This is certainly not to imply that midair encounters only happen there, but it probably reflects the far greater level of air traffic above that nation. Being such a large country, it is ideally suited to domestic air travel and so developed it more extensively and rapidly than anywhere else.

However, pioneer aviation has always been very much to the fore in Britain, where jet engines, the world's first commercial jetliner, and (along with France) the first supersonic passenger aircraft were produced. Consequently, given the relatively small size of the country, an unusually large number of encounters in the air have involved British aircraft.

Inevitably, because I live in the U.K., I have had the opportunity to study these to the best advantage. In fact, one of the earliest of modern-style episodes occurred on January 16, 1947—5 months before the term "flying saucer" was even invented by the U.S. media and when the memory of the ghost rockets in Scandinavia only weeks beforehand ensured that this case merited a military investigation.

At 10:30 p.m. that evening, an RAF Mosquito was on a night exercise above the North Sea and had traveled 100 miles off the East Anglian coast to be within Dutch waters. British radar then detected an unidentified target, and the jet, flying at 22,000 feet, was ordered to intercept. According to the official record, "a long chase ensued" and the target was followed all the way back to Norfolk, where it finally disappeared. During the pursuit, the airborne radar aboard the Mosquito established a lock-on with the same object, and the pilot was sufficiently concerned when the target appeared to head towards him that he was forced to take what is termed "effective controlled evasive action."

Although British files on this case are limited, it was apparently rated "unexplained" by the Air Ministry. A report was conveyed to the American government by London on August 8th when the U.S. started inquiries into the flurry of UFO activity over its Western states. Washington retained the information because this case was one of a dozen or so that involved British pilots (the others having American aircrews). That data was used by the U.S. government to justify the launch of its official UFO project at Wright Patterson Air Force Base in January 1948.

Oddly, the staff at the Air Ministry, or MoD (Ministry of Defense) as it was later to become, paid less attention to this incident and others like it reported by RAF personnel. Indeed, they did not even retain most files long enough for any of them to be consulted later. Archives on all matters are turned over to the Public Record Office (PRO) at Kew only after 30 years have elapsed since the final action on any particular case. The fact that many early midair cases were not handed over means that they were either routinely destroyed (the official MoD stance) or transferred to a covert location protected by the Official Secrets Act from any public release.

Because of this rule, even in 1998 you can access information only on incidents prior to 1968, as all later ones have yet to be declassified. Unless and until a Freedom of Information Act is passed by the British parliament, as it has been in many other enlightened nations such as the U.S. and Australia, this unsatisfactory state of affairs will continue to block our ability to investigate.

Thus, we do have a problem tracing the extent of and official response to midair encounters over Britain during the late 1940s and 1950s. Thankfully, some records are available via Kew, where I have spent much time scanning the shelves filled with information. In addition, I have personally been fortunate to meet and interview ten members of British aircrews who were involved in midair encounters up to and including 1957. They usually shared their experiences late in their lives because they felt the obligation to do so. Sometimes they remained unhappy with the attitude displayed by their superiors in London, who seemed to have ignored what had happened to them. Occasionally, they justified their decision to come forward because 30 years had elapsed since the event took place and, knowing the MoD rules as they did, they felt any restriction placed upon them by the Official Secrets Act was now at an end.

Perhaps unspoken, but no less relevant, was the fact that one or two of them were quite ill when they came to me, and they possibly suspected that they might soon be beyond the jurisdiction of the bureaucratic mandarins who sought to limit what they could say. This was an incident that may have lasted no more than a few seconds and which took place up to 50 years earlier. Yet the MoD was seen to be denouncing all such episodes and their witnesses by its act of suppression of the evidence. One can well understand the frustrations of aircrew members placed in this difficult position.

However, there is a further and very important source of information. This is Ralph Noyes, a retired MoD undersecretary who came to see through his 40 years of service that there was a serious problem regarding UFO reports and the way in which his government appeared not to be addressing it as professionally as he would have liked.

I have had many interesting conversations and exchanges of information with Noyes. I should make it emphatically clear that he does not believe in little green men and spaceships. He thinks that some kind of natural phenomenon with possible attributes of an intelligence may be behind what is being seen. Yet our defenses are so geared up to handling tangible enemies that they flounder in the face of such an abstract kind of problem. He draws an analogy with the rainbow—a clearly real phenomenon in the sky that one can see, photograph, and fly right through (thankfully without harm to one's aircraft). Yet this is not "real" in the sense that you can touch it or chip a piece off to study it in the lab. Science had to progress towards a knowledge of physics before we could understand what a rainbow was. For millennia, mankind feared this apparition in the sky because we did not understand the cause.

A more controversial analogy that Noyes draws from his association with the Society for Psychical Research (with whom he has been a leading administrator) is the poltergeist. He likens these "noisy spirits" that move chairs around rooms not to ghostly goings-on from the afterlife but to energies within our own psyche that act at random in a way quite impossible to predict.

So too are those aerial phenomena we face in this book. You cannot easily stake out their lair and wait for an opportunity to capture hard evidence. You have to be in the right place at the right moment, and even then you will probably fail to retrieve any kind of proof that will be persuasive to science.

No wonder the Air Ministry found these lights in the sky a nightmare it would rather not have to worry about. But Ralph Noyes did not have the luxury of ignoring these things. Shortly after entering the civil service, he landed a plum appointment as Private Secretary to Sir Ray Cochrane, the Vice Chief of Air Staff and Air Chief Marshal. This was between 1950 and 1953. Noyes was of similar status in the ministry for the next decade and saw all that happened during this crucial period. While he was there, the British government struggled to come to terms with the quickly overwhelming evidence that something "really was flying around," as one perceptive U.S. general bluntly put it.

Towards the end of his service, Noyes ran the British government department that, as a matter of routine, collated UFO reports for eventual transfer to the PRO. Thus, he had regular contact with what was going on at the start and end of his career. At his briefing for this latter job—in 1968, when the division was still fairly new—he was shown gun camera film obtained by RAF crew during the 1950s as it was vectored onto targets picked up on radar. Noyes says that the film depicted "fuzzy blobs and lights." He is adamant that there was nothing remotely like a solid spaceship from another world or anywhere else. Yet, rather intriguingly, this gun camera film has never been released by the MoD.

In fact, according to the outspoken Nick Pope, it was not even shown to him when he took the position as head of the MoD UFO data department in 1991. Pope, who has written a bestseller about his 3 years shuffling government UFO papers, was of civil service rank equivalent to a captain. Ralph Noyes was an air commodore. That he saw gun camera film, while Pope did not, emphasizes the importance of what he has to say. That the MoD still chooses not to release this evidence to the PRO, despite its now being well past the 30-year "sell-by date," is intriguing. Have they simply lost it or do they prefer not to have the public relations headache of admitting that their stance on UFOs is false?

After all, they have said repeatedly that they regard this matter as not having "any defense significance," as they usually phrase it. This is often taken by the media to imply that they mean there are no real UFOs. But it implies no such thing. The MoD disputes having any evidence of alien spacecraft, but, as we have seen so often already in this book, UFOs and their popular misinterpretation as alien craft are two very different issues.

I strongly suspect that the MoD does not want this distinction to be readily understood nor the public revelation that 40 years ago RAF flight crews filmed UFOs as they pursued them in state-of-the-art aircraft and traced anomalies on radar.

As Ralph Noyes told me, "The MoD is much happier investigating these matters quietly. They will never lie, so do not say that UFOs do not exist. Instead, they do not go out of their way to say that they do and emphasize (correctly in my view) that they have no evidence that aliens are coming here." Most people incorrectly judge this comment to mean that the MoD has no evidence for UFOs. But if the MoD were called to task, it could truthfully insist that this is not what it has said!

Further emphasis for this point comes from the French government. Their Minister of Defense, Robert Galley, openly stated on national radio in a March 1974 interview with France Inter that the government knew that UFOs were real, and they too had film evidence secured from military jets sent in pursuit. He has added to his comments in a 1993 interview after his retirement by saying, "If the French public could see the evidence that we have, they would be rather concerned." I suspect that such thinking dominates the motivation for its non-release by the British government.

UFOs exist. The MoD does not know what they are. It suspects they are not alien craft, but knows that it cannot disprove this theory. It also knows that this more extreme view will be adopted by the media and vociferous public opinion. As a result, silence seems a prudent step.

All over the world, the powers that be enforce a cover-up of information not because, as UFO buffs are so fond of suggesting, they have bits of spaceships and alien bodies locked away. Not even because they have evidence of an alien visitation. Put simply, it is because they do not know what lies behind this phenomenon and are afraid that such an admission would be perceived as weakness or indeed be rapidly and wrongly translated into support for alien starships by the UFO lobby.

We have a cover-up forged out of ignorance and a desire to find out what is really in the skies. We do not have a cover-up of fantastic guilty secrets—much to the dismay of the tabloids, I suspect. But there are probably other factors at work, as we will come to see a little later.

Noyes tells me that Sir Ray Cochrane was wont to assume that the question of UFOs had been resolved by U.S. Chief of Staff General Hoyt Vandenburg. If you recall, he was the man who rejected the "spaceships" interpretation of the early UFO project based on cases like the Eastern Airlines encounter over Alabama. Cochrane was often in direct contact with Vandenburg, as they held equivalent positions in their respective countries, and he was assured by the Americans that nearly all cases were examples of mistakenly identified objects, such as balloons and meteors. None were important.

But then everything changed very dramatically in summer 1952. For a series of incidents took place that were impossible for the Pentagon to ignore. They struck the U.S. capital, Washington, D.C., and they were seen by many witnesses on the ground, numerous pilots (both civilian and military), and tracked on both the D.C. Airport radar and military radar. There was no getting away from this one.

On July 14, a Pan-Am DC-4 crewed by long-serving and highly respected pilots William Nash and William Fortenberry observed six red coin-shaped lights that tagged the aircraft as it passed over the capital on its flight to Miami, Florida. They appeared to be reflecting sunlight.

Five days later, the first major radar contacts followed. They lasted from 11:40 p.m. on July 19 to after 1 a.m. the next morning. The long-range civilian aircraft radar at Washington, D.C., first spotted several unusual targets moving in stop-go fashion at up to several hundred miles per hour. Controller Ed Nugent brought in his boss, Harry Barnes, and they assumed that these must be military traffic from Andrews Air Force Base. He doubted radar defects but ordered the system to be thoroughly checked. Meanwhile, operators of the local radar at D.C. Airport, a separate system, reported that they had the same objects on screen. Controllers Howard Cocklin and Joe Zacko described for Nugent and Barnes the same motions of these objects that, at one point, were flying over highly restricted air space near the White House!

By now, Andrews military radar confirmed that they too were watching the blips that were not from any military traffic. A Capital Airlines DC-4 heading out of Washington, D.C., was asked to change course and go to take a look. The crew saw several strange lights that closed in and then streaked away, exhibiting the same sort of behavior that Nash and Fortenberry had observed earlier in the week. One light was tracked leaving the area at 7000 mph—quite an inconceivable speed for 1952.

Other aircrews reported visual sightings as they flew in and out of Washington, D.C., between 1 a.m. and 3 a.m., but these are probably unconnected. They spoke of blue/white streaks of light, and these were most likely meteors seen by people scanning the skies on the lookout for the now departed UFOs. UFOlogists will tell you that once a suggestion is given to people that they look at the skies, they see many things they never normally notice, because most of us rarely look upward in our daily lives.

A military interceptor flight had been sent up, but by then the visible glowing lights and the radar trackings had disappeared. Exactly a week later, at 9:30 p.m. on July 26, the whole thing happened again. Radars tracked fast-moving lights, and this time two F-94 jets were sent to the area right away. As soon as the jets closed in on what were seen by the crew as fuzzy lights, these vanished both visibly and on radar. When the aircraft left the area, the lights returned! This "game" went on for several hours until the phenomena vanished into the pre-dawn summer skies.

There had been many witnesses and the ground-to-air conversations had been overheard by the public, so that, by the time the F-94s were airborne on the final night of this "invasion of Washington," the media were swarming over the airport. However, the USAF kicked out everyone without security clearance. Captain Edward Ruppelt, then head of the USAF project investigating UFOs, explained in very candid terms why they did this: "They were positive that this night would be the big night in UFO history—the night when a pilot would close in and get a good look at a UFO." He added that this would be when the proof was finally obtained that UFOs were real, and the Pentagon simply did not want the media to be there when that event happened.

A major press conference was called 48 hours later to quell the rising storm. It was the largest since World War II and was chaired by Major-General John Samford, head of Air Force intelligence. He assured the public that the matter was resolved. The lights seen and radar targets tracked were what are called "angels" caused by a meteorological effect known as a "temperature inversion." It was all very simple really.

The result of this process is a kind of mirage in the sky produced in not dissimilar fashion to an effect easily noticed on a hot day down on the ground. You may spot what appears to be a pool of water on the highway ahead. In fact, this is a mirage image of the sky, caused by the way in which light rays bend at different angles depending upon the temperature of the air through which they pass.

In 1952, radar was relatively new and we were still learning about such things. It was a convincing explanation as far as most people were concerned. But it did not persuade any of the radar operators, who were the very people best able to judge. They always felt this solution was imposed as an excuse by the USAF to get the media off their backs.

Fifteen years later, when a great deal more was known about the capabilities of radar, the staff was reinterviewed as part of a study into UFOs at the University of Colorado. This used a million dollars of taxpayers' money. The air traffic controllers, radar officers, and pilots all said they did not believe that a radar angel or temperature inversion was responsible. They had seen such things many times since 1952 and these looked quite different from the phenomena that caused the Washington, D.C., "invasion."

Atmospheric physicist Dr. James McDonald from the University of Arizona was a specialist in the field of radar anomaly optics. He examined the weather data, characteristics of the radar, and visual sightings to conclude that whatever else was responsible, it was not some kind of mundane meteorological anomaly.

When news of these incredible events reached London in the summer of 1952, it produced great consternation in the Air Ministry. Noyes recalls Cochrane complaining to the Cabinet, "I thought Vandenburg had put an end to all this in '49."

Such was the impact that Prime Minister Winston Churchill issued a memo to his air minister. This, thankfully, has been retained by the PRO and shows a clearly disgruntled prime minister asking what "all this stuff about flying saucers" meant. He ordered an investigation. Sir Robert Coburn, Chief Air Ministry Scientist, was sent to Washington, D.C., as Noyes explains. Later, according to Captain Ed Ruppelt in his 1956 memoirs, several RAF intelligence officers came to his office armed with a long list of questions about how to set up a British UFO project.

Coburn returned to London and advised that something had happened over Washington, D.C., and, despite the public pronouncements, the U.S. government was not entirely sure what was going on. Perhaps, he told the MoD, there were radar anomalies and natural phenomena, but not, it was believed, some kind of invasion from either the USSR or outer space. Nobody actually knew for sure. Churchill was thus reassured, just as Cochrane had been before him, that most sightings were explicable and the rest were no direct defense threat. The U.K. had followed the Americans' advice that there was nothing to worry about. But the Washington, D.C. events had added to the confusion.

Even before Churchill could properly digest the implications of these opinions, something happened right on his doorstep that forced him to take action. Again, thankfully, the PRO files are available to trace the course of a NATO exercise over the North Sea called Operation Mainbrace. This involved ships and aircraft from the U.K. and U.S. The entire exercise, of several days' duration in September 1952, was plagued by sightings of strange things in the sky.

Ralph Noyes recalls how Air Chief Marshal Cochrane passed him the NATO signals and asked him to find out what was happening. As Noyes put it, "I referred it down to air staff and asked for a report. The reaction was more or less: Blimey, are our chaps now being taken in by hallucinations as well?" Noyes says that in retrospect he feels they should probably have done more than just pass the information along the channels. But nobody really wanted to believe that something was going on. The Americans kept assuring the British that nothing was!

Only a British report by Flight Lieutenant John Kilburn of RAF 269 Squadron in North Yorkshire could start out with the words "I have the honor to report the following incident...." But that is precisely how the first Mainbrace sighting on September 19 was forwarded by the base commander at RAF Topcliffe to the Air Ministry in London.

Kilburn and five other officers (another flight lieutenant, a flying officer, two sergeants, and an LAC) were on the ground watching an RAF Meteor descend into Dishforth, when Flying Officer Paris called the attention of the group to an object east of the jet. It appeared silver in the sunlight and was circular. It traveled quite slowly on a tracking course with the RAF plane, now descending through 5000 feet. Then it started a more vertical descent and, as Kilburn reports, was "swinging in a pendular motion...similar to a falling sycamore leaf." This is one of the first known accounts of the so-called "falling leaf" motion often attributed to these UFOs. It appears to suggest that whatever they are, they have relatively little mass and are, thus, carried by the wind currents. It may also be a feature of the aerodynamic properties of the shape, as you can simulate the effect by dropping a small dish into a bowl of water.

The RAF crew members dismissed their initial thought of a parachute canopy when the changes in direction and motion of the object were more clearly apparent. Indeed, now the Meteor changed course to fly towards the object, which appeared to respond as if aware it was being "locked onto."

Next, the object stopped swinging and descending and hovered, rotating on its axis, as the RAF Meteor flew past at speed. Then the UFO accelerated away at "incredible speed towards the west, turning onto a south-easterly heading before disappearing." The report adds, "All of this occurred in a matter of 15–20 seconds. The acceleration was in excess of that of a shooting star." The event took place before 11 a.m. on a clear, sunny day with "unlimited visibility" so that these descriptions clearly eliminate the other likely candidate for the object—a balloon.

Next day, September 20, a U.S. Navy aircraft carrier, the Franklin D. Roosevelt, was on an exercise off the coast between the northeast of England and Scandinavia. Suddenly, a round silvery object appeared overhead once more. It circled the ship and was seen by numerous personnel. The official photographer aboard, Wallace Litwin, was able to take three daylight shots of this UFO.

Only scanty information about the shipborne sighting was passed to the British. Noyes was completely unaware of the photograph until I told him about it. That photograph was kept hidden for almost 40 years by the U.S. government but was later released after pressure using the Freedom of Information Act. It was only then that it became clear why such circumspection was practiced. The vessel involved was the only ship in the world then equipped with nuclear missiles. As such, a UFO encounter in its vicinity was regarded as being of huge national security importance. Indeed, the ship became plagued with UFO activity during its active service life, according to later crew members.

Possibly the Americans may have suspected the UFO was part of a spying mission by one of its NATO allies, such as the British—hence, the desire to keep the matter to themselves.

On the following day, September 21, the NATO exercise continued its contact with UFOs. This time it was the turn of the RAF once again. Six aircraft over the North Sea saw another of the silvery objects. They tried to close in and it played "tag" with one Meteor before streaking away at phenomenal speed. The similarities between this case and the events over Washington, D.C. 8 weeks before were immediately obvious. One can well imagine why the powers that be felt as if this was evidence of a spying mission from some alien intelligence. By all accounts, this later discredited possibility was indeed entertained for a time in the Pentagon.

In January 1953, a top secret gathering of rocket scientists and government engineers convened in Washington. It was commanded by the CIA and set up a whole series of initiatives that were kept not only from the public but also from people like Captain Ed Ruppelt, the U.S. government's own UFO project head, and their science consultant, Dr. J. Allen Hynek.

Indeed, this dishonesty had such a major effect on Capt. Ruppelt that it led to him quit the USAF, take a job in the aviation industry, and, by 1956, publish his own UFO files while speculating, "Maybe I was just the front man to a big cover-up." I doubt Ruppelt was such a front man in the sense here implied. But it is easy to see why he would be so flummoxed. The CIA was simply paranoid about what might lie behind these sightings and neither Capt. Ruppelt nor Dr. Hynek had the kind of security clearance to be "in the know."

Aside from its dirty tricks against its own officers, the CIA ordered incredible tactics to be used against the public. We know this from several sources, even though it was kept secret for decades. The Freedom of Information Act has brought forth some data, and Professor Thornton Page, one of the leading rocketry experts who made the decisions for the CIA, had second thoughts about UFOs a quarter of a century later and in retirement came clean. He has confirmed for me that what I say here is true.

The CIA panel ordered the burning of the books so that any unsolved cases appeared to vanish. They discussed surveillance and monitoring of UFO researchers and groups in order to control their influence on the general public. Even more remarkably, they drew up a plan to get famous cartoonists like Walt Disney to make silly features about aliens and help change public attitudes. The CIA wanted these to move away from fear and concern towards lighthearted amusement! Such steps were taken for intriguing reasons. The CIA saw the subject as ripe for the manipulation of public beliefs by enemy powers who might use spurious UFO waves as a means of creating panic. These steps were definitely not followed because the authorities in Washington thought that nothing was going on—regardless of what they had told Winston Churchill 6 months earlier!

However, Churchill had already decided for himself that UFOs were no longer a topic he could ignore. After sending RAF intelligence staff to meet Ruppelt, the British UFO project was soon created. According to RAF personnel, this highly secret project was located at RAF Farnborough in Hampshire.

5 MILITARY CONFRONTATIONS

On January 13, 1953, just days after the CIA group met in Washington, letter FC/S.45485/Signals was issued by the RAF to all senior personnel on orders from the British Air Ministry. We can get an appreciation of its nature from a restricted memo dated December 16, 1953, that refers back to the decisions taken by that January circular. What is clear is that the newly initiated British research project at Farnborough had made a number of careful moves to restrict the flow of information, possibly taking tips from the CIA, which had just initiated similar tactics.

All senior air staff were informed that sightings by "RAF personnel are in future to be reported in writing by officers commanding units immediately and direct to Air Ministry (technical intelligence units) with copies to group and command headquarters." More interesting still was the comment that "the public attach more credence to reports by RAF personnel" and so "it is essential that the information should be examined at the Air Ministry and that its release should be controlled officially."

In other words, as it added, "personnel are to be warned that they are not to communicate to anyone other than official persons any information about phenomena they have observed."

This probably explains why we have official data on cases pre-1953, such as the Topcliffe encounter. They came before the new policy. But of the five British military encounters in this chapter dated between 1953 and 1957, the PRO only has a report about one of them and a brief reference to one of the other four, indicating that there ought to be a report somewhere. Such a report once did exist, because the reference indicates that it was used to brief a politician on ways to respond to questions in the House by an MP. Interestingly, the case where there are records available via the PRO happens to be the only one discovered by the media when it occurred, possibly explaining why the MoD had no option but to release the file many years later. They could not hide an event that was already in the public domain, but you can cover up events that nobody officially knows about!

The files that are missing from the public record describe cases never publicized at all—cases where the new Air Ministry edict was clearly adhered to by the personnel involved. Is there no present record of them because they were siphoned off into this new covert agency according to the new guidelines? Is their continued nonappearance simply because these files were "lost" or "destroyed" (the explanation suggested by the

MoD) or because those files of the UFO project created at Farnborough in 1953 are still subject to the Official Secrets Act all these years later? Either option seems tenable.

Fortunately, I have been able to gather evidence on these missing cases from firsthand sources—usually the aircrews themselves. In three of the missing four cases, they have kept their own copies of logbooks and other records and have been stunned when I could inform them that their original reports are absent from the PRO. Sometimes this absence is glaring, as more routine files from their base or squadron from the same time period are still there. When just the record of the UFO event has gone AWOL, the MoD claim that these were lost or routinely destroyed is suspect.

The existence of personal records held by the aircrew proves that the cases are real. More than that, they make it seem as if they were deliberately expunged from the public domain by the MoD in the hope that without such official confirmation we might doubt the word of the aircrew and suspect that such cases never happened. But why go to so much trouble if UFOs are the waste of time the MoD would like you to believe? They say with accidents that once is misfortune, twice real bad luck, but four times and you have the makings of a conspiracy. We can surely apply that saying to the case of the missing files.

These four missing cases did happen, and the even more worrying question seems to be that if these are the ones that we chanced to find out about through good fortune, then just how many others were part of that secret investigation at Farnborough but were never discovered? This evidence is naturally invaluable to any scientific investigation into the nature of strange lights in the sky. If the data is out there in some dusty filing cabinet at the MoD, being withheld for reasons other than national security, we surely deserve to see it.

One case about which a little detail has been known for some years concerns Flight Lieutenant James Salandin of the 604th Squadron. At 4:15 p.m. on October 14, 1954, he took off in his RAF Meteor from North Weald in Essex for a practice mission over the Thames Estuary. At 16,000 feet and in the vicinity of Southend, he spotted two unusual objects. They were circular and moving at great speed, as if inspecting two other RAF Meteors visible in the distance. It is not known if their crews saw anything. As Salandin was distracted by this sight, he momentarily took his eyes off the cockpit window ahead. When he returned his gaze, he was stunned to see a third similar object that was much closer to him. Indeed, it was heading right at him on a collision course!

According to Salandin, the UFO had a "bun-shaped top, a flange like two saucers in the middle, and a bun underneath." It was silver, reflecting the sun, and so large and close it overlapped his entire windscreen. For comparison, a 37-foot-wingspan Meteor at such close range that collision was imminent would not have had as great an angular diameter as this thing did.

The RAF pilot had no time to react. It was moving much faster than he was—probably beyond supersonic speed. Yet there was no sonic boom, a factor pilots have noticed with astonishment time and again during these aerial encounters. Before he could do anything to avoid smashing into the object, it seemed to alter direction slightly and rush past his right-hand wing. Note in coming pages just how often this happens. Why do UFOs never fly past the *left* side of aircraft?

So shaken up by this episode was the pilot that he had to fly around in circles for 10 minutes. As he explained to ground control, he dared not attempt to land until he had fully regained his composure. Only later did he realize that he could have filmed the distant objects and, if fast enough, he could have captured visual proof of the one bearing down on him. Aboard his jet was a gun camera. But he simply had too much else on his mind—a cry I have heard uttered plaintively by UFO witnesses in far less onerous circumstances than here!

We know what we do about this case thanks to the intervention of Derek Dempster, an RAF pilot, a celebrated aviation writer on topics such as the Battle of Britain, and a man who became very interested in UFOs. But, officially, the matter was hushed up. Intriguingly, almost 30 years later, in November 1983, UFOlogist Gordon Creighton told how he met by pure chance during a mishap on the London Underground a retired RAF officer who had been in Salandin's 604th Squadron at the same time. He claimed that they had all been instructed to steer clear of snooping reporters and especially UFOlogists. The incident was a "no go" area as far as the public were concerned.

We can see this policy in even greater evidence, and get some insight into what happened during the investigation at an official level, thanks to another incident that occurred in the period between the Air Ministry edict and the Salandin affair. Dating it has proven difficult, but I am reasonably certain that it happened in the period between February and June 1953.

I found out about it after doing a national BBC radio broadcast. A man, who would not talk on the air, called and left a message for me to call him back later. I did so and it was obvious that he wanted desperately to talk about an event then 30 years in the past. As he put it to me over the phone, "I am now retired and none too well. The 30-year rule has just expired on this matter. If you are willing to be discreet, then I will tell you all that I know."

I traveled out into the countryside to meet this man and, in the intervening days, he had become rather less keen to bare all. He told me that he had checked with his former base and, to his surprise I think, realized that there were still those who did mind him talking. He was never instructed to remain silent—or at least if he was, then it did not stop him. But it was clear that his "informal chat with my old employers," as he put it to me, led him to doubt the wisdom of ever calling me after my radio interview. Thankfully, he pressed on and I was eventually able to tape record his story before ill health tragically claimed his life not too long afterwards.

The man in question was Cyril George Townsend-Withers. He had begun his flying career in 1939, just before the outbreak of hostilities. He had a distinguished war record and, by 1953, was a flight lieutenant. His background in science and engineering caused him to specialize in radar and indeed, at the age of 47, he retired from active flying duty to take on a post as principle science officer for the Air Ministry, developing a number of state-of-the-art radar and aircraft in-flight systems as part of the experimental unit at RAF Boscombe Down. He was working here in 1953, test-flying new systems, when the UFO encounter took place. On retirement from the MoD, he had attained the rank of wing commander.

On the day in question, Cyril was asked to test some new ECM equipment. These are sophisticated electronic countermeasures to try to interfere with enemy radar. There had been some problems with ground interference during earlier tests so that Townsend-Withers, operating the equipment, and his pilot (also a flight lieutenant) were given a nearly new prototype Canberra aircraft to which no internal fittings had yet been applied. Stripped bare and thus remarkably light, the craft could fly very high and put the equipment through the motions well clear of any interference from below. Indeed, in doing so, they set a new height record for the Canberra by approaching 60,000 feet.

It was just after noon on a cloudless day as they circled high above Salisbury Plain on a northwesterly heading, when the radar picked up a target 5 miles behind them, pacing the jet like an echo. Cursing the return of the interference problems, they switched off the system, reset, and did a number of internal checks. This did not clear the target—as it did whenever there was an anomaly. Something really was following them. But that was virtually impossible at this height. The science officer clambered into the gun turret to investigate matters. This gave the clearest view to the rear. Sure enough, there was an object trailing behind. It was round and silvery, reflecting sunlight like a giant mirror.

Calling to his pilot, he requested they increase speed. Although they got to 260 mph, the object "just hung in there," so Townsend-Withers recommended "a big radius turn." Once they started on this, the object vanished from the radar, which was only operating in a rearward facing mode. However, it was not out of sight for long. It was now dead ahead of them. The pilot took the Canberra out of the turn and flew towards the glinting object. It was not moving, and as they closed the gap there were about 30 seconds when they were on a direct collision course. During this period, they had a perfect close-up view of the thing in the sky.

It was silverlike metal and very thin in body shape. Overall, it appeared to be a remarkably flat oval without any sign of wings or windows and with just a hint of a tail fin at the rear. Neither man had seen anything like it before—certainly not just sitting there at such great height. Both were familiar with weather balloons, often flying as high as the balloons did. This was not one of them.

As the Canberra flew towards the UFO, they were preparing to pull out and fly around the object. It never gave them the chance. At close range, it suddenly shot vertically upwards without acceleration, going from zero to immense speed in an instant. It climbed "sixty, seventy thousand feet as quick as you could say 'it,'" Townsend-Withers remembered. They lost sight of it "at an impossible height."

Back on the ground, they reported the incident, but Townsend-Withers was as surprised by the reaction of his superior officers as he was by the UFO. "Nobody seemed that interested," he said. The RAF pressed hard for reassurance it was not a secret Soviet aircraft, but the two men were adamant that this was absurd given what the UFO did. Nobody was interested beyond that point. The science officer could not understand it. However, he was instructed to work with the radar manufacturers. As he said, "We stripped the equipment and reassembled it. There was nothing wrong. Eventually, the Ministry accepted that there had been no fault with the equipment, and I expected a full debriefing about what we saw. It never happened."

I have heard this from other senior officers. Indeed, a USAF memo dated as early as 1947 and released under the Freedom of Information Act comments on the lack of "topside inquiries" about clearly credible sightings being made by aircrews. It speculates that the powers that be did not need to ask questions because they already knew the answers! At the time, this was taken to mean that the objects were secret American weapons. Later, the same logic was applied to the rather different theory that the U.S. government knew that they were alien spacecraft and had enough intelligence about them without grilling individual witnesses.

More likely, my view is that the British government, particularly as early as 1953, was still rather reluctant to accept that something was going on. In addition, it really had no experience in handling such reports. Indeed, Ralph Noyes, who was working with Air Chief Marshal Cochrane when the Salisbury Plain events occurred, merely says of such matters, "These things seemed like phantoms. We did not have a clue how to deal with them. Hardheaded military staff in the U.K. had come to regard the thing as a bit of an old wives' tale. They took a lot of persuading that it was otherwise. Besides, the real task at the time was to keep the Russians out."

However, Townsend-Withers was not satisfied by the apathy of his employers and started to ask questions. It was then that he stepped on some toes. Quickly, he discovered this was not an area to involve yourself in if you wished your career to progress. He did discover that there was a research team at Farnborough who were hand picked to study the evidence, and he heard whispers that they had a working assumption that alien craft might be coming to this planet. But it was made very clear that this was not for public discussion and he was not to dig further into that situation. Certainly, nobody from the unit ever interviewed him or his pilot.

What does this well-qualified witness believe that he had seen? He remained convinced until his dying day that he had had the privilege of viewing close up "a reconnaissance device from someplace else." That is as specific as he said it was possible to be. But he never accepted my suggestions that it might have been some new meteorological or atmospheric phenomenon, or a force of nature we did not yet understand. To him, it was an exotic craft and the powers that be had to know this fact. "To the best of my knowledge, this was a constructed object—a controlled device," was all he would say.

There were very probably other cases with RAF witnesses of the caliber of James Salandin and Cyril George Townsend-Withers during the first 2 or 3 years of the fledgling UFO project at Farnborough. I suspect that the reason why we have never seen records from this research site is because skeptics would be left floundering if the full extent of the evidence were made available from here. For whatever reason, the MoD seems to prefer that science in its public guise remains skeptical.

I was given a reason why this might be the case in 1980 when I was invited to Westminster to brief MPs and members of the House of Lords on UFOs. At the gathering, I took the chance to talk with leading politicians and civil servants. One of these was a former MoD chief of staff, then serving as a lord. His name was Peter Hill-Norton. Aside from his MoD post, he had also served as Britain's admiral of the fleet. His suggestions on this matter were worth taking seriously.

Lord Hill-Norton reminded me that the MoD interest in UFOs was not so much to find out what they were, but to "figure out what we can do with them." This was a twist I had never considered before. However, imagine that these things do have capabilities that we do not. It hardly matters why they do so, whether because they are visiting craft from some other place or because of some bizarre natural energy science has yet to understand. You need to harness the power of these objects before any other rival nation.

Think this through. The first country to solve the problem has a new energy source that might lead to a terror weapon. As the MoD officer said to me:

> We might be able to figure out how they can sometimes appear as radar invisible, or how they prevent shock waves at supersonic speeds, or control the power source or energy that lets them do things that we can only dream about.

Whatever the cause for these phenomena, the country that gets the answers first has a massive global technological advantage. Of course, this research is done secretly. That is the way of the world. So, I suspect, some of the caution about releasing information from secret government UFO studies stems from the fact that to make it openly available to science immediately loses that nation any initiative. All governments have their own security-cleared scientific analysts, and these are the people they want to have access to the data so that they might attempt to use the information gathered via UFO activity for either defensive or (I fear rather more likely) offensive purposes. You do not want your data discussed at the next scientific symposium and published freely where every nation ruled by a tyrannical dictator or terrorist group has the same insights as you do.

Altruism or selfishness, it is all the same and it adds up to the need for any nation to protect its UFO secrets. Aliens probably hardly even enter into the equation when the MoD is deciding what to do here, and no doubt there are plenty of smiles down Westminster way when UFO buffs and tabloid reporters constantly bang on the wrong doors! The real truth is probably more down-to-earth than little green men and all the more terrifying for that.

Whatever occurred between 1953 and 1956, August of that latter year was to prove a true turning point. At least two extraordinary midair encounters took place that were to leave nobody in any doubt that this was a mystery to be reckoned with. Neither case was publicized at the time, nor reported since. The MoD insists it has absolutely no record of either instance and assumes that it shredded the records in 1961 at the expiration of only 5 years, as was then customary with "unimportant" records.

Judge for yourself whether that seems likely.

We first heard about the "big one" 10 years later in the U.S. This was when U.S. Congress had devoted a large sum of money to a team of scientists to analyze the UFO official investigation procedure that had begun at Wright Patterson AFB in January 1948. A government scientist who had worked on the Manhattan Project to build the atom bomb was put in charge. He was physicist Dr. Edward Condon, a man who was outspokenly skeptical of UFOs. Between 1967 and 1969, he led a team of twenty university professors in Colorado to assess the seventy best cases from the USAF records. These were turned over completely for this study following pressure to do so led by future president Gerald Ford and the well-known cosmologist, Dr. Carl Sagan, who sat on a Congress committee in 1966.

Unfortunately, the publicity for this project reached the ears of an American serviceman who had been involved in a case in England in August 1956. He assumed all the records had been handed over because his government had promised to Congress that they were doing precisely this. His case had slipped through the cracks (along with how many others?). Until he spoke out, nobody knew of it.

From subsequent investigations, tracking down witnesses on both sides of the Atlantic, we have gradually built up a good picture of the events that took place in a case that was indisputably a most serious matter.

Late on the evening of August 13–14, 1956, three separate radar systems in East Anglia picked up unusual targets. The radars were at the USAF base at Lakenheath and Bentwaters in Suffolk and the RAF station at Neatishead in Norfolk. These observed fast-moving objects coming in from the North Sea towards land, and the fear inevitably was that a Russian invasion was under way.

One target proceeded inland and passed over Rendlesham Forest and Bentwaters base. The control tower staff saw it pass above them as a rapidly moving fuzzy glow. They called ahead to Lakenheath, which was on its path to the northwest, and they too recorded it heading their way.

Luckily, a USAF transport aircraft was flying near Bentwaters at the time and the crew members were able to visually see the object. They described it as a yellow ball of light with misty edges. They were at 6000 feet and the object passed below them.

This was the information obtained from the USAF officer from Bentwaters who told the Colorado University team what had occurred as he manned the radar. It was affirmed by other USAF staff members and, eventually, the records that never were appeared!

These sources also reported that, as this was happening over British soil, the U.K. took charge of the intruder response and that two aircraft were launched on an intercept mission. The USAF ground staff guided them from radar information and, as the U.S. file reports, these aircraft picked up the UFO on their airborne radar and visually. One RAF jet returned to base with a malfunction. The other had a "cat and mouse" game with the brilliant light that lasted until the UFO tired and flew away.

The British government refused to comment on any of this in 1967.

After the Colorado report was published in 1969, the American government took the opportunity to close down its USAF project. It did not, however, cease all UFO study as has often been alleged. We know this thanks to documents released by the Freedom of Information Act since 1976.

One of these is the actual memo that closed down the UFO project at Wright Patterson. Signed by Brigadier-General C.H. Bolender on October 20, 1969, it stated that "reports of Unidentified Flying Objects that could affect national security" were "not part of the Blue Book system" (probably explaining why the Lakenheath/Bentwaters case was not amongst the data released to the scientists under the false promise that they had all the best cases). However, even when the UFO project ended that December, Bolender insisted that these high caliber cases should "continue to be handled through the standard Air Force procedure designed for this purpose."

In other words, in the U.K., the secret Farnborough project (and its modern day equivalent) was studying all the best evidence immune from release of any of its data. In the U.S., Bolender admits there was a similar covert location, which contained the key data that affected national security. Reports fed out to the PRO in Britain today via the publicly acknowledged UFO team at the MoD tell just half the story, as do those given to the U.S. public via its Freedom of Information Act from Project Blue Book. They are mere sops and the best cases remain hidden from view. Ask yourself why.

Other U.S. records tell of scientific staff at the research and development division of the CIA working on UFO-related projects during the 1970s and 1980s, and of "Project Moon Dust"—an interesting military project whose full nature is not understood but whose files contain an ongoing collection of UFO reports from U.S. embassies around the world! All of the above postdates by decades the officially stated policy by the Pentagon (reiterated as recently as April 1997 after the Heaven's Gate cult of UFO believers and their mass suicide tragedy). This claimed that the U.S. government ended all interest in UFOs in 1969 when, very plainly, that can only be characterized as a lie.

Although Condon's report was used to close down the USAF Blue Book, the 1000-page study itself makes fascinating reading. At least one-third of the cases it reviewed were rated to be unexplained by the largely skeptical scientists after 2 years of research into them. Undoubtedly, the one they rated the most highly was this extraordinary affair in August 1956 in East Anglia.

Gordon Thayer, the radar expert and optical physicist who studied it most thoroughly, was no UFO believer. But of this episode he writes, "...this is the most puzzling and unusual case in the radar/visual files. The apparently rational, intelligent behavior of the UFO suggests a mechanical device of unknown origin as the most probable explanation of this sighting."

Condon's overall conclusions even added that "the probability that at least one genuine UFO was involved appears fairly high."

Even if this case were unique in the final Colorado University report— and it is not—nobody can read those words and say, as some have tried to do, that the Condon investigation disproved UFO reality. Their 2-year study provided some of the best positive evidence for a genuine mystery.

When news of the East Anglia "night of the UFOs" reached the British UFO community from the U.S. 14 years after it had happened, our own investigations soon turned up two significant leads.

First, a group of civilian witnesses, who had seen a jet aircraft and a glowing light in close proximity on the ground, was traced. From all that can be ascertained, this appears to have been the same event. The ground sighting occurred at Ely in Cambridgeshire and that location fits in with the details known about the flight of the intercept mission. The UFO was described, as by all the other witnesses to it, as an orangey-yellow or white fuzzy light.

The next breakthrough came in 1978 after the retirement of Squadron Leader Freddy Wimbledon. He decided to tell of his role in a major case. That case turned out to be this one. Wimbledon confirms that he was the man who ordered the intercept mission after the radar and visual sightings had been reported to his office. He was at first concerned about the possibility of an enemy attack but says that no conclusion could be reached about the outcome of the intercept once the results were assessed.

Wimbledon does recall that one of the aircraft used the correct security codes to identify a radar lock on (the code word was "Judy"), and he believes it had a visual sighting with an object that at first appeared in front of them and then, in an instant, flew directly behind!

However, the real fortune in this case came in January 1996 when I scoured the newly released data in the PRO at Kew. I came upon a note about the case that the MoD UFO office had constantly stated it knew nothing about. "You tell us about this one, we don't tell you" was how one MoD civil servant had put it to me when I quizzed her about their failure to find any evidence regarding such undeniably powerful events. Whatever the MoD chose to say, there was a memo dated May 2, 1957, buried away and hard to find. It was easy to miss because it was only part of an Air Ministry briefing given to a senior politician who was about to answer questions tabled in the House of Commons about UFOs. The questioner was an MP in whose constituency there had just been sightings.

The briefing file from the Air Ministry advises that there had been three UFO encounters during the previous year (which included August 1956) whose presence had been detected by radar. Very brief comments were given about each one, but it was sufficient to indicate that one was the Lakenheath/Bentwaters affair. Yet, interestingly, it suggested there was no visual contact from the intercepting aircraft, which did not gel with the American report of Squadron Leader Wimbledon's recall.

Of course, there must have been a larger file from which this memo was once prepared, and so the MoD clearly did have a report on the case in 1957. What has happened to it since then we do not know. Nevertheless, using all of this information, other data from the PRO, the resources of the BBC—for whom I was then making a TV documentary—and, it has to be said, a very liberal dose of good luck, one of the crew of the intercept was found. He was a now retired RAF officer, and I went to Kent to interview him. He agreed to put his testimony on film.

Even better news was that he had kept in touch with his old colleagues, and, within days, we had located two of the other three crew members aboard the two-man Venom aircraft involved in the intercept. One of these, the other navigator, also agreed to put his statement on camera. The missing crew member (one of the pilots) had emigrated some years before and was not traced.

Eventually, with the help of the BBC and the kind disposition of the USAF, I met up with both navigators back at Lakenheath and they were able to relive the incident. They had been scrambled from another base but flew over Lakenheath and Ely during the intercept. They did not recognize the name of Freddy Wimbledon; but this is not surprising, as he was not stationed on their base but was the night battle center commander for the whole of East Anglia that August evening, and the two jets simply responded to his launch order that had been issued from a remote protected bunker. Remember, at the time, there were fears that World War III was imminent!

We can be completely sure that these three men were aboard the correct aircraft, because both crews had retained their logbooks and these gave full accounts of their movements on the night of August 13–14 at just after midnight when the intercept occurred.

What was really fascinating was that none of these men were aware of the significance of the case. After filing routine reports upon landing, they had not been debriefed in any unusual manner. They had not been interviewed by the staff from any UFO project. In fact, until I told them that their intercept was hailed as one of the classic cases of UFO history, they did not even appreciate that they had been in pursuit of a UFO at all! They just considered it a peculiar radar target.

The aircrew agreed that this had been an unusual intercept, and they had all remembered it very well over the 40 years. It had been unusual because they were sent to intercept a target over land, when in all other instances the object detected by radar was still out over the North Sea, picked up by radar on its way towards the U.K. "Normally, if we were being sent to intercept while something was flying over Cambridge, it would already be way too late!" one navigator explained. Another oddity was the height of the mission. Spy planes do not come in under 4000 feet over land, as this object was doing. It would make them far too vulnerable to being shot down. The RAF crews had never before or since been sent on a mission so close to the ground.

There were a number of discrepancies between their accounts and the official version provided in the USAF files. But they all agreed with each other, so I am confident this is the correct sequence of events.

Neither aircraft developed a malfunction and had to leave the area. One Venom was launched first and saw nothing, so it returned to base. However, the second jet picked up the object before the first had left the area and, thus, it heard the intercept being described and participated indirectly in that sense.

The second Venom did indeed have a radar intercept of the target, but the navigator says that he never saw anything visually. Unfortunately, the pilot concerned has not been interviewed, and it is possible that he did see the object. But the other three witnesses seriously doubt that idea because he never mentioned the fact to them either during the mission or at any time afterwards. Was he perhaps the source of the claims about a visual encounter and is his subsequent silence evidence that he was the only crew member effectively gagged? Given the other men's stories, I find this unlikely.

As for the nature of the target, they came upon it while it was stationary and at no time did it move at speed to fly behind them, as the USAF record claims. Rather, what appears to have occurred is as follows: "We flew towards the object and, because it was stationary and we were moving so fast, the thing was behind us before we could react. We kept flying in circles attempting to home in on the target, but this was not possible. Eventually, low on fuel, we had to return to base."

There is an obvious source of confusion here. The UFO did appear to move from the front to the rear of the aircraft "in an instant," but not because of any intent on its part. It was, as a consequence of the target, hovering dead still in the sky combined with the fast closing speed of the RAF jet.

I did ask the crews whether they thought the target could have been a weather balloon hanging in midair. This would probably have been invisible in the dark. They noted it had been a very clear and well-illuminated night, and although a balloon was not impossible, they did not think they would have missed it. Also, the radar target was very strong and solid—not like a balloon at all. Finding one at 4000 feet that was neither rising nor falling also seemed to them to be rather unlikely.

However, what probably convinced them most that this case was more significant than a balloon was the information conveyed by the USAF ground staff at Lakenheath, which was guiding them by radio during the mission. "They kept telling us about the remarkable motions of the radar target before we had arrived. It was clear that they had never seen anything like this and that it had moved from the North Sea to its hovering position too fast for a balloon."

I also added that Philip Klass, an aviation journalist from Washington, D.C., who has written a number of skeptical books about UFOs, had suggested that the Venom pilot (he erroneously thought it was a single-seater aircraft) had mistaken the light of Orford Ness lighthouse off the coast 20 miles east of Ipswich. This brought great amusement as well as more sober comments, such as "But he has never talked to us" and "We were nowhere near Ipswich" or "We did not even see anything and this thing was 4000 feet up in the air." I am fairly confident that we can rule out Klass's attempted interpretation.

While these aircrews may not have been aware of the importance of that night, it certainly had an impact at the MoD. Ralph Noyes was not working for the air chief marshal by now and his new role had no direct contact with UFO data. But he heard about this case. He could hardly not have done so because, he says, "It was all over the MoD. Everyone was buzzing about that night." Furthermore, he states that:

> Coastal radar had picked up the objects and, at first, they were moving at 4000 mph. A response simply had to be made. Our first response was to check if the radar was showing false returns. It was not. The Venom was the fastest jet aircraft we had at the time. Two aircraft were simultaneously aloft and detected these objects on their own aircraft radar, and the pilot supposedly had a visual sighting. A game went on for 30 minutes. One object came to a dead halt and then made rings round our aircraft.

Noyes reported this account from personal experience before members of the aircrew were traced, and you can see how his recall of the matter generally fits in with their subsequent testimony. You can also see why the matter was so significant to battle-hardened MoD sources. It had multiple radar trackings from the ground, and visual sightings from the ground looking up and from the air looking down. The chances of some kind of illusion being responsible appear negligible.

Noyes states:

> Those events certainly caused a major inquiry and the Ministry buzzed with this story for weeks. Inquiries were held. Nobody was found to be to blame. Nobody had mishandled equipment. No damage had been done. No expla-

nation was found. Something had gone on and we did not know what. We had to assume retrospectively that it was a defense threat.

And yet, the MoD would have you believe that only 5 years later it destroyed all its records about this incident and now knows absolutely nothing about it.

You might find it even harder to believe this claim when you realize that 2 weeks later something similar happened all over again. Only this time, it occurred in broad daylight.

I first heard about this repeat run on December 30, 1991, when a man called Wilbur Wright wrote to say that he had enjoyed one of my books. At first, I suspected a joke, given that he was claiming to be a pilot and there can hardly be a more famous name in aviation history. But he was sincere, although Wilbur was a nickname that over the years had become adopted and now even figured on his headed notepaper. Wright was his real surname.

I exchanged information with him, then scoured the PRO looking for records to back up his story. A colleague, statistician Paul Fuller, lived near Wilbur's home in retirement and agreed to interview the witness. These are the sources used for this report.

Wilbur had joined the RAF prior to World War II. In 1944, while based at RAF Holme on Spalding Moor in Yorkshire, he had been walking on a country lane alongside the base, around midnight on a warm evening, when he saw something very odd: lights at very low altitude moving over the field to his left. They formed a large circle and were multi-colored. The whole ensemble was almost on the ground but rolled through the air towards him, rotating as it did so. A dark sphere appeared to surround the lights, but this was detectable only because the brilliant starlit sky was briefly obscured as this invisible sheath moved with the rotating ball. A sound like the rushing of wind accompanied the object as it gradually drifted across the field and vanished into the distance. This was clearly some quite bizarre natural phenomenon, the likes of which he would never see again.

A dozen years later, now a flight lieutenant based at Odiham on the south coast, Wilbur had put this experience out of his mind. On August 30, 1956, his task was to take Javelin number 627 on a mission practicing intercepts. Along with him were a navigator (Flying Officer Wallington) and a second aircraft with two crew members. It was a clear day with unlimited visibility, and they were flying over the Solent between the Isle of Wight and the mainland at 45,000 feet. Wright explained:

> We were flying west in line astern before separating for interception. The other Javelin was the target aircraft. We each turned through 45° in differ-ent directions, flying courses at 90° to each other. We were using airborne radar with a range of over 20 miles and a height indication. I was flying 627 north-west before turning southwest for interception when I saw a disk-

shaped object off my starboard wingtip. It was ahead of me. My navigator obtained a radar return at 19 miles. So I used my fingernail to get an estimate of the object's size. This led to later calculation of the object's size having a diameter exceeding 600 feet.

With this discovery, Wilbur alerted the other Javelin, which immediately saw the object. Then they called ground control and were quickly given permission to abandon the exercise and intercept the target instead. Although Wilbur did not know it at the time, MoD radar on the coast at Sopley near Bournemouth had picked up the arrival of the UFO from over the Channel. Wright continued:

> We turned north towards the object on our right wing, but it had apparently slowed right down and was now maintaining its position. The other Javelin had now caught up with me and was about half a mile behind. The second pilot confirmed both the visual and air radar sighting.
>   We both banked steeply and confirmed the object was at 15 miles dead ahead on radar. It appeared slightly larger in visual size. At full power, we then closed the distance to 10 miles on air radar and the object was now clearly seen as a metallic gray in appearance. I obtained a second size estimate using my little finger and the windscreen, and the diameter of this thing was exceeding 1000 feet. At 8 miles, the object suddenly climbed vertically too fast for our radar to track, but I estimated its rate of climb at 5 miles per second. Soon after it vanished.

If these estimates of size and speed are correct, then there was nothing flying at that time that could have caused this sighting. The speed and acceleration were way beyond any aircraft of 1956 and would rival a rocket ship of today. Aside from hearing confirmation of the radar contact at Sopley, the four crew members were told not to report the matter to anyone, their colleagues included, and to ask no more questions. However, they were to complete written statements for the Air Ministry.

Hunting for evidence on this case has been as frustrating as it was expected to be. Following leads from the pilot, all the records of his squadron (the 46th) were checked at the PRO. Air 27/2779 revealed details of the unit and contained photographs of the Javelins, the staff, and even Wright himself. There were references to various events that had occurred around the time of the sighting, plus notes about the medals that were awarded to Wright.

But there was nothing whatsoever about the UFO incident.

Even the official archivist for Odiham squadrons who agreed to search for records for me was surprised that this report was not there, because everything else seemed to be. This may well be further evidence that the UFO report bypassed the normal channels and went to the covert location from whence no files ever seem to emerge. It is a bit like a bureaucratic Bermuda Triangle.

Wilbur Wright was able to help me somewhat. He sketched the incident and provided a copy of his flight log in which details of his mission were recorded. So once again we have no reasonable doubt that this incident took place. It is just not in the archives of the British government, showing either their complete inadequacy or else the pretense of their claim not to have unreleased files located elsewhere.

Although Ralph Noyes does not recall the case being discussed at the ministry in 1956, he was shown evidence secured by a gun camera that was fitted to both Javelins in this incident. You may recall that when Noyes took the UFO desk job in 1968, the gun camera film was screened to him. Because the year 1956 was cited during his briefing, he had always assumed that the footage was taken during that Lakenheath/Bentwaters case. But the aircrew in that intercept denies taking any such footage. Now that we know there was a second intercept during that very month, we have a new potential source for this evidence that, you will not be amazed to hear, the MoD denies having any record of at all. Nick Pope, when head of the MoD UFO project between 1991 and 1994, claims that a major search was mounted examining all possible sources. There was no footage. Yet again came the suggestion that it had been "lost" or had "deteriorated" and so was "destroyed."

This gun camera film was kept between 1956 and 1968. We also know that in 1967 Home Secretary Merlyn Rees demanded the retention of all public UFO records, following a debate in the House of Commons; it seems improbable that such vital evidence would be destroyed in view of such a ministerial order. Even if the film itself vanished, or became unstable, surely some analysis of it was made and recorded. Are we to believe that all records have conveniently disappeared?

Was the film taken during the Solent episode? It may well have been. This is how Noyes described what he was shown: "It was a rather fuzzy gray spherical object.... Nothing like a flying saucer in popular imagination. Not a fully structured craft, but a fuzzy object behaving with the appearance of intent and certainly moving at great speed and using the kind of acceleration of which no ordinary vehicle should be capable." This sounds familiar.

Yet Ralph Noyes tells me that it was neither the Lakenheath nor the Isle of Wight events, but a third case, which followed a few months afterwards, that caused the MoD to finally shift policy. Unfortunately, whatever happened was not for him to know, as he was not then involved in UFO activity investigation. But he heard about the ramifications that were discussed in Whitehall.

This event was the only one of the cases in this chapter that generated open public discussion at the time. There were press stories and the Air Ministry hastily explained it away. However, the release of records on the matter to the PRO has emphatically shown that this solution was nothing but a sham. It was clearly invented to silence the media. The truth is that the ministry knew its explanation was a nonstarter even as it told the press that it was probably the solution to this case!

On April 4, 1957, several radar systems across northern Britain recorded the passage of an unknown object. It flew close to West Freugh in Dumfries and Galloway—one of the main RAF bases in southwest Scotland where today Stealth aircraft have been known to be located.

That the MoD took this case so seriously—more seriously than any other in this chapter, I am told—has always puzzled me because this was a radar-only encounter. To my knowledge, no visual sighting occurred. Or, at least, if it did then this has never been made public. Given the intercepts launched in Suffolk and over the Solent just months before, I am tempted to wonder if no such follow-up would have taken place during this experience. Is there a missing component to this 1957 case?

The reason why news of the radar tracking of the object reached the press is that some of the officers manning the radar stations were civilians. Indeed, such was the concern at West Freugh that a civil defense alert for a possible enemy attack was set in motion. This was hard to keep quiet.

However, the media got little out of the military. Indeed, the West Freugh base commander, Wing Commander Walter Whitworth, freely admitted to reporters, "I have been ordered by the Air Ministry to say nothing about the object." This was swiftly followed with the official ministry "suggestion" that the object was a weather balloon, which was gratefully endorsed as the answer in future statements. That rapidly killed the story and stopped the press from digging too deeply.

The disturbing truth is revealed by the records at the time. The radar at Balscalloch reported that the object was higher than 70,000 feet, and this was greater than the capabilities of any British aircraft. So there was great concern and the Air Ministry ordered that this news be covered up. That it was not a balloon was suggested by the evidence from the written statements of the radar crews. "It made a very sharp turn to the southeast, at the same time increasing speed," one said. A balloon cannot make sharp turns. It has to drift with the wind, which was not blowing southeast that day. Nor can it move at 240 mph, which was the speed at which the object was tracked leaving British airspace.

As the MoD report concluded, days after telling the public not to worry as the UFO was probably just a balloon, "There were not known to be any aircraft in the vicinity nor were there any meteorological balloons. Even if balloons had been in the area, these would not account for the sudden change of direction and the movement at high speed against the prevailing wind."

True. So why mislead people into thinking that this was the answer without sharing such damning evidence with them at the same time? That the MoD clearly did cover things up is proven by a then secret memo from the intelligence staff at the Air Ministry dated May 1957. It discusses the fact that the press had discovered the West Freugh case but not the two events that you have just read about. Those cases from only 8 months earlier had been successfully obscured.

The report says, "It is unfortunate that the Wigtownshire radar incident fell into the hands of the press. The two other radar incidents have not been made public and reached us by means of official secret channels. We suggest that the Secretary of State does not specifically refer to these incidents as radar sightings." It then proposes the careful wording of any public statements so that the government does not actually lie about these hidden cases while ensuring that nobody finds out that they have happened! Such paranoia must give good cause to believe that these cases were important.

These control tactics were also adopted in the U.S., where military midair encounters were happening every bit as often. A good example occurred on December 17, 1956, over Itazuke, Japan.

The starting point will seem familiar. Two pilots were practicing radar-controlled intercepts with each jet taking turns as the "target." As this was happening, a strange blip was picked up on radar and seemed to show an object the size of a B-29 bomber around 20 miles away. Ground radar was not tracking the object so the aircraft requested permission to investigate. One jet closed at 700 mph on the target, and at a range of about 8 miles a white fuzzy object appeared at the indicated position. The pilot locked on his airborne radar and continued to close, but then a mass of interference scrambled his radar and he lost the object. Using secret countermeasure equipment, he fought the jamming, and had intermittent radar trackings until the interference returned more strongly and he lost the object again.

The UFO was still visible and, at 5 miles, resembled a golden disk that was executing a turn. It was huge and estimated as at least 250 feet in diameter by the pilot. But then it shot away at phenomenal speed, heading vertically upwards. Radar became effective again as it left and noted a speed of 2100 mph as the thing flew skyward, but "this was an estimate since the rate of departure was faster than the onboard radar could track."

The comparison between this case and the one on the other side of the planet over the Solent just 3½ months earlier needs no elaboration. It is simply stunning.

Richard Hall, a UFOlogist with the American UFO group NICAP, received a report on the Japanese case a few months later via a friendly officer with the USAF in Asia. He sent the UFO group a then secret internal intelligence agency investigation report. But the U.S. government refused to comment and it was to be 20 years, in 1977, before its copy of the report was finally forced onto the public record through the Freedom of Information Act. This confirmed the events were real and established as correct all the details reported covertly to Richard Hall back in 1957.

But it did something else. The publicly sanctioned report withheld key details that were contained in the (as yet still unreleased) intelligence study. The USAF file seems to have been carefully phrased so as to boost the slant that the Pentagon was trying to put on the matter.

For example, the intelligence study leaked to Hall had noted that the failure of ground radar to track the object "should not be given much

99 4390

weight," explaining that a special system called IFF (Identified Friend or Foe) was used to track the aircraft and this meant the radar was not set to detect objects that did not use such electronic tags. The USAF evaluation nonetheless stresses the lack of ground radar support, as if to infer that airborne radar had to be faulty, because otherwise ground radar would surely have seen the same target. By twisting the facts, the UFO is publicly downgraded.

These moves to distort public awareness of UFOs should be judged in conjunction with the CIA study in Washington of January 1953 to which I referred earlier; one of their policy decisions was to order Blue Book to control public thinking on UFOs by downplaying the significance of any unsolved case and fiddling the facts where necessary to stress possible solutions, however unlikely those explanations may have seemed.

Very clearly those plans were put into rapid action on both sides of the Atlantic.

So, in the officially released U.S. file, we see the case explained away, ignoring the evidence ranged against that theory. Meanwhile, the intelligence study, which is not meant for public consumption, argues the matter very differently and indicates the true strengths of the data.

Precisely the same *modus operandi* seems to have been employed by the MoD when it sought to wish away the West Freugh episode in front of the press, while the unreleased evidence proves that the information made public was, at best, an extremely optimistic view of what had taken place.

Indeed, it is worth noting that in the data released to the PRO at Kew one usually finds the summaries and comments of uninvolved minions who sit behind desks in Whitehall. Rarely, if ever, are there copies of the intelligence staff investigation reports into the same cases. Given the evidence just discussed, we can be forgiven for suspecting that this is because those intelligence reports would give a truer and more alarming picture of what was really going on. Truer at least than the selectively edited version that the government chose to make public—often simply told to bureaucrats at the "UFO desk" who would not be expected to question matters too deeply.

CLOC Library
220 E. Main, Box 668
Magnolia, AR 71753

6 CIVILIAN STRIFE

Although governments could attempt to suppress information regarding military encounters in midair, only economic pressures could shield events involving passenger aircraft from public view. As noted, these pressures have grown over the years. But as the 1950s progressed, most of them were not yet formalized. As a result, we do have accounts of some remarkable cases. I will focus in this chapter on just two of them to give the flavor of what was taking place. But each represents dozens of other cases that are on record.

For example, on March 9, 1957, the delightfully named Captain Matthew Van Winkle was in charge of Pan America 257, a trans-eastern seaboard flight. Van Winkle was taking his aircraft down through what were drizzling skies, heading towards his destination in Miami, a couple of hundred miles to the south. He had deliberately steered his DC-6 aircraft away from its planned route, as one of Florida's bothersome thunderstorms was raging a few miles inland. In those days, pilots avoided such buffeting winds and unpredictable lightning bursts whenever possible, as their aircraft lacked the protection they have today.

Having moved a little out to the east in order to loop back in towards his landing, the captain was just about to call Miami tower and report his position when he spotted a bright light heading towards him from the east. He estimated it was coming from the coast and moving towards land at considerable speed.

His immediate, and quite rational, thought was that he had strayed too far off course and was in restricted airspace that he knew surrounded the coastal missile ranges at Cape Canaveral. In 1957, the space program was barely under way but military testing had begun here, and pilots were mindful to avoid it. Van Winkle assumed that a military interceptor had been sent to investigate why he was off the normal flying lane.

However, the closer the light got to the DC-6, the more it was obvious that this explanation would not work. He and his copilot were now looking at a round object with a tinge of green within what was otherwise pure white. It was brilliant like a magnesium flare and yet heading in what was undoubtedly a controlled flight. In fact, it was heading straight for the crowded passenger aircraft.

Terrified now that it was a missile launched against him, Van Winkle responded as any captain would, taking the aircraft out of the way. He made a steep climb and then had to perform an emergency maneuver in order to prevent stalling his engines. As he did so, the aircraft went through 1500 feet in a matter of seconds. However, it was successful and threw off the marauding "missile," to his intense relief.

Unfortunately, the act was not without consequence. The seat-belt order had not yet been given to passengers in preparation for landing, and some were not protected against the unexpectedly severe motion. Several were tossed about the cabin like rag dolls, and there were a number of relatively minor and a few more serious injuries sustained.

Van Winkle called ahead to Miami and asked them to have a fleet of ambulances standing by, while explaining the cause of the few seconds of terror in the sky which Pan Am 257 had just endured. The ground controllers were baffled. He had not strayed as far off course as he had thought, and there was no conceivable reason why a missile attack would have occurred.

Naturally, the FAA (Federal Aviation Authority)—then known as the Civil Aeronautics Board—had to launch one of its earliest "near-miss" inquiries of the type that today are becoming alarmingly frequent. This had the support of the military and missile ranges in attempting to discover what had taken place. But the investigation failed to do that.

There were no military aircraft in the area. No missiles had been launched at the time and so the pilot could not even have seen one accidentally flying past. Several other aircraft over Florida confirmed that they had seen a flash of light. From this, the eventual suggestion of the investigation was that Van Winkle had overreacted in the presence of a meteor. He had understandably responded with instinct to try to protect his passengers, but, in fact, the blazing light was miles away from him and never a threat.

As we have seen in cases such as the Montgomery, Alabama, episode from 1948, it is not impossible that this took place. However, Van Winkle never agreed, and had support from several of his fellow pilots who considered him a scapegoat used to cover up the fact that something really had zipped across the sky and put the DC-6 at risk. To them—and I dare say the passengers—Van Winkle was a hero and did not deserve to be chastised because the authorities could not figure out what was going on.

Unsaid in 1957—indeed, unsaid until the Freedom of Information Act released details some 20 years later—was that the U.S. government knew all about the sort of "green fireball" that had shot towards this Pan Am aircraft. They knew about it because such things had plagued their own secret research and rocketry facilities in the New Mexico desert during 1949 and 1950.

In fact, the reports had centered around Sandia Labs, Los Alamos, and White Sands, where research had begun into intercontinental ballistic missiles that were the first steps towards the firing of rockets into space.

It is important to stress that the many reports of these "green fireballs" in such sensitive airspace were not being made by local townsfolk who could not tell a meteor from a meat pie. They were coming from scientists at state-of-the-art facilities. They included Professor Lincoln La Paz from the University of New Mexico at Albuquerque. One of the world's leading experts in meteor activity, he had been brought in to investigate what kind of meteor these objects could be. He quickly saw one for himself and realized that they were not meteors at all.

La Paz convinced the government to invest large sums in a top-secret research experiment known as Project Twinkle. But it took the support of one of the Pentagon's leading scientific advisors, geophysicist Dr. Joseph Kaplan, to get the money. His report to Washington was that the evidence was "unsettling." The then top-secret reports on these matters spoke of high-level meetings headed "Protection of Vital Installations." The Pentagon was taking the threat of these green fireballs over such sensitive research sites very seriously indeed.

Twinkle used sophisticated cameras with diffraction gratings and spectrographs to analyze the light emitted by these fast-moving green spheres. This established the very strange nature of what was happening, including the fact that the green color came from a high copper content. Copper dust scattered on the ground beneath the fireballs' flight paths was found during the fruitless efforts by La Paz and his team to recover meteorite debris that would prove these things were natural phenomena.

One description of the green fireball was offered by a military pilot who saw one above the Los Alamos area. It was given to the UFO project staff at Wright Patterson (which was largely deemed not to have a need to know and was never a part of Project Twinkle). The pilot asked the USAF intelligence staff to imagine a fluorescent-green-painted tennis ball hurled at you from some distance at very great speed. It was an image that Captain Van Winkle would undoubtedly recognize.

The green fireballs were the subject of intense debate at numerous secret meetings convened at Los Alamos in 1948 and 1949. These involved some of the leading physicists of the day, such as Professor Edward Teller. Nobody knew what was going on. The discussion centered on whether these things were intelligently controlled—as feared by many, because of their apparent concentration around scientific research centers and the way they seemed to move elsewhere as soon as monitoring equipment was set up at one "hot spot." They even moved back as soon as that equipment was shifted!

Others felt that they were some unknown natural phenomenon—possibly a spinoff from the atomic energy research that was exploding bombs in the New Mexico desert. Teller suggested some rare type of ionized plasma forming in the atmosphere—a debate still raging today when regularly-occurring UFO phenomena are being seen, such as those in the Hessdalen Valley of Norway.

La Paz told Captain Edward Ruppelt some years later, after the project had concluded, that he was still not sure himself whether these things were natural in origin but, given their characteristics, he was doubtful of this. Even so, he "sure hoped" they were natural phenomena!

This was shortly before the Pan Am DC-6 saw one over Florida.

It cannot be irrelevant that this 1957 "green fireball" case happened in and around Cape Canaveral, where the center of attention had recently switched from the New Mexico desert. Here, the rockets that had been built to the west were now going to be flown spaceward, and this was to become the one place where all mankind's efforts to reach out into the universe would be concentrated.

The U.S. government must have known of this "coincidence" when it allowed the Pan Am captain to be pilloried. Only the government's desire for secrecy about these matters led to his being used as an excuse to silence the media. No wonder such tactics led to a greater and greater desire by disgruntled pilots not to speak out about UFO encounters.

There is a classic scene in the Steven Spielberg movie *Close Encounters of the Third Kind* where, almost in the first few frames, an aircraft encounters strange lights over a Midwestern town and is asked repeatedly by ground control whether it wishes to report a UFO. Ground control had tracked the object on radar behaving in extraordinary fashion, but after the flight-deck crew members have taken a few moments to consider the implications of going public, they emphatically state that they do not wish to report what they have just seen. The relieved radar operators express the same sentiments, so that another case is quietly buried from public view.

As with many other aspects of this Spielberg movie, that scene is based firmly upon reality. I have seen it happen within airlines and air traffic control centers. It is so common, thanks to the decision of power brokers, not to play fair with the public. They know that something strange really is flying through our air space, but they prefer to preserve the credibility of pilots and airlines, and possibly risk the safety of passengers, rather than openly say so or admit to what they know is behind the scenes.

Incidentally, green fireballs are an international phenomenon and are still being seen. Between 1980 and 1983, for example, there were many of them around Rendlesham Forest in Suffolk, which was a scene of a major close encounter involving military personnel. This is discussed in great depth in my book *UFO Crash Landing: Friend or Foe?* (Cassell, 1998), and you will see from this that the location has chilling comparisons with New Mexico 50 years ago. Aside from the adjacent Sizewell nuclear power plant, Orford Ness—focus of the recent British activity—was where radar was first developed and where, at the time the green fireballs flew, some top-secret research involving the NSA (National Security Agency) was under way. These experiments used high-intensity radiation and produced beams of energy that went all the way into space. They also had side effects that were causing intense electrical interference akin to the electronic pulse phenomenon following a nuclear explosion. This burst of energy can render all electronic equipment temporarily useless. On the Suffolk coast, the intelligence agencies were engaged in similarly disturbing research just as the green fireballs appeared there. Midair encounters took place in this location as well (see page 116). The August 1956 "Lakenheath" affair began here too.

Similar electronic scrambling occurred around New Mexico during their green fireball wave. Indeed, between October 31 and November 6, 1957, no fewer than thirty-six cases were recorded by police, sheriffs' departments, and emergency services. Cars and trucks lost power to engine and lights as a ball of energy flew towards them, crackling with power. Some witnesses reported hair standing on end, skin tingling, and heat pouring from the ball of light when it approached within a few feet. These occurrences were all concentrated around the area of Texas and New Mexico. One witness was an engineer at the local top secret missile plant and another two were security police guarding atomic silos.

On the night of November 2–3 (when no fewer than twenty of the thirty-six incidents occurred), thousands of miles away in the USSR, the first-ever launch took place of a life form from earth into space. Laika the dog stunned the world by riding on Sputnik into orbit. You can well imagine how this latest "coincidence" of both time and space established doubts in the minds of many who knew about the green fireballs as to whether they really were natural phenomena. The activities of these phenomena seemed suspiciously too well-designed and to be under intelligent control.

Decades later, when communism fell and ended the suppression of evidence on these matters, it was discovered that the Soviet rocket and space complex at Plesetsk was plagued by sightings of fuzzy, green, cloudlike masses that floated overhead during its own research. There is obviously a point when coincidence simply ceases to be a reasonable suggestion.

The same energy-sapping events have occurred in and around Rendlesham Forest during more recent fireball sightings. They were also recorded during the 1950s in the vicinity surrounding Captain Van Winkle's green fireball encounter in Florida. At West Palm Beach, just south of Canaveral, a classic episode saw a scout master attacked by energy bolts from an object hovering at rooftop height. This not only burned holes through his cap like "electrical spikes," but cooked the grass beneath his feet in a very strange way. The USAF investigation found the roots were charred, but the stems above ground were unaffected, suggesting a kind of microwave pulse was associated. This was something years from being understood by the science of the 1950s.

The research labs in New Mexico, the launch site in Florida, the USSR space center in Plesetsk, and the NSA energy research experiments on Orford Ness in Suffolk, England, were all affected by some phenomenon that glowed green, caused electrical tingling heat, and had the ability to stop electrical systems from functioning. It has to be accepted that there is a connection here.

Surely this is effective proof that something has been repeatedly witnessed that is directly connected with these research sites. Either it is—as UFOlogists have contended for years—a surveillance device spying on our most sensitive facilities, or it is a natural phenomenon. If it is a natural phenomenon, then we do not understand how or why it happens, but it is presumably a consequence of our dangerous research into high-powered propulsion and nuclear weapons. Perhaps we are destabilizing the balance of our own atmosphere in some way and creating some kind of briefly living powerhouse of plasma energy. This may be a more terrifying prospect than alien spy craft.

If indeed these energy balls are floating through our airspace—potentially into the paths of civilian aircraft, such as Pan Am Flight 257—then they are, in my mind, very disconcerting and desperately require open investigation. Any agency that is holding back data from the public on such matters is putting civilian lives at risk. That is completely unacceptable.

Little green men snooping from afar will be of huge academic interest. Little green fireballs charged with electrical forces that can cut out engines, scramble electronics, and churn out powerful heat waves are a serious threat to life on earth. They are especially dangerous to anyone who is flying through the air encased in a metal box that is kept aloft thanks to computers, electronics, and the very systems that are vulnerable to attack by this phenomenon.

That some of these midair encounters clearly involve a strange natural phenomenon is even better illustrated by perhaps the most documented civil aircraft encounter from the 1950s. It was reported at the time, because six flight-deck crews saw it, along with flight attendants and around twenty-nine passengers. All of this happened in daylight and lasted 20 minutes. Nobody could have stopped this case from entering the public domain even if they had tried, although there is indeed good evidence that there was an attempt to limit what the public came to find out.

There is a truly fascinating hidden story behind the brief press accounts of the day. This has been compiled thanks to recent interviews with the captain, his navigator, and the chief stewardess, all now retired, along with the meager details on the public record—hardly any of which have ever been released by the British government. Thankfully, the USAF did its own on-site study and so its data has been released through the Freedom of Information Act. The true story of the evening, when a BOAC Stratocruiser encountered something in the air over Canada, can now be told.

The Stratocruiser was call sign Sierra Charlie (G-ALSC) and was on a flight from New York to London on June 29–30, 1954. As was common in those early days of commercial air travel, the passengers were not tourists but businessmen, which explains why none were eagerly filming the phenomenon through the windows as many would no doubt be doing today. The navigator recalls that one passenger claimed to take film footage of the event, but the pilot doubts this really happened since that film has never surfaced. If such evidence was captured, it has been secured by the powers that be—probably the covert UFO research project then based at Farnborough. As you will see, it is quite possible that such a confiscation of evidence actually did take place.

Sierra Charlie was on Flight 510 from what is now JFK Airport in New York to London Heathrow. In command was Captain James Howard, First Officer Lee Boyd (a Canadian), and Navigator H. McDonnell. There were also engineers and radio officers on board this gigantic transatlantic aircraft. The flight left New York at 5:03 p.m. local time on June 29 for what was in those days a very lengthy expedition that would take 15 hours. As was not uncommon for a run that Howard had made dozens of times before, he chose to plan to land at Goose Bay, Labrador, to refuel and tackle the leg across the Atlantic with full capacity.

About 45 minutes after take-off, something unusual happened. Sierra Charlie was put into a holding pattern south of Boston. In those days of relatively free skies, this was extremely rare, and after the unexplained hold had lasted some time, Howard requested permission to continue, as his fuel was getting low. As he notes, the only likely reason for such a hold was unscheduled traffic ahead. Flights were carefully planned, and this was therefore very uncommon and not usually so long lasting. At the time, he never really connected this with later events, but now he wonders if it was somehow linked.

The Stratocruiser was soon given permission to reroute out of Cape Cod before rejoining the planned track well to the north. This meant that by the time it crossed the St. Lawrence River in Southern Canada, it was running a little late.

At this point, James Howard first noted that there was something off to the left of the aircraft and brought it to the attention of the others on the flight deck. All spent several minutes watching the phenomenon and trying to decide what it might be. However, none of them had seen anything like it, and—despite another 50 years of combined service between them after 1954—none ever saw anything like it again.

As they crossed the river, they were at 19,000 feet, with scattered clouds about 5000 feet below. It was after 9 p.m. local time and the sun was low in the northwest on its way towards setting. Howard describes what he saw in the following terms:

> It was a lovely summer's evening. Near Seven Islands, I was looking down to the left-hand side of the airplane and I saw through broken cloud that something was moving through the breaks. It was some miles away, but as we moved on into Labrador, we left all the clouds behind us and were in clear air. These things now seemed to be climbing up towards our own altitude while about 3 miles away. There was one large one and six small ones. Sometimes three were in front and three behind the big object. Then they would change position relative to the big one. The big one also appeared to gradually change its shape.

The captain adds that the large mass was sometimes like an oval, other times a triangle, and occasionally a sausage. It was "not a hazy object and had clean-cut edges. The color was dull gray."

One of the suggestions from the flight deck was that the small, dot-like objects were "flak," but this was soon dismissed when the retinue paced the aircraft. The prospect of a balloon or flock of birds, also mooted, went the same way, as the aircraft was traveling at 270 mph, and they had the object alongside them for 20 minutes. No birds could maintain station at that speed for what amounted to around 80 miles.

The navigator, McDonnell, reports how he was taking bearings on the thing. It covered a huge arc of sky, and you needed almost the width of your hand held at arm's length to cover it. The crew could not decide whether this indicated enormous real size or close proximity. They hoped the former! McDonnell also feels that the shape-changing effect was more an illusion caused by the setting sun reflected off the object's surface. He had more opportunity to watch it than James Howard, who had to concentrate on flying the plane, and he saw the effect was like shadows on a pencil, causing it to seem different in shape from various perspectives.

At this point, Daphne Webster, chief flight attendant, arrived on the flight deck because large numbers of the passengers on the left side of the aircraft had seen the thing and were naturally both curious and concerned to know what it was. She could not tell them and hoped that someone in the cockpit could. She had not expected the crew to be just as bemused.

Daphne was first attracted to the UFO by the commotion amidst the passengers. Looking out of the port side she saw "one big object, cigar shaped, and six smaller ones that were going around, under and over, and behind the big one in constant motion. Sometimes the shape of the big one stretched out."

When Captain Howard realized that the passengers were becoming slightly alarmed (the air stewardess notes there was some lighthearted banter about martians at one point), he decided to ask for a radio message to be sent to Goose Bay.

There was no airborne radar on civilian aircraft in those days, and so they had to rely on ground stations for guidance. Goose Bay claimed only to be tracking the Stratocruiser but agreed to vector a Canadian Air Force F-94 that happened to be in the area on patrol. Howard was switched to a military frequency and put in direct contact with the pilot of the jet fighter—code-named Pinto One—and asked to direct it towards the strange object.

The jet was seen to approach and fly directly over Sierra Charlie, heading towards the UFO formation. But even as it closed in, the flight-deck crew all saw the same change. Howard says, "The little ones seemed to huddle together into the big one and finally disappear inside. Then the large one appeared to go away from us—or, at least, it became smaller. Then it simply disappeared before the F-94 got to it." However, Captain Howard saw merely the latter stages of the whole event. McDonnell was the only witness to see the little dots enter the large craft (he says three went in from the top and three from below). This motion has since been likened to a mother ship and several babies, and the terminology has often been used in science fiction stories. But it is exceptionally rare in UFO events.

Indeed, I have only ever personally come across one similar case—where a large oval object was seen hovering about Werneth Low, a hill in the Pennines near Oldham, Lancashire. This was one day just before Christmas 1974 at 7:30 a.m., just as the sun was rising. The link with the sun may well be significant, given that it was setting over Goose Bay. As in the Goose Bay affair, the large oval changed shape to become a sausagelike object with one blunt end. From out of here, several small round objects were emitted by the large object "like soap bubbles being blown from a hoop." The woman who reported this to me lived in an isolated house on the side of the hill. There is little doubt that this sighting is very similar to what the crew of the BOAC Stratocruiser saw 20 years earlier—a case the Werneth Low woman had never heard about.

Back over Canada, the F-94 pilot confirmed having radar contact with the BOAC aircraft but never mentioned any radar lock-on with the target. In fact, he said very little to the civilian crew as he was vectored towards the objects.

With the UFO now gone, Howard had to focus his attention on descent into Goose Bay. They landed here about 25 minutes later, at 9:45 p.m. local time. Darkness was setting in as they did so.

Upon landing, the BOAC crew were almost immediately greeted by several people introduced as intelligence officers working for the USAF. Although all of the flight-deck crew and several passengers were briefly met, Captain James Howard and First Officer Lee Boyd were separated from the rest and taken to a room for a debriefing session.

McDonnell says that he saw Boyd and Howard led away by both Canadian and USAF officials and that after their return both men were reluctant to say what had happened. While the navigator awaited their return, the USAF took away his flight logs—something he had never known to happen in all his years with BOAC. McDonnell was quizzed about the precise bearings and headings of the aircraft. Later, the pilot and first officer merely intimated that they had undergone a "grilling."

Daphne O'Reilly (as she is now known) had to supervise the USAF questioning of stewardesses and passengers—none of whom were told anything about what was happening. "They glossed it over with the passengers" is how she puts it. There was a long questionnaire (probably the form used by Project Blue Book at Wright Patterson AFB) that the crew members were all asked to help fill in.

The instant "take-over" by the USAF in this case is interesting. The event occurred to a British aircraft while in Canadian airspace. Why did the U.S. government take command so quickly? This is one reason why Captain Howard wonders if the earlier hold near Boston was significant. He later received a letter from a doctor who was camping on a lake shore in northern Massachusetts along with his wife. They were north of the point where Sierra Charlie was held by American air traffic control. This was just south of the Canadian border and on the route the aircraft was prevented from taking before being diverted out to sea. In the letter, written after the doctor saw media stories about Howard's sighting, this man described how he and his wife had witnessed a very similar phenomenon pass over their New England campsite and move towards Labrador. It was making a soft buzzing or humming noise.

All these years later, James Howard is more forthcoming about the USAF intelligence interviews that he and Lee Boyd underwent. "The USAF seemed rather blasé about the whole thing, frankly," he notes. "The officer doing the interview gave me the impression that this sort of thing happened—if not daily, then weekly. He told me of several recent sightings over Labrador."

Because of all of this questioning, the flight was put even further behind schedule and it left Goose Bay at about 11:15 p.m.—after around an hour was added to its stopover. On the final leg across the Atlantic, Captain Howard prepared for what he expected was a new round of questions in London and wrote out a full report and drew sketches of what they had seen. According to McDonnell, they arrived in London from Goose Bay after a further uneventful 9 hours and 13 minutes. Touchdown was at 12:27 p.m. GMT. Howard was called away from the airport soon after landing by the Air Ministry, which presumably had now been notified of the events by either the U.S. or Canadian governments. This time he went alone.

It was some time before the two men flew together again, but when they met up in India, McDonnell asked Howard what the Air Ministry had told him. The captain reportedly insisted that he could not talk about the matter. "You know the score," he said to the navigator.

Yet, surprisingly, BOAC was not to order the crew into silence. Admittedly, the case was already too public by the time they were home in Britain, but the airline seems to have used it quite effectively to its advantage. Daphne O'Reilly recalls how she was asked to appear on U.S. talk shows, including one with comic book character Captain Marvel. The caped superhero crooned about little green men. She took it all as good fun and an experience to be remembered for the rest of her life. But it seems oddly out of phase with today's reaction by airlines, which would probably threaten to fire employees who put themselves and their company in such an embarrassing public light on TV.

Captain Howard also made a famous public appearance in which he sketched the events on a blackboard propped up alongside Sierra Charlie. The stiff-upper-lip commentator explained all of this to the accompaniment of cheerful marching music. Only in Britain could such a performance have been given—seemingly stage-managed by BOAC!

Perhaps the way in which this case slipped out of the airline's hands and provoked such merriment may have been a reason why impositions were later placed upon civilian pilots. Several have referred back to this case as a watershed. The public relations disaster many thought it proved for BOAC ensured other airlines would not do the same thing in future.

Indeed, Howard notes that he handed in his report early the next morning before senior staff was on duty, and the secretary gave it to the press before BOAC really had a chance to stop this from happening. He had never intended it to become a news story, but was trying to play it by the book and to be careful about any public statements—just as the Air Ministry had suggested he should do.

James Howard says that he was surprised no copy or findings from the USAF intelligence investigation ever found their way to the BOAC head office. He was perhaps expecting rather too much from military-civilian cooperation here, especially where UFOs were concerned.

Daphne O'Reilly adds some very interesting details about the interrogation by the British authorities. After being quizzed before they left Heathrow, she was later asked to go to the Air Ministry with Lee Boyd and James Howard. They asked her if she often saw things—whether she was psychic and if she had witnessed other life forms, such as fairies. It was a serious interrogation, she believes, but such questions in 1954 seem utterly remarkable.

After further questions by the government, all three were introduced to a Professor Black—a psychiatrist! He asked much about their eyesight and perception, and speculated about optical illusions and light refractions. There was an eclipse of the sun on the day that they landed, and some media sources connected this with the sighting. But the eclipse was long after the UFO had disappeared. Professor Black told the crew he was satisfied there was no connection.

Then, quite remarkably, the government requested Daphne and the pilots to undergo hypnosis! This would be the first time that such a technique was ever used following a UFO encounter, and 1954 was astonishingly early for any official investigation to think about using the idea. So far as UFOlogists have known until now, it was first employed 9 years later when a Boston psychiatrist, Dr. Benjamin Simon, hypnotized two witnesses and asked them to "relive their memories" of a UFO seen above the White Mountains of New Hampshire.

Daphne says of the process employed by Dr. Black, "We were all individually hypnotized and went through the encounter again this way. We were told that we did not have to do it if we did not wish to do so, and it was being suggested just in case there was anything that we had seen but we did not realize that we had seen it."

Regardless of how controversial hypnotic regression is today (and I am highly doubtful of it as a constructive way to investigate such cases), I do find it an incredible revelation that so long ago such a sophisticated method was being employed by a government department investigating UFOs. The questions about psychic abilities and the seeing of fairies are also bizarre, since only quite recently would they be considered valid lines of inquiry by the UFO community. In 1954, even UFO buffs would have found them utterly absurd. This implies a very sophisticated knowledge of UFOs.

Unfortunately, Professor Black, the files of whatever agency he was working for, and the outcome of his fascinating experiment are lost somewhere in the archives. No records have ever been released to the British public. They would be fascinating indeed if someone could find them lurking in a dusty filing cabinet.

The U.S. government scientific study into UFOs in 1969 also researched this case. If you recall, it found no evidence for anything important behind the entire UFO phenomenon and advised the closure of Project Blue Book. Yet it failed to identify one-third of the cases after 2 years of study by numerous scientists. Of the 1956 Lakenheath/Bentwaters affair, you will recall it found in favor of a genuine UFO. It did precisely the same with the encounter over Goose Bay.

In fact, the conclusion offered about this case by Gordon Thayer, the radar expert who spent months analyzing the evidence, was explicit. Thayer thought the phenomenon had to be some form of optical mirage, noting the shape-changing and grainy texture of the main object, and how it resembled "a swarm of bees," as James Howard described it in interview. However, Thayer acknowledged that there were serious problems with such an explanation, as the sighting had characteristics that he simply could not understand or explain. Nor did Thayer have the data from the Massachusetts doctor, an alleged sighting of the same phenomenon from a Canadian survey ship on Hudson Bay about the time the BOAC aircraft last saw the UFO, or indeed the possible recurrence of the same event over Werneth Low in England some years later, to take into account.

In the end, the scientist stated, somewhat exasperatedly, "This unusual sighting should therefore be assigned to the category of some almost certainly natural phenomenon, which is so rare that it apparently has never been reported before or since."

This seems to me to be just about as good a definition of a UFO as you are likely to get.

7 THE VIEW DOWN UNDER

In a case that was to have fascinating echoes a decade later, one of the earliest well-established midair encounters in the Southern Hemisphere took place on September 4, 1969.

By now, air traffic had become more commonplace and airlines' practice of preventing crews from discussing their encounters was having an effect. Although there were almost certainly many more incidents taking place, they were being reported in public less and less often.

Happily, that was not the situation here—perhaps because the airline concerned ferried cargo and there was less public sensitivity at stake. Straits Air Freight Express used Bristol freighter aircraft at the time to fly across Cook Strait in New Zealand, thus providing an easy air bridge between the North and South Islands. Around 7:30 p.m. that dark evening, such a routine flight was in the hands of Captain Ridgwell Cullum and his first officer (called Faircloth). They had left Wellington and were heading into Blenheim on South Island.

As they passed through 3000 feet, Wellington control came on to advise that they had "unknown traffic" 4 miles and straight ahead of the Bristol. They were heading north and about to turn west and then southwest towards their destination. At first, they saw nothing, but, as they completed their turn, a pulsating blue light was seen below and to their right. The crew estimated that it was some 2 miles distant at this point.

After calling Wellington, it was soon apparent to Cullum and Faircloth that they had both the Bristol and the UFO on radar, and the radar target corresponded with the blue light that seemed fluorescent in nature. From both visual observation and radar tracking, it was clear that the blue glow was moving unexpectedly slowly—no more than 70 mph. This speed still eliminated any thought that it was a boat on the water or a mirage effect of the lights of such a vessel.

The Bristol headed south—the same direction as the UFO—but, because of its relatively greater speed, it soon left the light behind. However, it was in view for 2 minutes and, as the plane flew towards South Island, the radar at Wellington was still tracking its steady progress. At around 9 p.m.—on their return cargo flight from Blenheim to Wellington—the pilot and copilot spotted what appeared to be the same phenomenon, closer to Cape Campbell and still heading south. Wellington radar confirmed that it was indeed the same object and that it had remained a clear airborne target for the past 90 minutes!

Cullum was a highly experienced pilot. He had trained in Canada, served with the New Zealand Air Force during the war in the European theater, and flown cargo with British United Airways before returning to New Zealand. He had had a quarter of a century of flying experience when he saw the blue light over Cook Strait and is as sure as he can be that it was an unexplained aerial phenomenon.

Being possibly the first case in New Zealand, it attracted media attention at the time, and Captain Cullum noted that he was put under no pressure to remain silent. Indeed, the New Zealand Air Force issued a plea for pilots to report future sightings to them, although one wonders how long such openness was to last.

The situation had certainly already become somewhat different in Australia. This had been due to a number of cases where problems had ensued. For example, Tom Drury, a senior figure with the aviation industry at the airport at Port Moresby in New Guinea, had taken film footage of a rocketlike UFO streaking into the sky above a beach in August 1953. This had been sent by the Australian government to the U.S., where the CIA promptly took command. Drury naturally trusted his government to look after matters, but found that a year later, when Canberra returned his footage and offered no explanation as to what he had filmed, there was something considerably awry. All the frames that had included the missile-like object had inexplicably disappeared. He was only sent back film that did not show the UFO at all!

It was many years before this man finally got some stills from his now missing film to prove that he had really captured the UFO as he had reported. He got these stills thanks to the intervention of industrial chemist and UFO investigator Bill Chalker, who managed to secure access to the government files prior to the imminent passing of the Australian Freedom of Information Act. The records revealed that, before the film mysteriously vanished somewhere between the Australian aviation authorities and the CIA in Washington, some stills from it were handed over to an interested researcher and he had luckily retained them ever since. Nobody knew that he had these stills, because the Australian Air Force intelligence officer who handed them over in 1954 only did so on the understanding that this man never speak of the matter in public! Then they lied to the witness when returning his film and maintained the cover-up of this film for a quarter of a century.

This was a plan to spirit away important visual evidence by the government of Australia and the CIA in Washington. Only luck ensured that it did not quite pay off.

In 1965, when another fiasco occurred, the memory of the New Guinea film was still strong in the aviation industry's mind. Then, on May 28, an Ansett ANA DC-6 was flying from Brisbane, ironically bound also for Port Moresby. At 3:25 a.m. the aircraft, call sign November Hotel (VH-INH), was over the Townsville area on the Queensland coast when strange lights appeared nearby and buzzed the aircraft for several minutes. This was immediately conveyed to ground control. The pilot had a camera and, while his copilot flew the plane and another officer watched the UFO, he took a roll full of excellent shots of the strange object. Soon after that, the lights passed in front of the DC-6 and disappeared. Meanwhile, Townsville control acted on instructions from the Royal Australian Air Force and orders from Canberra. The crew of the Ansett ANA plane was told that the film was to be left in the camera and not processed on landing in New Guinea, and the pilot was advised that he would be flown to Canberra where the film would then be properly studied by the appropriate authorities. Unfortunately, those authorities seem never to have bothered to enter their findings or release the photograph taken on board the DC-6 onto any public record. It simply disappeared. Fortunately, Townsville Airport control later contacted the police, who began an investigation in an effort to trace the vanished photographs that the crew of the DC-6 believed could prove UFO reality once and for all.

Once more, a promising case seems to have been effectively hushed up. Townsville control even told the police seeking the now missing photographs that the government had confiscated the 12-hour recording tape containing the ground-to-air communications with the Ansett ANA flight. Investigator Keith Basterfield has tried hard to get to the bottom of this mystery, but without success. The RAAF intelligence denies any knowledge of the affair. The crew of the Ansett flight has never spoken in public. The situation remains at an impasse.

One can well see why, in the light of such events, airlines and aircrews would become more and more careful as to what they reported.

Indeed, one man has put this into very sharp focus for us. For over 30 years, Graham Sheppard flew with British Airways and its predecessor BEA (British European Airways). He had two experiences while on the flight deck, but has only been able to talk about them in the past couple of years because he was prevented from doing so earlier.

The first event happened on March 22, 1967, when he was a junior officer aboard a BEA flight from Gibraltar to London Heathrow. It was a clear, starlit night as they crossed the Bay of Biscay and headed into France. Then they saw an unusually brilliant star in the sky ahead and debated which one it was. The third pilot had time to check a star chart but was baffled when no star was revealed to be in the correct location.

After about 5 minutes, the glowing light abruptly moved on a downwards flight path and began to pulsate blue and green with a fluorescent sheen. It then started to zip around the sky in loops at quite amazing speeds and was joined by a second light. They moved away to the left of the aircraft.

At this point, the captain called Bordeaux ground control, and they confirmed that they had unidentified traffic on radar 10 miles west of the BEA aircraft. Soon after, the plane flew out of range, leaving the lights behind.

About a year later, Sheppard was in the cockpit of a BEA Vanguard on a flight from Scotland to Heathrow. They were at 24,000 feet on a sunny day with only high clouds around, which they were above. They were flying over northwest England and under the control of Preston air traffic control when the control noted that a fast-moving target had appeared on radar and was heading straight at them from dead ahead. Within moments, all three crew members spotted a round or disclike object that passed almost level with them and to their right.

Sheppard, who was operating the radio and sat on the right, had the best view. He estimates it was traveling at 1000 mph and was far faster than the Tridents, BAC-111 jets, and other aircraft they were passing in flight on a regular basis. He thinks it was no more than a few hundred feet below and a quarter of a mile to the right, so he has no doubt about its strange nature. "I was looking down on a disk of about 30 feet diameter with a slightly raised center portion. No markings. It was shining in the sunlight. It was certainly metallic."

He reported over the radio to Preston control exactly what was happening and noted the curiosity that there was no shock wave created by its flight. At the proximity and speed, he expected that the Vanguard would be struck by one. Graham Sheppard certainly believes this was a constructed device of fantastic nature and under intelligent control—just as did Cyril George Townsend-Withers.

On neither of the occasions that Shepperd saw UFOs—like so many other cases, I suspect—was any official report filed. Sheppard says of the one in the Preston area that it would certainly have been investigated as an air miss had they suspected that the object was another aircraft. But this was "so otherworldly" that they all decided it was wisest to say nothing further. Air traffic control seemingly concurred, as they evidently did not file any account of their radar tracking, despite knowing it had been visually confirmed. As for the first sighting, Sheppard recalls how the crew members all sat down and discussed it after landing at Heathrow. The pilot left them in no doubt that this was not going to be turned into a report. He seemed aware that the airline would not favor this action and made sure his two fellow officers knew not to talk in public.

In 1993, Graham Sheppard decided that the climate had changed and he could talk openly about his two sightings. He spoke on local radio and agreed to take part in a *Strange But True?* TV documentary about UFOs, which we were putting together on the subject following my first batch of research. Unfortunately, British Airways was none too impressed by his decision to speak out. "Senior managers heard my radio broadcast," he explains. "On that same day, the airline took steps to stop me talking about it again. This was because it had commercial implications. It is a commercially-sensitive subject."

Sheppard was lectured by a senior staff member and told that he was a leading captain himself and so should behave impeccably. To talk about UFOs in public was not acceptable. The airline perceived it as "not to their advantage" to do so. It followed this ticking off with a written note adding that he did not have permission to discuss these midair encounters in public.

Not long afterwards, Graham Sheppard decided to move on and left British Airways. He still flies but is not under the same restrictions from his new employers, who, he says, have a lower public profile but still prefer not to be identified in connection with him!

Sheppard adds that "most sensible pilots choose not to talk about their experiences." He has talked with many aircrews who have seen strange things but are wary of the price they know they will pay if they dare speak out. He feels aggrieved that he cannot openly discuss matters he regards as important, but he understands the fears that major enterprises must inevitably have.

In his own way, Graham Sheppard is trying to break down the barriers and make it possible for all aircrews to talk about the things that have happened to them. Only then will we know the exact nature and full extent of what is going on.

Unfortunately, to bring about that new enlightened climate, *all* airlines have to make the decision to remove this subject from the taboo list. Nobody will take that first brave step alone.

8 CIRCUMNAVIGATION

Many of the cases discussed so far have occurred in the skies above the U.S. and the U.K. However, I want to demonstrate that this is a worldwide issue; these events occur all over the globe. During this brief circumnavigation, we will find cases from several new destinations while moving forward in time towards more modern days, lest you were suspecting—and not altogether unreasonably—that misperception was more likely in days when radar and instrumentation were less perfect than they are today.

"Ladies and gentlemen, if you look out of the starboard window…"

We will start our tour in Portugal on July 30, 1976, with a flight by a British Airways Trident, call sign Fox Golf (G-AVFG). Aboard the flight deck was a captain, whom we shall call Dave, and his first officer, whom we will simply term Carl, plus a second officer, Simon. You have already seen why such protection of aircrews working for British Airways is sadly necessary.

Dave had had 20 years of service and was considered a no-nonsense flyer. But as the passenger flight crossed the coast 40 miles south of Lisbon on a journey from London to Faro, air traffic control came on the radio to advise they had "reports of a UFO." A British Airways Tristar flying above Fox Golf was asked to keep a lookout and soon confirmed that it could see a light.

It was 9 p.m. local time, but the sun had yet to set and there was no cloud cover below their 29,000-foot altitude. Suddenly, as Dave later told UFOlogist Omar Fowler, to whom he agreed to speak to, "There was this brilliantly white, incredibly bright object… It was just sitting there."

Rather amazingly, Dave decided to tell the passengers and made a cabin announcement that those who could look out of the starboard windows would see "what we believe to be a UFO." As the crew and no doubt numerous passengers gazed intently, trying to see the bright object, a "long cigar- or sausage-shaped brown affair" simply appeared beside the light. Then a second one was formed next to it. Dave called Lisbon to back up the pilot of the Tristar, and the tape recorded him saying that "there is no way that this is a star or planet."

Simon noted that they filled out a standard Air Ministry UFO report form on returning to London the next day and, as far as he was concerned, it was the big light that was the riddle. This was several times brighter than any star, even at night. He said that the sausage shapes could, at a pinch, be regarded as aviation vapor trails seen in the gloom, but no others were forming that evening, and these did seem too short and too broad. But they had a non-sharp edge and were dark like the trails at sunset often are.

Carl, equally impressed by the light, called it a "dazzling headlamp." He was also baffled by how the oval shapes simply materialized, but agreed that the edges had a "vaporish appearance" and that their color was probably due to the setting sun.

There was an approximate 30-second gap between the appearance of the two "sausages." Aside from the two British Airways jets, a TAP (Portuguese Airlines) Boeing 727 confirmed the sighting as it crossed the same airspace. The objects appeared not to be moving.

As a former RAF pilot, Carl says that the response of the air traffic control intrigued him. Following this third sighting, the ATC operators became so excited that they debated the scrambling of military aircraft to go on an intercept course, but Dave cannot confirm whether this happened because he had to descend into Faro with his group of vacationers.

Upon landing, the crew asked the passengers if anyone had taken pictures of the phenomenon. Rather curiously, nobody said they had done so, although one man had viewed the big glow through binoculars and said that it seemed to be formed of "crinkled silver paper." Nor did any passengers go public with the sighting—even though the crew did so on landing in the U.K. Possibly the brief media interest had ended by the time the passengers returned to Britain—many, no doubt, after a vacation.

After just over an hour on the ground following the sighting, the Trident took off to fly back to London. It was now dark, of course, and so no sign of the sausages (or indeed the bright light) was observed when the aircraft passed through the same area at about 11 p.m. However, Dave decided to use the radar to study the location.

At the point where the UFOs had been seen, the Trident was climbing up from 28,000 feet towards its cruising altitude some 3000 feet above. Three main blips were detected in a cluster and the largest was much bigger than a supertanker ship (the radar could readily detect large ships when they flew over the Channel).

The radar targets were stationary and Fox Golf flew across them. Simon confirmed that the returns were very strong and that they came within 7 miles of the aircraft. Carl said they turned the cockpit lights down and had a beautiful view of the sky. If the returns had come from any ordinary aircraft, then they should have seen the navigation lights at that proximity.

This appears to be a very impressive case, where three experienced crew members, backed by two other aircraft, saw unusual objects and where radar later seemed to support their story. However, it is a good example of how all may not be as it seems.

Soon afterwards, this case was investigated in fine style by two UFOlogists—Peter Warrington, an amateur astronomer and radar specialist, and Philip Taylor, a mathematician working at the Royal Greenwich Observatory. They believe that they solved this encounter.

Taylor discovered that Southampton University had conducted an experiment using a high-altitude weather balloon. By tracking its position since launch, he believed that the winds may well have put it over the area of the sighting. The "crinkle foil" description through binoculars is relevant, because the bright metal foil used for the surface of the balloon would appear crinkled and so magnify the low sun like a giant mirror. Of course, this does not explain what the sausage-shaped objects were—unless they were, as considered by the crew, vapor trails from other aircraft.

As for the radar returns, Warrington had superb assistance from the radar equipment manufacturers. From this research, he suspects that the radar targets were unconnected and probably the echoes came from mountain ranges down below. He points out that the radar had two settings and, in mapping mode, was designed to show ground terrain, not aircraft-sized objects. Given the size of the targets reported by the crew relative to the 4-inch radar screen, he feels that the objects picked up were simply too enormous to be anything but mountains.

It is fair to say that the crew was not convinced by these theories.

Like a Rocket

Dan Air is involved in this next case. It occurred on August 28, 1978, near Natterheim in Germany, at 11:34 a.m. on a clear, sunny day.

The witnesses were the pilot and first officer of a passenger jet bound for Malta, and a nurse employed by the company. She was hitching a ride in the cockpit in order to take a vacation. They agreed to tell their stories when I worked with London Weekend Television to produce a *Strange but True?* special.

Lou Cockerill, the pilot, describes how they were at 33,000 feet and had just turned east heading towards Frankfurt when air traffic control advised that another aircraft was heading towards them at 35,000 feet. Both he and Paul Coomber, his first officer, looked out and saw the Boeing 707 pass by, but, as they were looking up, they caught sight of a different object high in the sky. They pointed this out to the nurse.

The object was extremely high—well above civilian traffic lanes—and appeared stationary. It resembled the moon but was far brighter than the moon appears in the daytime sky. The third crew member did not see it because he was busy working, and by the time he was free, the few seconds of the encounter had already elapsed.

Cockerill describes how an object now came out of the main "craft" and shot off in the same direction that they were heading. At first, it moved slowly, but after a couple of seconds, it accelerated like a rocket and, within moments, it was streaking away far faster than any missile he had ever seen. The captain was used to firing missiles, having done so while a military pilot prior to his civilian post, so he is positive this was technology beyond the level in our possession.

Paul Coomber had meanwhile been watching the main object as his captain followed the "projectile" outward. He said that the craft moved off in the opposite direction—also at phenomenal speed. The men scoured the sky for it, but it had completely disappeared during just a few seconds.

After a few moments of trying to decide what they had seen, the first officer got on the radio and called ATC, asking whether they had any radar trackings and to check for any unusual military traffic. It took some time for the control to come back, but evidently they had neither a radar return nor any advisements about military activity.

This is the kind of case that is very difficult to evaluate. Captain Cockerill says that he has from time to time considered whether they stumbled upon some military experiment—possibly the firing of a laser weapon. However, Coomber's report of the main object's heading away in the opposite direction with the sort of acceleration displayed by the smaller "projectile" seems very hard to square with that idea. Indeed, both pilots are adamant that nobody could have withstood the G forces exhibited within the objects that they saw.

Shoot to Kill

There are interesting similarities between this last case and a classic encounter that occurred 2 years earlier, on September 19, 1976. On that occasion, an Iranian Air Force fighter pilot saw a "rocket" launched by a UFO at very close quarters.

The event began at 12:30 a.m., when reports came into the command center from people in the Shemiran area of Tehran saying that a brilliant hovering light was drifting overhead. Deputy Commander of Operations B.G. Yousefi at first disbelieved the stories, saying the witnesses were just "seeing stars," but when he contacted Mehrabad air traffic control, he changed his mind. They told him that something was out there. He went outside and saw it for himself.

At 1:30 a.m., Yousefi launched an F-4 Phantom jet interceptor from Shahrokhi Air Force Base. The pilot soon saw the object for himself—a blinding light that pulsated colors, such as orange and violet, all in a rapid sequence. He locked onto the target and then, at a range of 25 miles, he suddenly lost all instrumentation and both UHF and VHF radio communication. Abandoning the intercept, he headed back to base. Communications all returned partway into his return flight.

Ten minutes later, a second Phantom was sent up, piloted by Lieutenant Jafari. An air force general was now in charge of the mission. The radar operator aboard the F-4 locked onto the object at a range of 27 miles and the pilot confirmed that he was closing on the UFO at 150 mph—indicating (given the rapid speed of the jet) that the UFO moved away from him at several hundred miles per hour.

Suddenly, the bright light shot away and Jafari put his jet into afterburner mode—breaking the sound barrier in his pursuit. The UFO was giving a radar return comparable to a Boeing 707 tanker aircraft as this bizarre chase continued south of Tehran and above a dried-up lake area surrounded by a desert landscape with sparse habitation.

Then there was a moment of sheer terror for Jafari as a small bright object appeared to emerge from the main UFO and head towards the F-4. Its speed was like that of a rocket. Convinced that he was under attack, Jafari immediately set in motion the computer launch of an AIM 9 (Sidewinder) air-to-air missile—the first time such a move is ever known to have occurred during a midair confrontation of this sort. Unfortunately, at the moment he attempted to fire and follow his shoot-to-kill orders, all electronics aboard the Phantom failed exactly as reported by the original interceptor.

At this point, according to the later report, "the pilot initiated a turn and negative-G dive to get away. As he turned, the object fell in a trail at what appeared to be about 3–4 [miles from him]. As he continued in his turn away from the primary object, the second object went to the inside of his turn, then returned to the second object for a perfect rejoin."

In other words, the "rocket" launched by the UFO had circled the F-4, stuck with it despite the brave attempts of Lieutenant Jafari to throw it off his trail, dogged the aircraft, and then flown back into the UFO. Jafari regarded this as a warning shot across the bows!

The F-4 regained all its instrumentation after the second object returned into the large light, but the pilot no longer considered an air strike even when a second projectile was released. This one went on a downward path at great speed and the two-man crew followed its passage, awaiting the explosion when it struck. Instead, it seemed to soft land and poured out a vast amount of light that illuminated several square miles of desert.

The F-4 spiraled downwards to mark the position of the object on the ground and noted a pulse of electronic interference on one bearing (150°). Exactly the same problem was reported by a civil airliner then coming into land at Tehran—some 50 miles away. But that crew saw nothing.

Jafari was shaken by the encounter, and his night vision was severely impaired by the brilliance of the glow. He had to be guided back to Shahrokhi and even then had to do several circuits before he was confident that he could see well enough to attempt a landing.

After a debriefing, the pilot and navigator were flown at dawn to the location of the now vanished UFO and the landing spot of the projectile. The helicopter landed by the only house within miles of the spot and found that the occupants had heard a loud noise (probably the F-4) and seen a brilliant light that they thought was from a thunderstorm.

Some years later, my colleague Peter Hough and I were approached by a British university lecturer who was married to an Iranian woman and had been living in the area at the time. During the night of the above encounter, he had been camping on a nearby mountain with a friend, and they had experienced a terrifying UFO sighting. It took him some months to share all the details with us, as his friend had told him they had been abducted by the "djinn"—Muslim mythological spirits from whence the word "genie" originates. The British man had been left with a terrible legacy that made him afraid of flying. He has always connected his nightmare on the mountain (during which he felt himself floated into the air by unseen forces) with the terrifying midair adventure that befell the two F-4 crews.

I should stress that the summary of the Iranian encounter and the direct quotations come from an impeccable source. In fact, they are from a DIA (defense intelligence) report submitted from Tehran to Washington by the defense attaché at the U.S. Embassy. This report was released under the U.S. Freedom of Information Act after UFOlogists got wind of this sighting—although there was a notable omission from the data released in public. This omission is an evaluation report in which the case is termed "outstanding" and "a classic" that meets "all the criteria necessary for a valid study of the UFO phenomenon." It adds that "the credibility of many of the witnesses was high" and urges further study.

In October 1997, I met with Dr. Richard Haines on a trip to Europe. He showed me drawings that he had managed to secure from aviation sources in Iran. These depicted the object as seen by Jafari and showed a strange, shape-changing canopy of light that at times rather resembled a colorful butterfly.

The Biggest One of All

The astonishing case below actually comprises two encounters exactly a year apart. So many aircraft were involved that suppressing the evidence was never an option. However, detailed investigation over the years has revealed some interesting facts.

The first event occurred on November 11, 1979, and involved a TAE Super-Caravelle aircraft on a charter flight from Salzburg, Austria, to Puerto de la Cruz on the island of Tenerife, off the African coast. This included a stopover on the Spanish isle of Mallorca. There were 119 passengers aboard. The pilot was 34-year-old Captain Francisco de Tejada, who had 8000 flying hours to his credit. His copilot was named Suazo.

Following the publicity, UFO researcher Juan Benitez conducted a detailed investigation and interviewed the crew. It was just before 11 p.m. and the jet was climbing through 24,000 feet after take-off from Palma. They were over the ocean some 40 miles out from Valencia when the ATC in Barcelona called and asked Tejada to switch to a frequency he knew to be used only in emergencies. Assuming that he was being called upon to assist in a rescue search, he did so, but found only a mass of noise on the bandwidth.

At that moment, the two pilots spotted two red lights in the south. They were heading towards the aircraft. Tejada says, "I have never seen anything like that speed." They flew past and behind the Caravelle. At first sight, they were estimated at 10 miles distant, but they had quickly come within half a mile and seemed to be "playing with us," as the captain put it. They moved around the aircraft in circles.

Wishing to distract the passengers, he advised them to put on their seat belts for possible "turbulence" and ordered the cabin crew to serve them a meal to ensure that nobody panicked at what was going on. Meanwhile, he began a steep bank to try to break away from the lights.

When this had no effect, he called ATC to report what was happening and requested permission to divert and make an emergency landing at Valencia. The autopilot had by now failed. The red lights followed them towards the coast but "laid off" at a greater distance behind the TAE jet. They touched down just before midnight, and several airport personnel, readying themselves for an emergency, witnessed red lights above the end of the runway. This included the airport director and senior air traffic controller.

The press accounts of this case really only take the matter this far. But the Spanish Air Force took control of the situation and completed a detailed file on the case after a thorough investigation. This was secured many years later by the persuasive efforts of skeptical UFO investigator Vicente Juan Ballester Olmos, who is an engineer.

The official records reveal that when the TAE plane landed, the (somewhat angry!) passengers were bundled off to a hotel without any explanation as to the real reason why their vacation in the sun was being interrupted. As this was happening, the Spanish Air Force was reacting with the launch of two F-1 Mirage fighter jets from Los Llanos Air Base near Albacete.

Although nothing had been recorded by the civilian radar during the encounter with the TAE aircraft, military radar and the long-range civil radar at Barcelona had by now picked something up as the interceptors were sent airborne. This anomalous return was tracked as an object dropping 12,000 feet in 30 seconds—a rate of descent that would have been disastrous for anyone on board.

According to the records, one Spanish Air Force pilot saw lights, but Benitez claims that the other filmed the UFO with a gun camera. If so, there is no data regarding this on record.

This extraordinary case—so far as I know unprecedented—was confirmed by the Deputy Director of TAE (Alfredo Espantaleon), who told Benitez that "the plane was forced to land at Valencia and we know that the UFOs were also seen by other eyewitnesses on the ground, as well as by pilots of several military aircraft. Even the Spanish transport minister, Salvador Teran, was forced to admit as a result of this case, 'It is clear that UFOs exist.'"

However, this was not the end of the midair confrontation—because it happened all over again, on a far greater scale, exactly one year to the night later—November 11, 1980.

On this occasion, no fewer than seven civil aircraft were involved in the midair adventure. Four were Iberia Boeing 727s (three on internal journeys—Flight 810, from Asturias to Barcelona, and 1800 and 1831, on the Barcelona-to-Madrid shuttle—and a fourth, Flight 350, en route from

Barcelona to Athens in Greece). There was also a French Air Taxi commuter plane that was flying from Mallorca to Marseilles. Transeuropa Airlines Flight 1474 was outbound from Mallorca on its way to Bordeaux. Finally, there was a British vacationers' package tour—Monarch Airlines Flight 148—crossing the Spanish skies, bound for Alicante. All of these aircraft were witness to what took place.

Captain Ramos was pilot of the Iberia 727 heading for Barcelona with Flight 810. At around 6:40 p.m., as darkness fell but with traces of twilight still visible at 31,000 feet, he was headed southeast towards Maella when something appeared. He had ample opportunity to view it as his copilot was flying.

Ramos described the sight as follows: "We saw a green light and we thought it must be the green light carried by a plane on starboard wings. But this supposed plane was coming straight at us...it was getting closer and closer and was like a sphere—or rather like an enormous soap bubble." He adds, "I made an instant reflex movement. The second pilot had switched off the automatic pilot, and I pushed the controls forward and we dived. I did a dive of about 300 feet."

The captain estimates that the object took just under a minute from first sighting to passing right beside them. At closer range, they could see that the soap bubble was emitting other lights. Both pilots and two flight-deck engineers witnessed the whole frightening experience.

After the trauma had concluded, Ramos called Barcelona ATC to ask if they had other traffic that could have narrowly missed collision with the 727. They reported that the only aircraft nearby was Monarch 148, and that they had just reported a massive green light that had flashed across their path.

Overhearing this conversation, Transeuropa 1474 called in to say that they had seen the object as well while flying northwest over the ocean towards Reus near the Spanish coast. They were well out over the Mediterranean at the time, and more than 100 miles from the location of the first two aircraft.

The Iberia flight heading to Athens saw the UFO to its south. The Air Taxi saw it northeast of its route, which was over the ocean between Spain and France. One of the two Iberia shuttles was still on the ground awaiting take-off when it saw the green sphere.

Such a combination of sightings from that kind of wide area and at a range of heights from 0 to over 30,000 feet establishes that this object—whatever it was—had to be traveling at considerable height, probably many miles high in the atmosphere.

Juan Benitez again investigated, and claims that there were witnesses on the ground at Barcelona (where Iberia Flight 1831 had its encounter) who saw the green sphere come down at a steep angle, buzz the runway, and then "bounce off" and away at a sharp angle of ascent. If true, this makes the identification of this object very difficult to establish, because no obvious solution (e.g., a meteor) can change direction in flight in this way. It is also eerily similar to a later, British case, where the same thing occurred at a U.K. airport (see p.162).

Unfortunately, we have no record of these Spanish ground witnesses—only a comment by one (that Benitez reports) saying that "it is totally impossible for a machine that does all these things to be anything else but controlled by some type of intelligence."

Or is it? That is worth pondering, because you will see that the now infamous 1995 British Airways encounter over the Peak District has chilling similarities to this one. You may well have also noticed the links with the green fireball stories once again and wondered about possible Spanish defense establishments that might be in the area.

However, we must always seek a rational answer to such cases, if there is one. That is why the words of Vicente Ballester Olmos should be heeded. I interviewed him in August 1995.

He told me how in 1990 he began to coerce the Spanish defense authorities to release their data on UFO activity. The colonel in charge of the Air Safety Division was responsible for them—an interesting, if not surprising, choice for such a task. It stems from the sheer number of midair encounters within the Spanish records.

Ballester Olmos persuaded the defense authorities that "UFOs are a scientific problem and nothing to do with national defense." Their research supported that view, and so the government was willing to turn over its findings for proper study. What a shame that so many other nations, such as the U.K., have not adopted this kind of enlightened attitude.

As of May 1991, the Air Safety Office had fifty-five cases over Spain. This increased to sixty-six by 1995, when the number of actually released files totaled forty-nine. The missing ones apparently contain "sensitive" data. The released material involves some 1108 pages—so the case reports are on average more detailed than the feeble scraps of paper that are released to the PRO in Britain each year—all 30 years old as well, of course! They are available today via the library of the air force in Madrid.

Because the Spanish cases are nearly all newer than the most recent case ever released by the British MoD—and many considerably so—follow-up civilian investigation has been easier. This has enabled research to be carried out into events such as the midair episodes of November 1979, although the 1980 file has yet to be made public.

Ballester Olmos and his team have concluded that only seven out of seventy-one separate UFO incidents in these forty-nine files should be considered unexplained. The November 1979 midair encounter is not one of them, in his view. The files reveal that whenever a UFO is clearly reported by a pilot, radar often fails to show an attendant object. Although there are radar trackings, these often do not coincide with the sighting in time or space.

Data for the sixty-six files to 1995 (including the seventeen not released) indicates that in seven cases radar tracked an object, something was seen, and military jets were subsequently scrambled. As this occurred in a 30-year period over Spain, one can gain some insight into how often these remarkable things may be occurring on a global scale each year. There must now be thousands of midair encounters on record somewhere and the cases in this book represent only a small fraction of those.

As for the TAE encounter, Antonio Fernandez, working with Ballester Olmos, believes that the files allow identification of the red lights that caused this holiday jet to be diverted. He believes the crew mistook a reflection of the burn-off from the oil exploration rig that was located north of the coast of Algeria. No doubt Captain Tejada would be unlikely to agree, and, if the same red lights were really seen by a Mirage fighter crew used to operating in that area, this may alter matters somewhat, as may the alleged radar trackings.

With regard to the events one year later, that was clearly some kind of gaseous natural phenomenon akin to the by now rather familiar green fireballs. A meteor burning an ionized trail or space junk reentering the atmosphere are both possible. The real key here is whether there really were ground observers who saw the "soap bubble" change course and "bounce off." If so, then it was no ordinary meteor—that is for sure.

A Load of Hot Air?

Italian UFO researcher Antonio Chiumiento received word of this case via a friendly pilot. It took him some time to persuade the witness to talk and only then on the understanding that the details would not be published. This situation persisted for several years, until the witness retired from the air force and felt able to go public. Then the matter was pursued—first by the UFOlogists arranging for questions to be asked in Parliament, and finally by pressuring the Ministry of Defense for answers.

The witness was Senior Warrant Office Giancarlo Cecconi of the No. 2 Wing of the 14th Jet Fighter Group. On June 18, 1979, he was flying a G-91 aircraft used for aerial surveys. Because this was his mission on the day, he was equipped with several special cameras that pointed forwards and sideways, and took eighty photographs per minute.

Cecconi had been taking pictures over the Apennines. He was between Rovigo and the Abano Terme hills in northeastern Italy when his ground control asked him to contact the radar operations room at Istrana Air Base. They told him of a low-flying unidentified return. Would he investigate?

It was 11:30 a.m. on a clear day, and he went in pursuit. Istrana told him that the object kept appearing and disappearing on the scope. But he soon made out a large dark mass ahead. It was oblong and seemingly opaque. He flew by within 200 feet, getting a perfect view and taking photographs. There seemed to be a white "dome" on top. Within the next few minutes, he made several turns and took many separate images of the device.

Down on the ground, air traffic controllers at his home base in Treviso were watching the object through binoculars and radioed that they could see a faint bluish trail being left in the wake of the slow-moving thing.

Then, between one turn and the next, the object had simply vanished. Try as he might Cecconi could not find it again. The ground observers in the control tower had also lost sight of it, and it never appeared on radar at Istrana again.

Upon landing, the film was developed, and perfect close-up views were obtained of the object. When Chiumiento first met Cecconi, he was allowed to see (but not to keep) one of these photographs and confirms that it showed the object that the pilot reported.

After 31 years in the air force, Cecconi retired in 1983, and the story could finally be told in public. The Italian government—rather like its Spanish counterpart reported above—was becoming more liberal and willing to publish its official UFO files. So it seemed quite acceptable for him to talk.

In 1984, in response to this new official attitude, Chiumiento persuaded an Italian MP to press for the release of the photographs. Finally, on November 2, the Ministry of Defense responded and confirmed details of the sighting but added, "The object in question, which was detected immediately, was photographed with the cameras aboard the aircraft and was unequivocally identified by photo interpretation personnel as a cylindrical balloon constructed from black plastic bags."

Cecconi was stunned by this claim, saying that he saw and filmed an object that could not have been constructed by any state on earth! He added, "On the basis of our knowledge of physics, it would never have been able to be airborne." However, the photographs were not released to prove the argument of the Ministry of Defense.

But then, a year later, a skeptical magazine article on UFOs did appear and supplied a "solution," complete with three photographs of a small black cylindrical object recognizable as a toy balloon. The Italian government had released these pictures to the magazine. Such balloons are sold all over Europe—in the U.K. they are even marketed as UFOs!—but they are no more than a foot in length.

It seems improbable that an aircraft could fly around one of these very small objects, as Cecconi did, without realizing what was happening. Equally, the radar tracking surely could not pick up so tiny an object, and the sighting by ground observers from so far away seems doubtful as well.

More significantly, the pilot himself denies that these "toy balloon" pictures depict what he saw, and Chiumiento says they are different from the one photograph he was shown back in 1979.

In some support of the claim by these two men that the real photographs are being withheld stands the official air force file on the case. This was eventually released in 1986 but had none of the photographs as published by the magazine. It pronounced the sighting as unexplained!

This was to be the first, but by no means the last, that we would hear of the "toy balloon" story. During the 1990s, it was to take on increasing significance as more and more air misses featured small, dark, cylindrical objects that did indeed seem remarkably similar both to the thing over Italy in 1979 and also to the officially released photographs, which were said to show this toy balloon.

Indeed, there is a case that is remarkably similar in many respects. It also occurred over Italy, but this time the aircraft was a Dan Air Boeing 737 heading from London Gatwick to the Greek island of Corfu. The date was June 21, 1982, and it was at 11:15 a.m. on a bright sunny day.

The same team that "solved" the Portuguese Trident encounter—Peter Warrington and Philip Taylor—tackled this one and managed to get some help out of Dan Air. They established that the 737 was carrying 130 passengers and crew but only four were witnesses. These were the two pilots, and two passengers on a goodwill visit to the flight deck at the appropriate moment.

The aircraft was flying southeast on heading 125° and was descending from 27,000 feet to 19,000 feet in the early stages of its landing at Kerkira on Corfu. At the controls was Captain Schwaiger, and his copilot was David Robinson. They were out to sea, east of the Brindisi beacon on the southeast toe of Italy.

Schwaiger first saw the object and pointed it out to the others. It was initially below them, but, as they descended, they drew level and then passed it. At first, they speculated about a falling tire from an aircraft above, but this was soon dispelled by its stationary nature. In all, it was in view for under a minute before the descent path of the 737 took the UFO out of sight above them. The object had a rectangular shape and was shiny black. There were no appendages, but there was a small "bump" on top in the middle.

David Robinson says that the sun was shining brightly here, while Schwaiger says it gave the appearance of a dent, or protuberance, making it look almost like a doughnut. There is no doubt that there is a considerable similarity between this object and the one that Officer Cecconi saw further north and 3 years earlier.

As there was no radar coverage east of Brindisi, the crew did not report the matter over the radio, but only upon landing back in London—where they filled out an "air miss" form.

Warrington and Taylor thought the most likely solution here was a balloon. They established that weather balloons were released from Brindisi at 5 a.m. and 11 a.m. each day, but that, by plotting the course of each one, neither was likely to be anywhere near where the sighting occurred. In addition, this object did not resemble the typical weather balloons in use—which were conical and silver.

The UFOlogists understandably did not consider the possibility of a toy balloon, and it seems very hard to imagine one of these making it to 25,000 feet and 40 miles out to sea. If such balloons can do this, then they are certainly some toy!

The other option considered by the investigators was the fact that a NATO exercise ("Deterrent Force") was taking place south of Italy at the time. They speculated as to whether a target drone used in aerial practice might have drifted into the air lanes. During a similar NATO exercise 2 years earlier (June 27, 1980), an Itavia DC-9, call sign Golf India (I-TIGI), met a still unexplained fate off southwest Italy. It was at an almost identical height (25,000 feet) and heading as Flight 870 from Bologna to Palermo, towards Sicily, when it crashed into the sea near Ustica, killing all seventy-seven passengers and four crew members. Radar had detected an unidentified target moving at high speed on a path that crossed just in front of the aircraft moments before the aircraft disappeared. Tests on the wreckage proved that the DC-9 either collided with something or was damaged by a midair explosion just outside the aircraft—leading to inevitable suggestions that either an air-to-air missile from the exercise got in its way or else it tangled with a target drone. Of course, the unidentified object may have been precisely that—yet another UFO.

It is certainly very likely that Giancarlo Cecconi and the Dan Air Boeing 737 both met the same kind of object in 1979 and 1982. As you will later see, the same phenomenon was also very clearly almost struck by several aircraft over Britain and various other countries during the next few years. These unidentified missiles have become a source of considerable concern for the aviation "air miss" investigators. One hopes that they are not all off-course target drones! Nevertheless, it is worryingly possible that the potential of a terrible accident in the wake of these numerous midair encounters was foreshadowed in June 1980 off the coast of southern Italy.

Russian Sausage

Rather harder to categorize are the cases typified by this next example. I take a slight detour from the normal path because, as far as I am aware, the aircrew saw nothing during this episode. The report comes from a passenger. But it seems reasonable to suspect that an incident may well have been logged by the pilots and then obscured by the then typical Soviet bureaucracy.

It was July 5, 1984, and the aircraft was a Russian state airline Tupolev on a flight from Leningrad to London. At around 2 p.m., the Aeroflot plane was cruising at 35,000 feet when the object appeared. The person who reported it to me was a retired experimental atomic physicist who was returning to the U.K. on the flight. He saw what appeared to be a "thick black pole" sticking vertically out of some fluffy clouds. It was at a strange angle and the thought flitted through his mind that it was a rather tall building until he realized that it was impossibly high.

The scientist, who asked me to protect his identity, called it to the attention of several fellow travelers, one of whom was an aircraft inspection engineer. All were completely baffled. The pole resembled a sausage stuck in a plate of mashed potatoes at an oblique angle, and it was in perfect view for around 3 minutes until they drifted past and it began to be covered by clouds. One woman exclaimed to him, "That's a mighty long telegraph pole!" Unfortunately, no photographs were taken, as Aeroflot banned cameras from its aircraft.

I have myself seen the shadow from an aircraft traveling across clouds, and I did wonder if this was such an effect. However, the witness was insistent that this was not the case and said the outline was very solid. The angle at which it rose from the clouds is also difficult to explain. Possibly it was an illusion caused by the peak of a mountain, but, if so, it was sufficiently odd to have fooled several people.

As explained, there have been a number of almost identical reports—for example, an American Airlines aircraft in which passengers and crew saw precisely this kind of object after take-off from Los Angeles heading east. This implies that it is not something so easily resolved.

As with the infamous remarks made by the Colorado University team about the object seen by the BOAC Stratocruiser, perhaps it is some kind of novel phenomenon of natural origin akin to a mirage that science as yet fails to record. Just as, sadly, science may miss out on a great deal because the phenomenon is reported under the stigma of the word "UFO."

Time for Another Lozenge

A further example of the dark cylinder shape was recorded by Olympic Airlines Flight 132 on August 15, 1985. This was on a trip from Zurich to its native port of Athens, Greece, with Captain Christos Stamulis in control. There were sixty-one passengers aboard.

Flight 132 was over the Swiss border heading for Italy at 4:05 p.m. on a bright day. The Boeing 727 was on airway Amber 14 at 24,000 feet and was preparing for a further climb, when a strange object rushed past it. Stamulis later estimated that it came within 300 feet of the jet.

He says that the object was "missile" shaped and perhaps a few feet long. It traveled at great speed and appeared dark brown or black against the sky. He called Milan Linate control to report the matter and said that he thought it was over too quickly for any passengers to have seen anything.

The affair was examined as a near miss. Investigations revealed that a Swiss military exercise was under way that day in St. Gotthard and air traffic had been rerouted around there. However, the exercise had concluded before Flight 132 flew nearby, and the Swiss government was adamant that no missiles had been used during the exercise.

Since the dark object came from the Italian side of the border, the authorities in Rome were quizzed but denied any knowledge of a rogue launch or scheduled activity that might have been involved. NATO also had no explanation to offer. Both Swiss and Italian radar failed to detect an anomaly, but one of the radar staff added that an object that small traveling at the reported speed would almost certainly not be detectable in any case.

The Olympic pilot told the inquiry that he believed it had to be a missile, despite their failure to find one. But this has been the belief of many other pilots who have had identical close encounters since 1985. While it is possible to accept that a very rare stray missile would put a passenger jet at risk, it does seem inconceivable that this would occur as often as these numerous reports seem to indicate. If that is indeed the answer, then a major air safety scandal lurks behind the news. In my view, there are simply too many cases worldwide for us to believe that aircraft and missiles are rubbing shoulders so often.

Another example occurred only 3 days after the Swiss encounter. This one, on August 18, 1985, was near Söderhamn in Sweden and involved a Cessna plane with four qualified pilots aboard. They were heading for Gävle at around 3000 feet, with Per Lundqvist in control, when a dark "cruise missile" shape perhaps 15 feet long was seen heading straight for them. It was described as being dark and metallic, and it reflected sunlight. Small protrusions like fins appeared at the rear. It seemed to be hugging the course of power lines down below. The Cessna pilot dived after it and gave pursuit, but the object rapidly outflew them and disappeared.

Because of the obvious danger to civil air traffic, a military investigation took place. It was suggested that a real cruise missile test was intercepted. However, after 6 months, the Swedish defense authorities found no evidence to prove that this came from any identifiable source.

Exactly the same diagnosis followed on June 25, 1987, when William Cantrell and Delta Airlines Flight 1083 from Pittsburgh to Atlanta encountered something near Charleston, West Virginia. The FAA (Federal Aviation Administration) report was obtained by researcher Stan Gordon. It notes how the Boeing 737 with sixty passengers aboard encountered a small missile-like object heading straight towards the aircraft and then passing by within 500 feet.

Cantrell described the object as about 5 feet long and "homemade" in appearance. It seemed to be on a descending path as it flew close to the passenger jet. However, at 29,500 feet, any suggestions of a toy balloon do seem hard to swallow. This is especially true since Cantrell said the object's speed was very high. It was also moving against the wind, which strongly argues against a balloon. The Pentagon found no missile launches that could be responsible, and this case became just another unexplained statistic.

These three midair encounters with missiles between 1985 and 1987 were very much the start of a huge wave of such events. The cases are remarkably consistent in nature and must involve the same phenomenon. This spate of activity, which we shall look at in more detail in a later chapter, is being hidden from the public. There is no deliberate conspiracy here, but every major airline in the world seems to have had at least one confrontation, and so commercial factors really ought not to be an issue. None is more prone to these episodes than any other.

Perhaps the airlines are unaware of the frequency of such events. However, though I am sure that they do care deeply about passenger safety, an unwillingness to openly discuss the evidence must be compromising that position. Something disturbing lies behind these consistent reports, and it is vital that we find out what that something is.

9 "It's Really Getting a Bit Frightening Up Here"

The quote for this chapter title comes from a New Zealand cargo aircraft pilot during a midair encounter. But it could probably have been uttered by almost any of the aircrew members whose stories we tell in this book.

It is certainly appropriate to Vladimir Kuzmin, who described his encounter to Dr. Richard Haines when he was able to visit fellow aviation scientists in Novosibirsk within the former Soviet Union. Kuzmin was an aerobatics instructor and on December 24, 1989, he was test-flying a Czechoslovakian-made L-29 jet trainer. It was around 3:15 p.m. on a bitterly cold day typical of the weather around Chelyabinsk east of the Urals.

The pilot had taken the aircraft to around 26,000 feet and was about to descend towards the airport when he saw something several hundred feet below him. He now executed some descending 360° turns, spiraling down around the object to view it carefully at close range.

It should sound rather familiar to you after the previous chapter—being dark gray in color and cylindrical in shape. But he had never seen anything like it before, despite 16 years as a flight instructor. During all of the turns, it appeared to remain stationary. Ground control could not see it either on radar or visually, indicating its relatively small size. They did confirm, however, that there was no other traffic known to be in the area.

This rather typical sighting of what are supposed to be toy balloons had one most unusual difference. Kuzmin says that he felt a strange sensation from the object—a "sense of presence." It was an uncomfortable feeling, but it was not psychological. Rather, it had a physical origin, possibly some energy associated with the phenomenon. Later events seem to prove that diagnosis.

After climbing back up and initiating another diving turn past the object, the pilot was stunned to find that it had completely disappeared. He had been watching it for more than 8 minutes and found the way it vanished rather disturbing. He continued on his downward path and landed at 3:45 p.m. But, by then, he found that his face felt rather strange.

Upon checking in a mirror, it turned out to be red as though scalded by high temperatures. Only the part not protected by his leather flying helmet was affected, indicating that it was a result of some "exposure" during the encounter. The skin felt sensitive to the touch but was not like a sunburn.

Dr. Haines inspected the pilot's helmet, plus the cockpit and windscreen of the L-29. This was designed to cut out ultraviolet radiation from sunlight and so this was clearly not the cause of the physical effects. The scientist suggests that a type of microwave energy might have "cooked" the pilot's skin from its inner surface outward. The effected skin did turn flaky 24 hours later and gradually returned to normal. This microwave effect was recorded in the West Palm Beach, Florida, case if you recall—below the site of the Pan Am midair encounter.

Clearly, no toy balloon could possibly be responsible for such an effect even if such a thing had been on sale in the USSR (and it was not). Yet the encounter over the Urals appears to describe exactly the same kind of object as in those cases where the toy balloon theory is proffered as the definite answer by aviation authorities. Does this suggest that a different and more disconcerting natural phenomenon may lie behind all of these cases—a phenomenon with potentially destructive overtones?

There are plenty of other examples of this same type of radiation effect. In one case that I investigated, two witnesses at Paco de Arcos in Portugal were burnt in similar fashion by a glowing object that passed above them. This was just after 9 p.m. on December 25, 1980. The weather was not warm enough for sunburn—as it most definitely was not over the Urals almost exactly 9 years later—and it was, of course, pitch dark over Portugal in any case! Yet the person whose skin was more adapted to sunlight (a native Portuguese man) suffered less severely than a visitor from Britain.

Four days later, two women and the grandson of one woman were seriously "cooked" by a radiating object that hovered low above their car in Huffman, Texas. The emitted radiation heated up the metal door handle of the car and induced eddy currents into the wedding ring worn by one of the women, badly burning her finger. The severity of this attack also led to eye disorders and nausea of the type known to be introduced by microwave radiation. One of the women stood outside the car for some time and she suffered by far the most serious effects. In fact, she was made so ill she spent weeks in the hospital suffering what were clearly radiation effects. She lost large chunks of her hair in clumps.

In another case, on January 8, 1981, at Trans-en-Provence, France, a small egg-shaped object landed in daylight on the terrace of a farm. It left a ring of affected soil underneath. In France, a team of scientists at the Space Center in Toulouse operate a government-funded UFO project and have laboratories around the nation on standby. Trained gendarmes are even instructed when to call in the scientists, as they did in this case. Plant biologist Professor Michel Bounias spent months working with the aero engineer in charge at Toulouse, Dr. Jean Jacques Velasco. They could not explain what had happened to the soil. It had been affected by radiation akin to microwave energy, and this was certainly related to the object that landed because the effects exponentially decayed from the mid-point of the circle left behind. Yet the changes to the chlorophyll content of the plants in the ground, as compared with those outside the ring, were impossible to reproduce by any known force. The detailed scientific report issued from Toulouse has attracted some valid criticism but still strongly infers an unknown phenomenon behind some UFO reports.

So there is a formidable database that indicates how a radiating energy source is associated with some of these UFO phenomena. Thankfully, it leads to medical problems in very few of the midair encounters.

Another common type of physical event associated with UFO reports has also been alluded to before—the way in which electrical systems can be prevented from operating. We have seen car-stop events in Midwestern America and the nightmare endured by an Iranian Air Force pilot while trying to launch an air-to-air missile, plus several other rather worrying midflight incidents.

Here is another example that also takes us to a new part of the world—China. Obtaining reports from this nation is very difficult, as a hard-line communist regime still controls the state and UFO data is regarded with deep suspicion by the authorities, as it was in the former Soviet Union. What we do know comes from scientific sources who sought to identify the phenomenon witnessed over a large area on August 27, 1987.

It seems that Chinese Air Force pilot Mao Xuecheng was ordered to fly from Chongming Island at around 7:35 p.m., although he was not told why. The suspicion has to be that the military had either reports or radar returns of an unknown target. He crossed the Yangtze River, and at 7:57 p.m., while passing over Jiangnan, Mao saw a strange object off to his starboard side.

Mao reported that the object was descending. It was a yellow/orange color and not unlike a hat in shape. A spiral trail coiled away from its rear. The main body of the object was rotating but the trail was not. Within 2 minutes, it crossed his path (he was flying south) and headed out towards the China Sea. It now appeared to climb and increase in speed.

He had changed course and endeavored to catch the UFO, but even at 600 mph had failed to get near to it. Mao saw it now head off towards Huansha and disappear after another minute or so. The pilot then radioed through for permission to land.

On the ground, in Shanghai just south of Mao's intercept point, there were many witnesses. A typical report, at Pudong, spoke of a large "basin" crossing the sky southeastward and emitting pulses of bright light. At Zhongguxiang, one witness gave a graphic description of the trail as being "coiled like a watch spring." He added that it passed through clouds and these glowed in eerie fashion even after it had disappeared.

This suggests a form of plasma energy, and it has been reported on several occasions. Indeed, during some cases, the object has been said to punch holes in clouds as it passes through them. This implies that ionization of the atmosphere is associated with the UFO. I recall one case from Exhall in Warwickshire where the UFO moved from power lines and parted the clouds as it flew upwards.

Other cases involve car interference. For example, in New Mexico on November 4, 1957, James Stokes, an engineer working at a government research center investigating the physics of the upper atmosphere, noticed that his radio failed. Then his car engine stalled as "a light-colored egg-shaped object [was] making a shallow dive across the sky." It flew past the shocked driver, who got out and felt a strange sensation (like that described by the Russian aerobatics instructor). His skin was tingling and his hair began to stand on end as when affected by an electrostatic field. Returning to his car, Stokes found his battery churning out steam, but his engine was working again. The UFO was now flying through the sky and cutting through clouds "like Moses parting the Red Sea"! When he got home, the engineer found that his skin had a "burn" and was very red and sensitive to the touch.

The stunning consistency of cases such as these really strikes a message home to any skeptic. The British UFO Research Association has amassed sufficient examples to produce a catalogue of over five hundred cases—surely demonstrating that a physically real phenomenon is involved in some of these encounters. It would seem that the phenomenon behind these UFOs generates electrostatic and microwave radiation and appears to ionize the atmosphere through which it passes, creating brightly glowing trails of plasma and having unexpected effects, such as causing clouds to disperse.

Certainly the ground witnesses around Shanghai during the August 1987 encounter often noted such features. The weather bureau, observatory, and university were flooded with calls from people wanting to know what had just moved across the sky. The meteorological bureau chief, Shu Jiajin, even saw it for himself.

These scientists tried bravely to come up with an answer but knew it had been visible for too long for the most obvious source (a meteor) to be feasible. They eventually suggested a missile launch from "some western country" (none were likely to be foolish enough to send one over a hostile land). Astronomers at the observatory had another theory—merely noting that it might be "some natural phenomenon arising from the earth's own atmosphere." Which it very probably was, although this hardly gets us far in deciding what sort of phenomenon it might be.

After moving out to sea, the object appears to have passed over Shengsi Island. This is sparsely populated, mostly by fishing families, but here there were numerous reports of electrical interference in homes. Lights failed, and clocks and watches stopped as if magnetized. The island was plunged into darkness, a report notes. Everyone rushed outside, and almost the entire population of the island saw the UFO—burning brighter than Venus, spinning fast, and issuing spirals of energy. The local electricity board confirmed that there was an unexpected power outage that lasted about a minute during the passage of the object.

Of course, the most common type of physical evidence for these aerial encounters comes in the form of radar trackings. We need to take a closer look at how useful these can be. A remarkable example occurred on the night of May 19, 1986, over Brazil. Numerous aircraft, both civil and military, and several ground-based and airborne radars were involved. You cannot get more evidence than in this case. But did it prove there was a genuine anomaly up there?

It started at about 9:10 p.m. on a clear, starlit night when a Xingu executive aircraft was approaching São José dos Campos on a flight from Brasília. The pilot was Osires Silva, who was president of the state oil company and of the aeronautical outlet Embraer—owners of the jet. With him was Alcir da Silva, a pilot with the company who had 6000 flying hours to his credit.

Osires Silva was a qualified aircraft engineer and first saw a light that was behaving oddly. The aircraft was at 2000 feet, descending under control of São Paulo regional air traffic center, but the two men quickly turned the plane to face the light more clearly.

The UFO was described as "brighter than a star, emitting a constant red-orange light" but pulsing every 15 seconds or so. The object was in the northeast over the Serra da Mantiqueira region between Brasília and Rio de Janeiro. Over the course of the next few minutes, further colored lights were seen, and Silva turned on his airborne radar and picked up confirmatory echoes.

However, ground control soon became concerned about the "pursuit" set in motion by the Xingu, now merrily chasing these lights all over the sky. They ordered the men to make for a landing. São Paulo had a large volume of air traffic in the area and the presence of reported UFOs was already complicating matters. A rogue jet flying after them was not wanted by the ground control.

Silva later noted that the big red object "did not look anything like the flying saucers seen [in the media]. It was a circular light. It was moving at speeds of up to 950 mph."

By the time the Xingu touched down just before 10 p.m., the radar system for the area was already on alert. Screens at both São José dos Campos Airport and the regional center at São Paulo had picked up about a dozen unidentified returns. The same was true of a military radar to the north at Anapolis Air Force Base. Valdecir Coelho, radar controller, said that in his 14 years of service he had never seen anything like the returns they were picking up above the mountains.

Even the air minister, Brigadier-General Octavio Lima, was very frank and explained days later why they ordered the Xingu to land. "Since the UFOs had saturated our radar system in São Paulo and were interfering with air traffic, we decided that we must send up [military] planes to pursue them."

This they did. Three Brazilian Air Force F-5s were scrambled from Santa Cruz Air Force Base near São Paulo. Two were airborne at 10:23 p.m. and the third half an hour later. Lieutenant Kleber Marinho was one of the first F-5 pilots. He was sent towards a target 35 miles from him, but he could not see anything. Radar control advised that the blip was rushing towards him at speed, but still nothing was visible. Finally he saw a distant light and tried to chase it, but reported that it was "like attempting to reach a point at infinity." Running low on fuel, he returned to base.

Captain Mario Jordão had a better view. He closed the gap on one target to 12 miles and says that the object was a bright light pulsing white and green. He finally had to give up when the light shot off towards the ocean.

At 10:50 p.m., the military decided to take no more chances. Three Mirage fighters were loaded with AIM-9 Sidewinder missiles and launched from Anapolis Air Force Base near Brasília. However, by the time they had reached the area to the south, the UFOs had begun to speed away towards the coast. Only one Mirage pilot, Captain Armindo de Freitas, saw anything.

He was scrambled towards several targets, which at first were 20 miles away, and then closed in 2 miles behind him and tailed the Mirage! He explained, "I was warned by ground control that the contacts were approaching me. Then they were following me. I had to lower my plane, because the lights had descended, but, from that point on, they began to climb vertically. This was my only visual contact, but I could see them on my radar at a distance of 12 miles dead ahead." Visually, they were simply bright lights.

Hugo Freitas, manning the radar at Anapolis, called the rather concerned Mirage pilot to report at one point that thirteen of the targets had lined up and surrounded his aircraft—six going to one wing and seven to the other. These made twisting turns through right angles at great speed, making it very difficult for the Mirage to get a good view. "No planes I know can make turns like that at 700 mph," the Mirage pilot noted.

One of the F-5 pilots saw this close encounter on his airborne radar. But soon afterwards all of the targets disappeared both on radar and visually. The last contact was around midnight, when a Brasília airline pilot, Commander Oto, was en route from São Luis to Brasília and observed "an object like a ping pong ball. It seemed not to reflect, but to have light of its own. It followed my plane at 40,000 feet."

It was quite impossible to contain such a big story, and the president of Brazil decided to order the full public declaration of all of the evidence about this case. As a result, the air minister, Octavio Lima, observed that "it is not a question of believing." The evidence, he felt, spoke for itself.

The Brazilian defense authorities made several suggestions—from radar echoes caused by meteorological mirage effects known as temperature inversions to electronic warfare experiments by a foreign power. But they admitted that these were just guesswork. In truth, as Lima said, "We have neither answers nor technical explanations for what happened."

Here we have perhaps the sort of case that ought to be definitive. Yet it is not. Numerous pilots saw things. Ground and airborne radar detected objects as well. Yet often there was no direct correlation. A radar detection had no attendant visual image, for instance, or vice versa. This behavior, plus the fact that these targets were around for some hours, is more characteristic of radar anomalies and atmospheric deceptions, known as angels, than it is of solid targets akin to unidentified aircraft (terrestrial or non-terrestrial). UFOs are normally rather transient things.

Yet there were several occasions when all three modes of perception—ground radar, airborne radar, and the eyes of the pilots—simultaneously recorded something. This alone does not prove that UFOs were involved. Some kind of illusion generated by an inversion layer could distort both radar signals and visual stimuli, such as bright stars or ground lights.

Is this what happened here?

The official investigation appears not to have found such an easy solution. Instead the chief of the air traffic control system, Ney Siqueira, effectively opted out of the debate by saying that they could merely emphasize the facts in their report and leave judgments about them to others. As far as they were concerned, they had labeled the contacts as "unidentified aerial movements." Of course, as I suspect you may be able to appreciate, in many respects it does not really matter what these phenomena were. The fact is that they clearly put air traffic at risk—if only because aircraft were scrambled out of their way and military jets were aloft, cavorting around amidst civil airlanes, armed with missiles and ready to shoot.

Undoubtedly, given the tension that night, they were not immune to the sort of mistake that could have seen the worried military pilots interpreting a passing jumbo jet as one of the UFOs that they all believed were posing an immediate defense threat.

We have to find out what is causing these crises. If they are unknown phenomena, we should identify them through careful scientific analysis. In that regard, the decision by the Brazilian government to openly and swiftly publish its data on this case is greatly commended and such a policy ought to be more widely adopted. For even if these events were the result of some kind of anomalous atmospheric process that can create spurious targets on radar and fuzzy light distortions in the sky, their capacity to wreak chaos for air traffic control is obvious. And, sadly, so is their undoubted ability to lead one day towards an inevitable disaster.

If, indeed, they have not already done so.

On May 29, 1984, the Soviet Union announced the creation of an official UFO study program. It had operated a covert project for many years, as we know thanks to the release of files after the fall of communism. So why did it suddenly choose to make this odd public announcement? The timing may have been very significant.

Indeed, the story featured a reference to an earlier, rather reckless official *Pravda* statement that "all objects that fly over the territory of our country are identified either by scientists or by those who stand guard over the security of our homeland." This also may not have been unimportant.

The case that really convinced the USSR that it had problems occurred on March 17, 1983, when air traffic control at Gorky observed a light gray, missile-shaped object heading across the evening sky in their direction. It was at 3000 feet and moving at 125 mph in a strange path that took it southeast of the city and then back north. It was tracked on radar, and the matter was taken seriously.

Gorky was a highly sensitive area with many secret research sites. This object was considered to be potentially hostile. The air traffic controllers attempted to establish radio contact but received no response to their demands that the UFO turn away from its course and land. On orders from Moscow, the object was allowed to proceed northwards where, at 25 miles, it simply vanished off the radar screens. It was, of course, yet another of those mysterious missiles or flying lozenges.

The man put in charge of the newly-created Soviet investigation was cosmonaut and scientist Dr. Pavel Popovich. He noted that the Gorky case involved highly-qualified witnesses and ground radar observing an object for 40 minutes. This, he said, was too important to be ignored.

Six months after Gorky, another unidentified target was picked up by Soviet radar. This was also heading for top secret airspace—over Sakhalin Island. Warnings were sent on military frequencies, but there was no response and the object continued on its path. This latest intrusion was regarded gravely, and an interceptor was sent up. In the dark, it failed to identify the outline that it saw ahead—a long, dark cylindrical shape. The Soviet pilot fired an air-to-air missile and blasted the target out of the sky. That target was Korean Airlines Flight 007—a Boeing 747 packed with passengers. The aircraft had strayed off course and had its cabin lights turned low.

This terrible disaster stunned the world. There were outcries against the shooting down of an unarmed civilian aircraft in such a callous manner. Yet, rather curiously, there was not the massive official outcry that you might have expected. I personally felt that the matter was rather too rapidly forgotten. In isolation, this seems difficult to understand. But what if this tragic affair could be seen by the powers that be in a broader light than that afforded to most ordinary folk? What if they knew full well that mistakes like this were almost inevitable because unknown aerial phenomena were passing through our airspace and being tracked on radar all the time? These were almost bound to provoke some kind of response and occasionally result in tragedy.

Did the downing of KAL Flight 007 follow as a consequence of the UFO that overflew Gorky only months before? Was the fact that this second incident appeared to the Soviets like a rerun secretly taken into account by other nations? Once its terrible mistake was realized, was the creation of the UFO Project by the USSR a sort of public atonement?

Certainly the sequence of events in that 1-year period from Gorky through Sakhalin Island to the creation of the Popovich commission may well be relevant. This might indicate that UFOs are not of incidental interest to those involved with air safety. Regardless of their origin, they could be fundamental to the protection of the lives of hundreds of people. Thankfully, there are signs of a dawning awareness. But the bureaucratic machine grinds slowly and the impact of bad public relations where UFOs are concerned—not to mention military consideration—keeps on getting in the way.

On November 17, 1986, a Boeing 747 owned by Japan Airlines found itself the latest victim to be thrust into the middle of the UFO war zone. JAL 1628 was a cargo flight from Paris to Tokyo which traveled on a dog-leg flight over the North Pole. En route from a refuel stop at Reykjavik in Iceland to Anchorage, Alaska, it was to confront something that was cer-tainly not Santa Claus.

At the helm of the giant aircraft was Captain Kenju Terauchi. Also aboard were First Officer Takanori Tamefuji and Engineer Yoship Tsukuda. All were to witness the events and to file a report on landing at the Alaskan port. The American FAA was to immediately launch an inves-tigation, then abandon this after a few days. However, it had no intention of making its findings public. No doubt it hoped that the JAL crew would follow the time-honored practice of not talking in public where UFOs were concerned.

Only the crew did not. They talked to family and friends back in Japan, from whence news of the incident filtered out around 6 weeks later. Then the FAA was asked for answers by the story-hungry media. Paul Steucke of the FAA's Anchorage office tried to explain that nobody had meant to hide the truth. "We just did not do anything with it," he said. "We were not keeping it a secret. We just did not announce it." This no doubt happens more often than not in situations where the aircrew maintains its silence.

Faced with what was a brief press interest in this case, the FAA made noise about an investigation and did reopen its study—seemingly on orders from Washington. Of course, by then the press had lost interest, which was probably the expectation. UFO stories are news for only a short while and then something new comes along to distract the public's attention. Only UFOlogists were sufficiently interested in the truth about JAL 1628 to real-ly push for answers. This account will attempt to tell you what did happen.

It was about 6:14 p.m. Alaskan time as the 747 crossed Fort Yukon at 35,000 feet. The sky was sharp and clear with many stars and a full moon visible. Terauchi spotted three lights ahead of the jumbo and pointed these out to his colleagues, thinking another aircraft was on the same path ahead. They resembled the glow of an exhaust and were colored yellow and amber.

After some debate, the cockpit lights were switched off to rule out reflections from the windscreen. But the lights were still out there and nobody could figure out what they were. By now, they knew that no aircraft should have been in their path. Terauchi even altered course slightly to ensure that the lights had indeed moved relative to the aircraft. This proved that they were really out there in the sky.

At about 6:22 p.m., with the lights still visible, they called Anchorage control to report the sighting. Terauchi was a veteran pilot with 30 years' flying experience. He was genuinely perplexed by what they were seeing as all the staff at ground control confirmed.

According to the testimony of the crew, there were two strange "strip lights." They formed vertical banks of color, seemingly made up of myriad lights. These were ahead of the aircraft and fairly small—hence, the original suspicion that they were lights on an aircraft exhaust. All crew members had good views of these lights.

Yet there was a third object, and only Terauchi saw that one. This was enormous. He claims that it dwarfed his 747 and was "twice as big as an aircraft carrier." He described its shape as like a walnut without the shell. However, he only saw its dark outline for a few moments through his side window.

Using rather emotive language, which might provide a key to his perception of what was taking place, the captain spoke of "two small ships and a mother ship" and was free with his speculation about them being extraterrestrial. Coupling these inferences with humor (he joked that the aliens may have been after his cargo of Beaujolais wine!), Terauchi may have come across as somewhat excitable, although no doubt he had every reason to be so, under the circumstances.

By now, rather keen to evade the objects, the 747 got permission from Anchorage to descend to 31,000 feet and try to escape. It failed to do this. The UFOs remained in proximity to the jet.

This seems to be important information, because it demonstrates that whatever they were seeing was one of two things. It was either something very close that was matching them step for step—a dangerous prospect that would inevitably have fueled speculation about alien devices. Or else it was something in the order of miles in diameter and a very long way from the aircraft—such as a glowing phenomenon in the furthest reaches of the upper atmosphere. These are the only reasons for its lack of movement as the aircraft descended.

The 747 now turned over Fairbanks to head towards Alaska. As it did so and began its full descent into the airport, the UFOs were lost from view. They were last seen at around 6:51 p.m.

On board the jumbo was color weather radar equipment. As already noted when discussing the British Airways Trident encounter above Portugal, this kind of system is not adapted to pick up targets like other aircraft or UFOs. It exists to warn pilots of massive cloud systems and so will really only pick up very large reflective objects in the order of magnitude of thunderstorms and mountains.

Neither of the two "strip lights" in front of the aircraft—emitting red, yellow, and occasionally green light—was ever seen on the 747 radar. But Terauchi claims that the massive object was. It appeared at about the 11 o'clock position—close to the two smaller lights. This return gave a huge green circular blob as a target during the few minutes when he visually observed it.

A green target on color weather radar indicated a fairly weakly-reflective object. It is not what you would expect from an alien spaceship twice the size of the *Ark Royal*. This was not likely to be a mountain reflection either, as during the Portuguese Trident case. There were no ground targets of sufficient size to cause this problem. Rather it suggests a cloudlike mass was being picked up on the system, possibly a reflective cloud and maybe even one generating ionization high in the atmosphere.

What of the ground radar? There were two separate systems—one civilian, at Anchorage control, and one military, at Elmendorf Air Force Base. Both were fed from the same primary source, although the civilian radar had a filter that cut out interference from things like temperature inversions and normal ground clutter. The military radar did not have this, being primed to pick up any return as opposed to just aircraft.

Both of these radars did see another target close by JAL 1628. It was estimated as 5 miles distant at its nearest point, yet there has been huge debate over what was actually detected.

It was 6:26 p.m. when the FAA called Elmendorf to see if their radar had anything besides the 747, as Terauchi was saying there was something on his weather radar at 8 miles. The FAA radar did have a weak secondary target near the JAL flight, but it kept fading in and out. The military radar backed this sighting up. There was a target 8 miles from the jumbo. However, within seconds it simply vanished.

This intermittent appearance seems to have continued until just before JAL 1628 last saw the lights. Then the radar at Elmendorf picked up two blips, one of which was the 747, but the other had fallen behind the now descending aircraft. As the 747 came in for a landing, the unidentified target remained high in the sky and then disappeared.

Acting on this radar information, the FAA requested both a military Hercules transport aircraft and United Airlines Flight 69, which passed through the area around 6:45 p.m., to look out for unknowns. Neither aircraft saw anything apart from the JAL jumbo, despite the United 747 being vectored into a position where it should have been able to see the target that the ground radar screens were now reporting. However, that target vanished from radar permanently almost the moment that the United jumbo was flown into place ready to see it!

So what was the object on radar? The only comment by the military at Elmendorf was by Captain Robert Morris, who said that they interpreted the second image as "random clutter or weather interference." When Walt Andrus of the Mutual UFO Network pursued this theory with Paul Steucke at the FAA on January 2, 1987, he said they had given up any expectation of finding useful data. Elmendorf had reused their radar tapes a few days later and so this evidence was not even available to the FAA inquiry. While the civilian controllers at Anchorage had seen a target fading in and out during the sighting, this failed to appear when they regenerated the radar pictures by putting the FAA tapes through a computer program. As such, Steucke was of the opinion that this had merely been a radar echo of the 747, as was sometimes known to occur, and that its signal was simply too weak to be reproduced when the electronic reconstruction process was used.

That was the line given by Washington to the media. It quickly killed interest in the case. Although the pilots were considered sincere and competent and clearly saw something they could not identify, there was really nothing that could be done by the authorities because the anticipated radar confirmation did not pan out.

There was only one problem—and it was not recognized by the media. Half the vital radar evidence was simply not available for study because it had been destroyed by the military, despite a supposed FAA investigation leading to its retention. Also, the civil and military authorities disagreed as to what their controllers had seen. Was it weather interference or an echo of the jumbo jet? Without any permanent record, we were never going to know.

Interestingly, the same day that Walt Andrus pressed Steucke on this matter, the FAA decided to reopen its investigation. The official reason given—by Steucke himself, in fact—was that the event "was a violation of our airspace." But he added that "no one considers it realistic that we can identify the object," although they would try to discover the source.

Despite this seeming assurance about the poor nature of the radar evidence, it is interesting to note the comments of the radar controllers who were on duty at the FAA facility at Anchorage that night. Sam Rich, one of the team speaking on behalf of himself and two colleagues, says, "All three of us thought there was a track."

This seems to fly in the face of the official FAA position that only one radar operator saw anything and that he had simply mistaken an echo of the 747.

Rich further notes that Captain Terauchi was clearly distressed and had a "quaver in his voice." They turned their radar from long range to closer proximity to look for the target that the JAL pilot was describing and found it "near the plane about where he said it was."

Rich agrees that the radar target was not a strong one, but states also that none of the operators who saw it thought it was an echo of the 747 transponder signal. He also confirms that he spoke with the military radar controllers at Elmendorf, and they were clearly watching the same track as Anchorage.

Moreover, the controllers are familiar with areas of the Alaskan sky where double images of aircraft do occasionally appear. But JAL 1628 was not near any of them. Rich adds that the FAA banned the air traffic controllers from speaking in public until after the press interest had died down. This rather suggests that the FAA members were afraid of its becoming clear that they really did not have a good explanation for the radar returns.

As for Captain Terauchi, the only JAL crew member to speak out, it is difficult to know what to make of his story. He was clearly sincere, and in fact insisted on taking both drug and alcohol tests on landing, and to be given a polygraph (lie detector) test. He passed all three.

Yet on January 11, 1987, he claimed another UFO encounter while passing over Alaska at 7:30 a.m. on a JAL cargo flight from London to Anchorage! With Terauchi were two different crew members. The copilot confirmed seeing lights that passed below them, but chose not to speak in public. The engineer told the FAA that he was "uncertain" whether he saw anything at all.

Terauchi was anything but uncertain. He told the ground controller, "I see irregular lights. It looks like a spaceship." However, he insisted they were nothing like the objects seen in November.

This time, neither the Anchorage nor Elmendorf radar picked up any targets other than the 747—not even an echo! However, the FAA was reasonably sure this UFO was probably what is termed a "bounced light effect"—a mirror-reflective mirage caused by lights on the ground being seen from the air through a weather phenomenon known as a temperature inversion layer. There was one in effect that night at 23,500 feet, and this can distort objects in quite spectacular fashion.

What was seen during the earlier encounter where there was, at least, some evidence of radar confirmation? Aviation writer Philip Klass, a tenacious UFO skeptic, tried to show that the JAL aircraft merely saw the planets Mars and Jupiter. Both were in roughly the same part of the sky, but it seems improbable that such an experienced pilot would mistake these commonly seen lights in such a huge way. To make the theory work, Klass must also establish that the radar targets were irrelevant.

I think it could be significant that auroral displays are common over polar regions. This phenomenon was not the aurora borealis as such, since Terauchi and crew had often flown the route and seen the rippling curtain of colored light many times. However, the glows of an aurora are caused by charged particles of ionized gas high above the earth creating green, yellow, and orange colors. Perhaps on November 17, 1986, there was a rare type of high altitude ionized cloud that chanced to create a very unusual sight.

Indeed, some fascinating films have been captured by recent space shuttle flights from earth orbit. One incident in December 1996 aboard STS-70 involved several minutes of film that showed slowly drifting glowing clouds as bright as the periodic flashes of fierce thunderstorms.

These masses are about the size of the object that Terauchi claims appeared on his 747 weather radar, and are very high in the atmosphere—so high, in fact, that they would rarely be visible except from orbit or, rarer still, from high-flying aircraft.

I suspect the shuttle footage is scientific evidence of a not too common and barely understood atmospheric phenomenon in which huge clouds of glowing, powerful ionizing radiation can drift at speed across the edge of our atmosphere. The JAL jumbo crew may have seen this effect from below rather than from above.

However, once more we have found that a case that appears to offer real hope of strong evidence actually provokes more questions than answers once you start to dig deep. Of course, we cannot disprove that JAL 1628 encountered an alien spacecraft—as its pilot appears to believe. But his theory does seem needlessly extreme in such circumstances. Surely a glowing mass of colored lights and a briefly perceived dim outline of a large dark shape—all of which appear to have remained more or less stationary in the polar skies for half an hour—are more suggestive of a natural scientific anomaly?

But then, who knows what an alien starship would look like?

Certainly not the film crew from an Australian TV station who found themselves amidst the same terror that confronted JAL 1628. This case may offer us the best chance of all to analyze the value of radar evidence, since it has been subjected to more scientific study than any other UFO event in history. It has just about everything—visual sightings from the air and on the ground by multiple trained witnesses, radar trackings, and film evidence of the objects that were seen. If this case cannot provide us with proof of something genuinely unexplained, then it seems unlikely that any midair encounter ever will!

The scene of this remarkable series of events is one that we have already visited during an earlier look at a midair encounter. Then, a cargo aircraft crossing Cook Strait between New Zealand's North and South Islands encountered a strange light also picked up by radar. But this 1969 prelude bears little comparison with the dramatic events of December 1978.

Kaikoura, south of Blenheim on the South Island, is today a popular tourist spot where boat tours take you out to go whale watching in the fierce seas. But the mountains inland and the scattered villages surrounding the foothills, such as Clarence, had been host to numerous sightings of strange lights in the sky as the antipodean summer months of late 1978 approached. These pulsated red, green, and white and even led to speculation amongst local farmers about vanishing sheep being kidnapped by aliens. All such views are typical of what follows sightings of lights in the sky in today's social climate.

Then, on the night of December 20–21, the dam broke.

It started just before midnight, when Warrant Officer Ian Offendell was working at the air base at Blenheim. His job was security and he was driving around the perimeter in a van, checking that all was well. But then he saw three lights in the sky that he assumed was a freighter aircraft coming in to land. So he stood to watch it arrive, except that the lights remained in the sky and did not begin to land. Puzzled by this sight, he went to the base control tower to ask what was hovering over the coast. They had no idea, but the duty officer went with Offendell to see for himself and then put a call through to the radar control center at Wellington on the far side of Cook Strait.

On duty here was John Cordy, a man who had worked at busy airports, such as London Heathrow, but who was now enjoying the more relaxed traffic flow in New Zealand. Cordy was in charge that night and had a junior, Andy Heard, working with him. They were awaiting the arrival of a DC-8 that was on its way from Sydney, Australia. It was still many miles away from their airspace. Nothing much else was going on at the time. So when they spotted unusual radar returns off the coast near Kaikoura, they had more opportunity to pay attention than they might normally have done.

Cordy admits that he and Heard joked about UFOs because they were much in the news. This was because an Australian pilot had just vanished after reporting a close encounter.

He notes, "We just sat there and watched them quietly because we had no aircraft to talk with and nobody we could ask to take a look." The blips were "moving in a random but purposeful fashion. They were making little circles and going backwards and forwards." As there were coastal hills to their south and over 80 miles between them and either Blenheim or Kaikoura, they did not consider going outside to try to take a look, as they knew it would be futile.

After an hour or more of these unusual targets appearing on screen, the duty flight service officer, Bill Frame, called from Blenheim to report what he and Offendell were seeing out towards Cape Campbell. Cordy told them that they had been watching odd radar returns in this area for quite some time.

As the men talked, it was soon obvious that the military personnel at Blenheim were seeing visually what Cordy and Heard were watching on their radar screen. There were three primary targets—a large central one flanked by two smaller ones. If they seemed to move north on the radar, Offendell and Frame saw them move north. If they went out to sea, the radar confirmed that they were doing this as well.

Cordy kept trying to think of an explanation, but had never come across anything like this. The blips seemed too strong and were moving too logically to be spurious returns. Besides, the two experienced air force personnel who were watching them confirmed that they were really there. He knew they were not aircraft, because they had checked every possible source—needing to know if anything was up there, as Wellington airspace would get busy later in the night with much inbound international traffic. Also, these objects were moving in too tight a circle to be manned aircraft.

However, there was another problem. From time to time, the targets stopped moving and were stationary on the radar screen. This ought to have been impossible, as the aircraft radar system employed something called a "moving target indicator." This MTI was designed to cut out stationary returns, which objects like tall buildings might provoke.

Back at Blenheim, two of the objects had separated from the large one and climbed higher in the sky. Then beams of light were seen to come down towards the ground. These appeared to move across the sky as if searching for something. Offendell relayed this news to Cordy, asking for an answer. Cordy had none to offer, but the warrant officer had already concluded that "it was a controlled craft of some description." Because it did not seem to be from New Zealand or any of New Zealand's allies, he then began to suspect that it had to be extraterrestrial in origin.

Later in the night, police on the coast called the air base to discover if they had any helicopters flying. They had received similar reports from people out near Clarence that "searchlight beams" were playing on the water and on the beach, moving around as if probing the area.

Eventually the three lights being viewed from Blenheim had lined up in formation again and drifted off southwards and out to sea. Ian Offendell said he had had enough and went to bed.

Unfortunately, that luxury was not available to the air traffic controllers at Wellington, especially as traffic was now increasing. Even when Andy Heard's tour of duty ended and he had the chance to go home, he told John Cordy that he was staying on to see how things checked out. Like his boss, he knew that this was something he might never witness again.

In his later report, Cordy was to try to justify what kind of targets they had been seeing. He said that the images were exactly the same as an aircraft return and there was nothing about the blips that suggested an angel (spurious return). He did not think they were solid objects, in the same sense as an aircraft, but he could not say what form of object the returns really were.

The DC-8 arrived at Wellington, but did not pass near Kaikoura in doing so and reported seeing nothing. But finally an opportunity arose when a cargo aircraft took off from Auckland and headed south for Blenheim. Cordy asked the pilot to look out for the lights, as strange returns were still on radar out to sea. The crew saw nothing.

By 1:20 a.m., that aircraft, a Safe Air Argosy freighter (Alpha Echo), was scheduled to take off from Blenheim to fly south to Christchurch. At the controls was Captain John Randle, accompanied by First Officer Keith Heine. Randle reported seeing "several bright yellow-white lights" out to sea off Kaikoura as they turned south on departure. At the time, Cordy was tracking lights moving at about 1200 mph in the area indicated. Cordy adds that Captain Randle said the lights were projecting beams downward, causing reflections to shimmer on the ocean. He stressed that these were definitely not distress flares. Heine tells us that there was one large white light out to sea to the east. It was so strong that it was lighting up clouds. He likened it to a parachute flare, and was indignant at suggestions by skeptics who later insisted that this was the planet Venus. In 1995, Heine said that after flying commercially for 30 years he had seen Venus rising high in the sky and under all sorts of atmospheric conditions. He knew what it looked like. Nothing he had ever seen was remotely like the object out to sea off Kaikoura that night.

Cordy and Heard had been watching on radar an object that crossed the strait southeastwards from Wellington at a steady 140 mph. Then it slowed down and stopped off the northern coast of North Island. It remained there for 40 minutes.

The only possible thing that the controllers could think of to explain this was a weather balloon. They called the release station to discover that their last launch had burst and fallen to earth an hour later. In any case, the tracked speeds of this object were far too high, especially when the long-time stationary target streaked away at almost 200 mph. Indeed it appeared to see the passing Argosy and move towards it, tailing it at some 15 miles' range. But John Randle did not see anything that might correlate at this point. Indeed, Keith Heine says the voice of John Cordy conveyed the proximity of the object as it started to move towards them, and things got rather scary for a time. It was initially said to be on a collision course but quickly tracked behind the Argosy.

Frustrated by their inability to figure out what was happening, the operators at Wellington pulled apart the radar to try to find something wrong with it. But it was working perfectly and tracking all the identified air traffic as normal. As Cordy explains, if there had been any doubts about the capacity of the radar, then they would have immediately taken it out of use. It is too risky to try to control air traffic with equipment that is not 100%.

After these adventures, Randle and Heine decided to change their return journey flight plan from Christchurch to Auckland. Normally this would route inland over Nelson, but they decided to head east towards Kaikoura instead. By now, virtually all air traffic and ground staff in New Zealand that were on duty were aware that they were living through a real "night of the UFOs."

The Safe Air Argosy reported further brief sightings at 4:06 a.m. as it flew through the area heading north to Auckland. Cordy asked Randle to do a circuit, and he told of "dancing lights" by the Clarence River mouth. But there was a further drama described by Heine.

> As we were tracking towards Kaikoura, we saw a light that was coming towards us very, very quickly. I recall Wellington radar talking about returns they were getting, and Captain John Randle said that he was seeing them on the aircraft radar by his side. They were coming rapidly towards us for some minutes. Then they suddenly vanished. It all happened so fast.

Heine has since concluded that the only explanation that satisfies him is that the object seen visually and on both ground and airborne radar had to be some kind of secret American military technology. Nothing else could move like this thing did. He does not believe in alien spaceships.

An hour before this frightening episode, a second Safe Air Argosy (Alpha Foxtrot) was at 13,000 feet heading south on its way towards Christchurch. By now, 3:00 a.m., they were aware of the UFO activity reported by Alpha Echo and knew that Wellington radar would be asking them to keep their eyes open. In charge were Captain Vernon Powell and First Officer Ian Pirie.

Powell called Wellington to ask if there was an aircraft on a parallel course. Cordy told him there was no aircraft, but radar was tracking an object where he was seeing a big reddish/white light. As they headed south, the light faded. They told Wellington. Cordy confirmed it had vanished from radar at the same moment. This happened a couple more times—the object disappearing and then reappearing, both visually and on radar. Finally, they left the light behind to head into Christchurch.

Approaching the airport at 3:28 a.m., something incredible happened. The onboard radar was in mapping mode to chart the coast, but suddenly, as Captain Powell reports, "We had a very bright radar echo...whatever this was produced a very bright image and the tail of it stayed bright between sweeps." The object swept across the radar "at alarming speed, leaving a trail across the scope." They had never seen any effect like this on the screen before. Powell, with 35 years of flying experience behind him, reckons that its speed was so phenomenal it seemed "ridiculous"—thousands of miles per hour!

Even as the captain yelled out what was happening, Ian Pirie was looking out of the cockpit and watching a brilliant flare of light streak across their path at incredible speed. Christchurch radar had not detected anything. Wellington radar was too far north to do so.

Vern Powell says that he later received numerous reports from people living in the Kaikoura and Christchurch areas who had seen things in the sky that night. Many were too afraid of ridicule to go public with their stories. One of them was a medical scientist who held a major government position at the time. He asked Captain Powell to come to his Christchurch home to talk about his sighting, but only on the understanding that his identity be protected.

Powell had seen various other things during his flying career, notably a number of the "strange green fireballs" that are by now rather like old friends. But there had never been anything as extraordinary as the night of December 20–21, 1978.

With so many people involved and the air transport community of New Zealand buzzing with the news, it was not surprising that the media featured the story. By chance, reporter Quentin Fogarty of an Australian TV network, Channel 10, was on vacation in the country. Before leaving Melbourne, he had agreed to cover any New Zealand stories that might break during his vacation. When the UFO sightings occurred, the TV network called Fogarty on Boxing Day to suggest he get some footage to accompany their planned report on the matter.

Fogarty knew that the Safe Air Argosies flew the route from Auckland to Wellington to Blenheim to Christchurch and back north again each night. Their cargo was newly printed newspapers—hence, this nocturnal flight plan. So he came up with the idea of flying aboard one of the aircraft and filming the scene from above. This was just for background shots to accompany his news report. That report would include witness interviews. With his normal film crew back in Australia, he commissioned a local team, David and Ngaire Crockett, to take care of filming and sound work.

Safe Air was very cooperative, and on the night of December 30–31, 1978, the news team crammed aboard the freight hold of Captain Bill Startup and First Officer Bob Guard's Argosy.

Fogarty recorded a set-up piece amidst the rumbling noises of the flight as they headed south over Cook Strait. He told how they were approaching the Clarence River, the scene of most of the sightings 10 days earlier. As they were about to do a second take, Bill Startup popped his head down into the hold and urged the three of them to come onto the flight deck. They all clambered into this noisy, cramped, and dark environment. Startup pointed down towards the lights of a small town (later found to be Kaikoura), and above there were several strange lights floating in the sky.

I have either met or communicated with many of the people involved in this affair, including Quentin Fogarty, Bill Startup, and John Cordy. During trips to Australia and New Zealand, I have studied the whole footage. The witnesses described how the lights pulsated red and white colors and lit up the ground or the sea over which they hovered. At first, Fogarty stood entranced watching them. Then he realized what a scoop had fallen into their laps.

The ever alert Crocketts were already filming through the tiny window, desperately trying to get the camera to focus properly on the distant lights. Davy said that he could only see lights that looked like stars through his lens, but the excitement of the aircrew suggested that more was going on.

Meanwhile Fogarty started babbling an off-the-cuff commentary recorded by Ngaire. As Fogarty talked, his words expressed the awe that the people on the flight deck were feeling. He spoke of how frightening it was getting and uttered the perfect sound bite, "Let's hope they're friendly," which later became the title of his book about that night. It was to concentrate on the amazing media furor that followed, while Bill Startup and Bob Guard told their own story in a very different kind of book.

The reporter was to express disappointment when the film was later processed. It did not capture the brilliance of the lights, the way they pulsated, nor the size they seemed to convey to him. In fact, the film really shows a camera struggling to focus properly on what are just little lights— rather as the cameraman Crockett said they were. The fact that the flight deck was overcrowded, that the cargo plane was not set up for passengers, and that the heavy vibrations made filming through a tiny window very hard, indeed all contributed to the problems. But, overall, you are left to wonder how much expectation, excitement, and the inevitable tension of the night ensured a heightened sense of anticipation. Cameras do not suffer from excitability in the face of close encounters. That they recorded rather less than the witnesses recall seeing for themselves is interesting.

After landing at Christchurch, the team from Channel 10 was supposed to offload and drive back north, stopping at Blenheim and Kaikoura to film ground witnesses. But Fogarty urged the Safe aircrew to let them fly back to Wellington. Ngaire Crockett absolutely refused to go back up in the air. So local reporter Dennis Grant, who had overheard the radio transmissions, took her place.

More strange lights were seen over Kaikoura during the return leg. This most spectacular footage was captured using a 200 mm telephoto lens, with some of Fogarty's choicest commentary included.

There are various odd shapes on the many minutes of footage, but these are mostly artifacts caused by the camera's zooming in and out of focus. One scene shows a light moving at high speed in a loop-the-loop when stills are extracted. But this is a result of the camera shaking.

Truthfully, there are plenty of lights on the film. Some are probably ground lights, such as aircraft beacons. Others are probably stars and planets in the sky. A few may be unidentified. Crockett was pointing and shooting at anything out there, but in the end (at least to my eyes) there are no spaceships or any solid, structured craft that is clearly visible. Anomalous lights are about the full extent of it. That is so very often how it turns out, of course, in UFO encounters.

To be honest, I have my doubts as to whether anything truly bizarre was filmed that night, although it may have been. That said, Wellington radar was also tracking unknown targets over Kaikoura as the film was being taken. So perhaps this is being a little unfair.

Very quickly the film footage was flashed all over the world. It became an enormous story for a few days, and, in Fogarty's book, he concentrates on the media fiasco that developed as a result. Optical physicist Dr. Bruce Maccabee flew from Washington to investigate the evidence and was persuaded that something important was recorded. Yet the witnesses have very different ideas as to what that might have been. These range from some kind of alien craft to a secret U.S. weapon to Quentin Fogarty's opinion that the lights were a form of psychic phenomenon. John Cordy accepted that the radar trackings could have been some kind of optical effect but felt they were too strong and long lasting for that.

However, the skeptics had their own ideas. This case generated more explanations than any other on record. Some of these solutions were absurd, such as Santa Claus and the wonderfully daft suggestion of moonlight reflecting off a cabbage patch (not many of those out at sea, unfortunately!). Others could be quickly disproved, such as Venus (it had not risen at the time and planets do not turn up on radar). But the most logical explanation and the one that seemed quite feasible for a time was a fleet of Japanese squid-fishing boats that used brilliant floodlights. Sadly, these were traced 150 miles away at the time in question and could not have been the cause of the sightings.

Perhaps the most telling evidence that something genuine might well have been seen was the fact that Davy Crockett persuaded Safe Air to take him up again during the first week in January 1978. They flew the same route—as indeed did many other Argosies over the coming months. The strange lights filmed on December 20–21 and New Year's Eve 1978 did not reappear despite the cameraman's having far better equipment, such as infrared film and a massive telephoto lens ready to stun the world anew.

If the objects filmed had been some kind of mundane phenomenon—such as stars, planets, fishing boats, or cabbages—then, surely, they would have been seen by these aircrews on a regular basis and picked up on Wellington radar many other times. The fact that they were not seems to enhance the strangeness of the events on these two nights in 1978. But once again we have no proof of exotic flying craft—simply mysterious lights in the sky.

10   FATAL ENCOUNTERS

"This is Echo India Alpha Oscar Mike—with you... We are at 12,000 feet, descending, spinning rapidly."

With those poignant words, an Aer Lingus Viscount (EI-AOM) fell from the sky into the cold waters of the Irish Sea just before noon on March 24, 1968. The crash claimed the lives of sixty-one people, but to this day nobody knows why it happened.

Although we can certainly learn a good deal about strange objects in the sky from the study of midair sightings, there can be no doubt that fatal encounters offer the most evidence. This is inevitable because the aviation authorities go to extraordinary lengths to trace the cause of any disaster in the hope of ensuring that it can never happen again.

Aviation is probably the safest form of transport yet invented, because of the decades of safeguards built in by so much thorough investigation. But it does not mean that the causes of all crashes are quickly identified. Sometimes they never are. Over the years, there have been a number of incidents in which, for want of a more appropriate term, a UFO was intimately involved and may even have been the direct cause of the tragedy. Of course, it should be remembered that by UFO I do not mean that an alien spaceship has been shooting our aircraft from the skies. Rather, I mean that some unknown object, whose origin has not been traced, was flying near the plane and seems to have been responsible for the accident.

Precisely what this "unidentified flying object" might have been during a fatal encounter will undoubtedly point us towards possible solutions during midair contacts where the outcome is rather happier. Thankfully, it most often is. As you will see, we may not be on the trail of just one culprit, the elusive "UFO" of modern folklore, but a range of phenomena that trigger close encounters.

It is a fallacy to assume that UFOs will provide a single answer. IFOs (identified flying objects) do not. They turn out to be all things—from weather effects to misidentified aircraft and balloons. I am equally confident that there are several different types of UFO that could be involved in aerial contacts.

The episode in which Viscount Oscar Mike fell from the sky is a case in point. The Aer Lingus plane was en route from Cork in Ireland to London Heathrow and had turned southwest at a cruising height of 17,000 feet to start its relatively short journey towards England. Captain O'Beirne had been ordered to switch from Shannon Air Traffic Control to the

London ATC. But something happened in the few moments between that instruction and the brief snatch of conversation heard by radar staff in England. Seconds after the pilot uttered those terrible words, the aircraft smashed into the ocean and sank.

A 2-year inquiry began immediately. The captain had an impeccable record. He had logged more hours on Viscounts than any other Aer Lingus pilot. Oscar Mike had just had a full inspection and was considered to be in perfect working order. The weather was calm and fine and seemed in no way likely to be a cause of the disaster. It all added up to a huge mystery.

But then came the statements from eyewitnesses at Hook Head—the closest land to the point where Oscar Mike met its fate. Quite a few of them had seen what appeared to be a cloud of debris following an explosion. This focused immediate attention on the possibility of a bomb. In later years, the activities of the IRA may have made that a strong possibility. But, in 1968, the troubles in Ireland were only simmering and, in any case, no trace of an on-board explosion could be found when some of the wreckage of the Viscount was hauled up from 250 feet down on the ocean bed. Finding signs of a bomb is one of the easier tasks that befall air accident investigators, and so they were as sure as they could be that there had not been one aboard Oscar Mike.

So what else might have been responsible? The accident investigation found six witnesses who saw what they took to be a second aircraft heading towards the area where the crash occurred. Others said they saw a dark cloud over Carnsore Point, out of which emerged a dark, cigarlike shape. This seems to have been at the time and place above the Irish Sea where Oscar Mike was falling to its doom.

Speculation has followed ever since that the Aer Lingus aircraft had a midair collision with either a missile or a target drone launched from Britain. The terrible accident was then covered up by both the MoD in London and the Irish government, although why this would occur seems hard to understand. Certainly such a revelation would have rightly provoked concern about these exercises. Yet ultimately, if it were a terrible mistake, things could have been learned from it and the obvious necessity of military training would have ensured that this would continue with added prudence.

Even in civilized nations cover-ups and conspiracies can occur, but it does seem hard to imagine that the cause of the destruction of a civil airliner would be deliberately hidden for 30 years if it were as tragically mundane as a straying missile or drone—especially when valuable lessons were thus learned.

The only known source from which such a launch could have occurred was on the coast of southwest Wales. However, the staff at RAF Aberporth denied any test launches and was supported by the local Catholic priest, James Cunnane, who swore that key men from the site were taking mass with him that day until after 11 a.m. They thus could not have returned to base early enough to down Oscar Mike. One man was controller of the self-destruct mechanism and no launches were permitted without his presence.

But then, as we have seen, strange missiles still get in the way of air traffic with alarming frequency all over the world. They surely cannot all be an incredible series of clumsy misfires.

So, if the eyewitnesses are correct, was there another unidentified object that could have collided with the Viscount? If it was perceived to be a UFO by the MoD and Irish government, did they choose expediency in saying nothing further?

Certainly any suspicion of UFO involvement might shed light on the fact that local fishermen, recruited to help search for the wreckage, told journalist Clive Gammon that they felt they were steered away from the correct spot for months afterwards. They knew where the aircraft had fallen, based on what local folks had seen that Sunday morning. Yet they were told to search in areas where the plane had not crashed. Predictably, they found nothing—until long after the furor had died down, when the search was ending and they started looking in the right place. Within half a day, they found Oscar Mike.

However, even when the wreckage was located, they report, the RAF salvage ships seemed remarkably reluctant to bring up the debris. When they also found bodies over the coming years, snagged by their fishing nets, they were told to throw them back. This does not square with the aviation industry's normal practice of pursuing all leads to learn the truth.

Nor does it fit with the final report on the crash of Viscount Oscar Mike published by the Irish Inspector of Transport, Richard O'Sullivan, on June 30, 1970. He stated that "the conclusion that there was another aircraft involved is inescapable." Unfortunately, as he added, "No aircraft have been reported missing." Thus, the origin of the object in the sky that may have collided with this civilian flight seems forever shrouded in mystery.

That this kind of mystery can happen today is demonstrated by a case that occurred in Poland on August 11, 1994. The scene was the Dolina Olczyska Valley, where two climbers got into difficulties that afternoon 6000 feet up the Krzyzne Pass. As is usual, the Tatran Voluntary Rescue Service swung into action, and a Sokol helicopter, Sierra Echo (SP-PSE), was launched with two pilots and two rescue workers.

A rescue was successfully conducted and the women climbers were delivered to the railway station for dispatch to safety. The Sokol then left for its base at Zakopane but never made it. Instead, on the return flight, it plunged vertically to the bottom of the valley, killing all four people on board.

Thankfully, the investigators had unexpected assistance in this case. A tourist filming on top of Mount Nosal, a high peak in the area, actually videotaped the disaster. Yet, far from resolving what took place, this footage provoked intense debate. Even before the footage was available the investigators were puzzled. Other eyewitnesses had said that the Sokol was traveling normally and then hit something in midair. They could not see what this was but the impact was obvious and destructive, causing the helicopter to fall like a brick out of the sky.

Border guards in this mountainous region close to Slovakia also witnessed the accident and were equally bemused by the way in which the crash occurred. R. Lesniakiewicz of that team became part of the investigation, along with aviation officials and representatives from the manufacturers. They were stunned by what the video depicted, for it confirmed all the eyewitness testimony. The helicopter had clearly collided with something in midair, just like hitting a wall. The only problem was that the film showed no visual evidence of any other object with which Sierra Echo might have come into contact!

After a year of study, Lesniakiewicz attempted to persuade his colleagues that there must have been a UFO present and that this was a phenomenon that was not always visible. The others on the commission refused to accept this suggestion, but struggled to come up with an acceptable alternative.

It is known that some air crashes have been caused by "wake turbulence"—tornadolike spirals of wind that are created by jet aircraft. These can persist for some miles behind the jet and flip over nearby small aircraft like toys. This is why there is a legal space separation requirement for landings, and this was nearly doubled to 6 miles in 1995. That came when the dangers caused by wake turbulence were revealed as worse than expected after several terrible crashes to small business planes landing behind Boeing 757s.

However, there were no other aircraft involved in the Polish case. So other options were considered. These included CAT (clear air turbulence) and wind shear—sudden, very dramatic vertical air currents that have enormous ferocity. They can also smash an aircraft into the ground and, despite being very rare, are believed to have felled some aircraft during as yet unexplained disasters.

However, CAT is thought to destabilize an aircraft rather than simply cause it to fall like a brick, and this ought to have been more obvious from the eyewitness accounts and the video footage. The evidence does instead support the idea that the Sokol simply flew into a solid object that was hovering in its path but that was unseen or camouflaged because of the dark backdrop.

Lesniakiewicz noted that there had been numerous sightings of strange light phenomena at night over the Tatran Valley area, and there were some in the days surrounding this accident. This suggests that the location is what UFOlogists call a "window area," where some kind of natural energy manifests itself with unusual frequency. Is it possible that at night this may be readily visible as a glowing mass of energy, but during daylight it can appear as a dark mass that is difficult to see against a mountainous background? Or could it even be completely invisible at times? There are grounds for suspecting that possibility.

Dr. Michael Persinger is a neuroscientist at Laurentian State University in Canada. He has spent 20 years studying UFO data and attempting to prove that they result from what he terms "transients."

These are intense electrical fields that can create glowing forms when they ionize the atmosphere. But the transients are not themselves visible and may be completely unseen in most other circumstances. When they are detected, it is often because their radiating energy fields can cause witnesses to feel tingling sensations, and to develop pounding headaches and watering eyes. When these fields come into contact with power systems, they have been known to cause serious energy malfunctions.

Persinger has even built a machine to create artificial transients in his laboratory and has successfully proven the validity of his ideas to the satisfaction of many researchers. Is it possible that a transient could have caused the Sokol to lose all power and fall from the sky?

If so, then this was clearly not what happened to a Britten Norman Trislander owned by Kondair—a freight company based at Stansted Airport in Essex. On the night of August 24, 1984, it struck a metal UFO over Rendlesham Forest, east of Ipswich, and nearly paid a terrible price for this still unresolved incident.

I first heard about the matter a few weeks later when a friend wrote to me. He was an air traffic controller who knew that I was investigating a remarkable series of UFO encounters in that same forest in December 1980. Something had crashed from the sky and irradiated the area. I was discovering that strange experiments involving an energy beam weapon under testing were probably involved.

My contact was able to secure a copy of the preliminary investigation by the Accident Investigation Branch of the Air Safety Board. From this I pursued the matter and spoke with the airport and the airline, and eventually was in contact with the pilot.

From all of these sources, I could piece together an account of what took place. At 12:55 a.m., some 17 minutes into a flight to Amsterdam and while flying at 5000 feet, the pilot of the Trislander noticed a sudden bump. This was transmitted through the controls and lasted only a second or two. In the darkness, it was not obvious what had happened and there seemed no immediate cause for concern. However, within moments, the pilot realized that he had lost the right-hand engine.

A Trislander has three engines, and this allowed him to continue on his flight without any real problems. He did consider the safety aspect as he was about to head out over the North Sea, and he pondered whether he should turn back, but the other engines seemed to be working fine. As he pointed out, the same fortune would not have been his had he been aboard a single-engined aircraft.

The Kondair cargo plane managed to reach Schiphol Airport and landed safely, although one of its engines was windmilling and the pilot had to come in asymmetrically. It was only after he got onto the ground that the full extent of the damage became apparent. There was substantial impact to the left propeller, control runs, cables, and right engine controls. Without doubt, something had struck him a very heavy blow, and he was lucky to have stayed up in the sky. Gaping holes had been punched right through the fuselage at one point as well as on part of one wing. Near these impact points were found pieces of metal that were foreign to the aircraft and presumably were left behind by whatever had struck it.

Naturally, it was important to find out what had caused this near disaster. But that was easier said than done. The accident report noted that radar tapes had clearly recorded the Kondair aircraft, but that "no other aircraft or identifiable objects" were seen to be in the area. I found this a fascinating choice of words, as it implied that "unidentifiable objects" could well have appeared on tape—otherwise why differentiate here at all? However, neither the Civil Aviation Authority nor the MoD was willing to comment further, and the staff at Kondair simply did not know what this comment meant as they had not been informed.

The accident team noted that they immediately suspected a weather balloon, although the rather flimsy nature of one of these seems hard to square with the extent of the damage to the not insubstantial aircraft. The study of the damage indicated that whatever had hit the Trislander had probably first struck the smashed propeller and bounced off here into the fuselage, causing the metal fragments to be embedded.

But what was this object? The option of a "radio sonde" device was considered. This is a small piece of equipment usually attached to weather balloons to help them send back radio information about the weather. However, no balloons were found to be either missing or in the area at the time, nor could the metal pieces be matched to equipment used by such a balloon.

After getting flight details from the traffic director at Stansted, the airline confirmed to me in early 1985 that they were still unsure what had happened and noted that the largest hole in the side of the aircraft was 4 inches wide. Their flight had been struck by something very hard.

When I heard from the pilot, I had my first chance to see the recovered fragments and was surprised to find that these were decidedly terrestrial in form—in fact, quite literally nuts and bolts. They certainly appeared to me to be manufactured.

In fact, they were described by accident investigators in less terrestrial terms: i.e., "two short cylindrical sections (one of which was magnetic) and something like a valve." These ought to have allowed specific identification of their source but did not. The pilot merely commented to me that he assumed that it was a weather device of some sort—possibly hundreds or thousand of miles off track—and that its foreign origin belied the inability of the aviation authorities to identify it.

Perhaps that was the case, but I could not help wondering about two things. First, if this was indeed a large balloon with metal equipment attached and it struck the aircraft over land at just 5000 feet, then it must have fallen to earth over Suffolk. Yet nobody appears to have found it despite the promotion of the possibility by the aviation authorities. The other reason for my caution was that I knew just how many strange things were going on over Rendlesham Forest—a spate of green fireballs and a large mysterious triangular craft had been seen hovering over the woods in the months before this accident. That Britain's only proven case of an aircraft struck in mid-flight by a UFO should just chance to happen in the same place seemed quite a coincidence if the cause was just a weather balloon. For one of those could have hit an aircraft absolutely anywhere and the odds of doing so in this strategic spot seemed remote.

The interim accident report published in 1984 concluded by stating that the powers that be were baffled by their failure to identify the object but were sure it was not any British device. They then asked, "Has anyone got any ideas?" A year later, in their final summation, the aviation authorities indicated that they had even enlisted the help of both the MoD and defense command to see whether space junk might have hit the plane in some freak accident. But this had not really solved the mystery either.

The truth is that nobody knows what hit that Kondair Trislander, but all concerned know that they were very fortunate indeed to have avoided a catastrophe.

Yet, perhaps the greatest puzzle revolves around a case that is a classic modern detective story. It is also an incident that, as it stands, strongly suggests that UFOs can and do cause aircraft to disappear. Indeed, it is the case that was in the news only weeks before the encounters over Kaikoura, New Zealand, and it explains why Australian TV chose to send in Quentin Fogarty to make a film.

The incident occurred on October 21, 1978, when 20-year-old Frederick Valentich of Avondale Heights, Melbourne, set off to fly to King Island in the Bass Strait. His aim was to pick up a load of crayfish for his friends. He flew alone aboard a hired Cessna 182, code sign Sierra Juliet (VH-DSJ).

Valentich was keen to become a commercial pilot and was taking classes to gain further flying certificates. He had been turned down by the RAAF because of poor school grades but had flown with the Air Training Corps at Sale where he had shown interest in UFOs. Indeed he was fascinated by the subject and was following keenly many reports on a wave of sightings over southern Australia at the time. He had just seen the movie *Close Encounters of the Third Kind*, in which a pilot vanished while flying at night over water and was returned by aliens years later not having aged a day.

Some sources claim the pilot took his UFO scrapbook with him on the flight to King Island, although his father Guido Valentich denies this and says that his son's interest in UFOs stemmed only from his desire to learn more about unusual weather phenomena for his meteorology exams.

Whatever the case, Valentich filled up the Cessna with several times the required fuel that afternoon, ready for his short hop across the ocean. He filed a flight plan that saw him estimate landing on King Island just before dark. Then he left the area of Moorabin Field in Melbourne, for reason unknown, and returned to his aircraft an hour later—thus rendering his carefully logged flight plan useless, and certain now to arrive at his destination in the dark. Valentich was not an experienced night flyer.

After takeoff, he was in sporadic contact with Steve Robey, the air traffic controller on duty that evening. Robey treated this as a routine flight and knew Valentich could handle the trip. Because it would be flying below 5000 feet, the Cessna was too low for radar coverage during the 20-minute passage of the straits after crossing the coast at Cape Otway. But this was not unusual for smaller aircraft, and pilots had training to navigate the route.

Before Sierra Juliet headed out across the ocean after reporting he was over Otway, Robey asked Valentich if he wanted to adjust his SAR time. This "search-and-rescue" estimate tells aviation authorities how long after the expected arrival at a destination they should start to worry about non-appearance and consider an aircraft as missing. It is standard with all flights, but the one filed by the Cessna was now useless because of the curious decision by the pilot to put off his departure at the last moment. Valentich agreed, evidently somewhat grudgingly, to the ATC suggestion to adapt his SAR time.

A few minutes after that, as Sierra Juliet was around 6 minutes into its crossing of the Bass Strait, the young pilot asked Steve Robey if there was another aircraft ahead. Robey was puzzled. He had no record of one as low as 5000 feet and immediately started to make inquiries to see if any military traffic might be up there that Melbourne had not been told about.

Several minutes of taped conversation followed between Valentich and Robey. They constitute some of the most astonishing on file anywhere. The pilot kept referring to an "unknown aircraft" that was "traveling at speed" and that kept crossing his path, flying overhead and hovering in close proximity. He asked several times for Robey to tell him what it was—"Is there any air force aircraft in the vicinity?" By now, Robey was certain that no known craft ought to be anywhere near the Cessna.

Valentich told how the bright light, which he described as green, was "playing some sort of game" by circling his small aircraft at speed. Throughout this period the 20-year-old pilot was maintaining composure, only beginning to show tension towards the end of the encounter. Then he seemed a little unsure whether he was flying south or north (although he quickly corrected the error and reported accurately) and stammered of the light, "It's not an aircraft, it's...," trailing off and not concluding his sentence.

The pilot was also now reporting problems with his engine. This was, he said, "rough idling" and he described to the controller in Melbourne more details of the falling revolutions per minute. Robey asked what Valentich intended to do. He told him that he would carry on and try to reach King Island where, Robey later realized, the pilot had not even followed standard procedure for night landings and called ahead to request that the small airfield turn on its lights.

Then, a somewhat shaken Valentich came over the radio to tell Robey, "That strange aircraft is hovering on top of me again... It *is* hovering and it's *not* an aircraft...Delta Sierra Juliet, Melbourne..." The young man's voice trailed away into the night.

All that followed were a few seconds of noises that some experts say sound like metallic scraping sounds, but which Robey says to him resemble some sort of radio interference like a carrier wave. Then silence. Sierra Juliet was never to be heard from again.

Despite a major operation using many civil aircraft, ships, and a military Orion search-and-rescue flight, no trace of the Cessna was ever recovered—not even fuel residue on the water. However, the waters are deep and aircraft lost in the area before had disappeared completely. This was not in itself a mystery. Of course, none of those other aircraft had vanished while allegedly being hounded by a UFO.

Naturally, a massive investigation was mounted. Indeed it was to be almost 4 years before the aviation administration published its report in May 1982. This reached no conclusion, saying only that "the reason for the disappearance of the aircraft has not been determined."

Not that there was any shortage of theories. Some again thought the Cessna had encountered space junk or a bolide that by a billion-to-one fluke had struck the aircraft, but the long duration of the sighting as recorded by the air-to-ground communications makes this very unlikely. Others suggested that the pilot had become disorientated and flown upside down, seeing his own reflection in the water as strange lights. But the Cessna could not have survived for 6 minutes flying like that.

Possibly Valentich did get confused and mistake distant lights, such as the Cape Otway lighthouse. But Steve Robey disputes that theory. He says that Valentich "would not have been able to speak to me on the radio [as coherently] as he did if he had lost control. He *was* in control of the airplane just prior to my losing communication with him." Moreover, Robey says that the information about his engine malfunction was consistent with the aircraft and indicated that the pilot was thinking clearly despite the danger he was facing.

Some more exotic theories have been suggested. One idea was that Valentich ran foul of drug smugglers and crashed after getting tangled in a net they were using to trail cargo to the mainland. Smuggling aircraft had been known to fly low with a net held beneath the water so that this could be released if they chanced to be intercepted by the authorities. However, such missions nearly always occurred late at night (not at dusk) and rarely attracted attention to themselves by displaying bright lights. In any event, Valentich was flying too high for such an encounter to make sense.

One theory taken seriously by many was that the pilot engineered his own disappearance by faking a UFO story. In truth, he flew on—perhaps to Tasmania. He certainly had the fuel to do so. But no evidence has ever surfaced that he was involved in illegal practices or had any reason to wish to vanish. He had a happy home life and plans for the future. In any case, it is not easy just to hide an aircraft. After many years, no clue has ever been found to suggest that Valentich is alive and well somewhere else, although such a possibility can never be ruled out.

However, there are those who wonder if the pilot set up a UFO hoax and, during his preoccupation with this ruse, lost control of his aircraft and crashed. Once again that can never be proved or disproved, although if this is the case he surely missed his vocation and should have been an actor, since he certainly fooled Steve Robey.

Of course, the most obvious interpretation is that Valentich saw an unidentified object as he reported. It paid close attention to his aircraft and may have led to an engine malfunction and a loss of radio communication. Then he inevitably crashed. What happened next rather depends on whether you believe (as some members of the Valentich family under-standably hope) that the UFO was an alien craft. For then the young man might have been "rescued" by its crew. On the other hand, if you perceive a UFO as a random, natural phenomenon, then the pilot presumably went down with his plane.

Steve Robey, several decades on, is unsure of what happened, but, as a pilot of 30 years' experience himself, he feels that Frederick Valentich was honestly describing what he saw: "I am convinced in my own mind that he saw something strange. Whether it was a UFO or not, I just do not know."

There is some evidence to support that possibility. UFO activity was reported that afternoon and evening over the Bass Straits area between the mainland and King Island. At 2 p.m. at Currie on King Island, a strange cloud was seen floating from which a ball of light emerged, headed out to sea, and then circled back into the cloud. Within 15 minutes of the Valentich encounter, a further strange phenomenon was recorded by Roy Manifold, who was on vacation at Cape Otway. He was taking sunset pho-tographs out over the Bass Strait using a tripod-mounted camera and shooting in 20-second bursts. Two of his photographs depict a strange, cloudlike mass out over the water, although opinion among experts is divided as to whether this was an optical effect or something really out there at the time.

Dr. Richard Haines has also devoted a good deal of time to this case and is one of the few people who, because of his association with accident investigations, has had access to the full official details banned from pub-lic release. He believes that there are four options to consider. The pilot could have faked his own death. He may have become confused by ground lights and crashed. He could genuinely have encountered a UFO. Or he might have fallen prey to the nefarious activities of the American intelli-gence agencies!

This last idea is extraordinary and is based upon investigations by Dr. Haines. He wonders if the young pilot was sounded out while serving in the air corps at Sale and chosen as a candidate for an experiment because of his access to a light plane and his interest in UFOs. The sources of this interest were the Defense Intelligence Agency and National Security Agency, which, Haines has found, were very active at a top secret base called Pine Gap in the Australian outback. According to Haines, the staff at Pine Gap was conducting experiments in the projection of high-intensity beams into the atmosphere using lasers. These were the early stages of efforts to create a "Star Wars" weapon that might shoot down incoming nuclear missiles.

Quite remarkably yet again, this ties in with the research that was occurring during the same period (1978–84) over Orford Ness in Suffolk, England. During that time, green fireballs were seen and the infamous Rendlesham Forest close encounters took place. It was also when the Kondair Trislander was struck in mid-flight and nearly went the same way as Cessna Sierra Juliet. The NSA was coordinating the British project under the code names "Cold Witness" and "Cobra Mist."

Can it really be coincidence that the locations where this research was taking place always seemed to involve powerful UFO activity? It is just the same in the case of the link between green fireballs and midair encounters over New Mexico and the Cape Canaveral regions discussed earlier. The things being seen in these areas suggest atmospheric ionization. Is that resulting from laser weapons? Also, can it merely be coincidence that the aim of the weapons was to interfere with electronic power systems and computer guidance, and that precisely such interference was noted in all of these locations?

Indeed, over East Anglia in October 1983, 10 months before the Kondair incident, two RAF jets fell into the sea during separate incidents on the same day when all electrical systems seemed to fail. One navigator managed to eject and told how the plane suddenly dipped for no reason and flew straight into the North Sea. A baffled MoD spokesman speculated about a "Bermuda Triangle" effect. But, of course, unknown to him, a few miles away, the NSA was beaming energy weapons into the sky, and in December 1980 had successfully deflected the reentry path of a Soviet nuclear-powered satellite that was heading into the earth's atmosphere. Also unknown to him, but presumably not to the UFO team at the MoD, green fireballs were especially active in the area around Orford Ness in October 1983.

I find more than coincidence at work here and so take this idea of Dr. Haines quite seriously. The possibility that a similar kind of experiment might have been tested in full view of Frederick Valentich, perhaps in expectation that he would report UFO activity, is not as absurd as it seems. Possibly the energy weapon worked better than it should have done and caused the pilot to lose control of his aircraft.

As with all of these actual collisions, the evidence remains open to debate. But there is certainly an indication that something quite disturbing is taking place and, if nothing else, it proves that there is very good cause for concern when we see the alarming rise in the number of midair sightings. Just how long will it be before the next one ends in tragedy?

11   SQUARE TRIANGLES

It would be wrong to think that UFOs must resemble the saucer shapes seen in Hollywood movies. The term "flying saucer" is actually the result of a simple mistake back in 1947. A witness, Kenneth Arnold, was describing the *motion* of what he saw as being like "saucers skipping across water" (or flat stones skimming over a lake). He was not alleging that the things he saw were saucer-shaped. However, the media reported the sighting as being of "flying saucers" and created a misconception that remains to this day.

It is fascinating that—despite considerable pressure from almost every alien movie, TV program, and space advertisement ever made—people do not see fleets of saucerlike objects when reporting UFOs. You would expect that if these phenomena were the result of hallucinations or wishful thinking, people would describe what they have been conditioned to see. That they do not do so is very powerful evidence that a real phenomenon underlies these strange things in the sky—albeit one that is confused by the effects of human psychology and sociology.

As you have seen in this book, pilot reports, just like reports from other cross sections of society, feature few sightings that resemble the "traditional" saucer. Instead, any database of sightings will tell you that balls of light are far and away the most common description, and that cylindrical or egg shapes are the next most common type. Between them, these account for 80% of all UFOs.

Triangular shapes have always been seen on a more frequent basis than "saucers." A U.K. database of three thousand cases to 1995 shows this type as producing 9%, as opposed to 2% for reports of saucerlike objects. But there has been a further marked increased since then. Triangles account for over 20% of the sightings in 1996–97.

Obviously there are vital lessons to be learned from this information.

Indeed, the first big wave of triangle sightings took place in the autumn of 1978 when a large, slow-moving, and silent black shape was seen over Leicestershire. Because it resembled the incredibly noisy Vulcan bomber, the object of these baffling sightings earned the nickname of the "silent vulcan."

Near Leicester in October 1978, a piece of film captured and showed little more than three white lights in a triangle moving across the sky. Opinion among UFOlogists was divided. Some felt these reports were the result of alien invaders, of course. But one or two, even then, did suspect that some kind of secret earth-built aircraft might be involved. This was particularly so when the sightings were noted as focusing around the RAF base at Alconbury.

The "silent vulcan" soon spread its wings and was seen far and wide. For example, there was an astonishing wave of activity in the 48 hours between November 26 and 28, 1978. Witness descriptions varied from the triangle to other popular comparisons, such as the jellyfish and manta ray.

At Portslade in Sussex at 5:20 p.m. on November 26, the object passed over, making just a quiet humming sound; 35 minutes later, a nearly identical object was reported at various points between Coventry and Nuneaton. As in Sussex, two huge headlights were at the front. Just 35 minutes after that, what might have been the same object yet again was spotted at Whaley Bridge in Derbyshire—a location that was to take on added significance 17 years later when a British Airways crew had its own encounter here.

It was as if one gigantic triangle had passed the 250 miles from the Sussex coast to Derbyshire on a northerly flight that took just an hour. A similar sighting occurred in the early hours of the morning at Sproston Green in Cheshire only 34 hours later. Again the witness, a security engineer on a night delivery run, called the object a "manta ray" and got out of his van as it moved in silent majesty over his head at an estimated height of just a few hundred feet. He said that time seemed to stand still as it passed over, giving him an eerie feeling, and his two-way radio in the van was filled with static as it did so.

At first, researchers began to suspect that some of these cases resulted from aircraft heading into Manchester Airport. Both Whaley Bridge and Sproston Green are on different flight paths into that airport, which is very busy at night, and people unfamiliar with the area might well mistake incoming jets. However, it did seem hard to imagine this was the answer in so many strange cases.

Incredibly, the UFO group NARO was able to establish that aircraft from a certain famous airline were performing an extraordinary tactic on taking late-night cargo trips into Manchester. They were throttling back the engines, as noise abatement laws required, and in some cases quite literally "gliding" in with cabin lights turned off. The result was a rather eerie view if you chanced to be just a few hundred feet below one of these near-silent aircraft as they swooped like eagles over your head.

Although we proved this theory in a very effective manner—by having one UFOlogist in the radar room at Manchester Airport as others were on a hilltop watching the plane come over their heads—we have agreed not to identify the airline involved. This is because they were breaching aviation rules and stopped their pilots from adopting this tactic pretty quickly after this unique CAA/UFOlogy investigation!

However, while some of the sightings within 20 miles of Manchester were probably late-night gliding cargo jets, this was clearly not an explanation that could be widely applied. Many of the sightings were occurring elsewhere in the world and not during the early hours—the only time of day when these tactics were considered "safe" by the pilots. In any case, the triangular shape was the real puzzle, as this did not fit any known aircraft.

On August 31, 1980, a spectacular case occurred in which dozens of witnesses spotted the by now familiar triangular or manta ray craft heading northwest across Derbyshire. Many of them were in the Ashbourne area—a town that was to continue to have sightings of triangles for the next decade. But there were again reports out towards the western edge of the Peak District National Park at Buxton and Whaley Bridge. It seems hard to imagine that this is not a significant pattern.

Living in a village just outside Buxton, I have often seen aircraft coming in late at night, heading for Whaley Bridge just over the hills. I have never mistaken one for a UFO. However, because of the height of the land (between 1000 and 2000 feet) and the low height of some incoming planes, these can seem much lower—as indeed they are, relatively speaking. Because you are out on the moors miles from Manchester Airport by road, it is quite common for people passing through this area not to realize what they are watching. Locals, however, would be very unlikely to be fooled, in my experience and most of the witnesses to the sighting on August 31, 1980, were indeed familiar with the area.

Although I did consider a rogue case of a gliding aircraft in the Ashbourne sightings, this was never proven. And there was a bizarre sequel just an hour later at Golborne near Wigan. Here, several witnesses reported a large object surrounded by an orange cloud or mist that seemed to drop "missiles" towards a reservoir.

On its own, this case was intriguing. Coupled with the completely independent multiple-witness sighting over the Pennines shortly beforehand, it became all the more significant. However, the strangest aspect of all was how the witness at Wigan, who made the initial report (and then clammed up), was seemingly pursued by a strange figure. This man impersonated a scientist from the Jodrell Bank radio telescope and seems to have successfully prevented the witness from telling her full story.

It was as if someone somewhere were taking the report rather more seriously than it appeared to merit. Does this suggest that the MoD knew full well what had flown across northwest England that night and was desperate to ensure that witnesses did not speak out about it? Was it a secret aircraft, perhaps? The full story of this bizarre sequel to the August 31, 1980 case is told in my book *The Truth Behind the Men in Black: Government Agents—Or Visitors from Beyond.*

More clues came to light as time went by. We noticed that many of the flying-triangle sightings concentrated in "strategic" locations—exactly as had worried the scientists at Los Alamos back in 1948. There were encounters over power stations and oil refineries, such as at Partington near Manchester, Bold near Warrington, and Pitsea in Essex. This all soon began to look like anything but coincidence.

A surprising number of the reports were in northwest England and, if you plotted their locations on a map, seemed to point towards the

Wigan/Preston area as being the center of activity. Some UFOlogists began to speculate about the possibility of a local battery factory working in conjunction with aviation sources to try to develop a silent aircraft. Was this being tested late at night in the full knowledge that if seen by witnesses it would be misreported as a "flying saucer"?

If so, then this effectively guaranteed that few aviation experts other than those charged with a "need to know" would figure out what was going on. Only UFOlogists had access to the data, and most of them erroneously believed that little green men were flying alien spacecraft. That may have been the entire point of deliberately engineered misinformation. It is very easy to get UFOlogists to believe dumb things.

Perhaps the most remarkable incident occurred on February 24, 1979, between 2 a.m. and 2:45 a.m., when an object was seen to land in a quarry at Bacup in Lancashire. A man and his wife tending their sick teenage son were the witnesses. The man rushed off to get his brother, secure a camera, and climb up towards the hilltop quarry. But when he got there he saw no UFO—only two police officers who had witnessed the events from their patrol car and had also gone to investigate. Meanwhile, the UFO had evidently departed at great speed towards the west. It was seen at various points en route at Wigan and St. Helens. Witnesses included taxi drivers, firemen, and late-night travelers. But also in evidence was a fast-moving jet aircraft that defied all the aviation rules to cross civilian territory at a low height and a speed that employed afterburners. The fearful racket was heard by many from the Wirral Peninsula to the Lancashire coast.

At Scarisbrick near Southport, this jet fighter roared overhead so loudly that it shook doors and windows and did damage to a caravan park. The local MP, now TV talk-show host, Robert Kilroy-Silk, even asked questions in the House on behalf of his constituents. Eventually, the news emerged that the jet was an American Air Force F-111 on a routine flight.

Kilroy-Silk seems to have accepted this version of events offered by the Civil Aviation Authority. But he knew nothing about the many sightings across Lancashire that night that all fitted neatly together like a jigsaw puzzle. Once you see this interlocking evidence from more than a dozen independent witnesses, it is obvious that the F-111 was sent in pursuit of a UFO that had headed westwards from the Rossendale Valley towards the coast near Blackpool. It must have been tracked on radar. The jet came into the region from the south, and the two courses plotted on a map were set to intercept just out into the Irish Sea.

In fact, the key to this case comes from the security guard on the Central Pier in Blackpool. For he saw and independently reported both the jet and the UFO. The jet raced out to sea, causing the pier to shake as in a heavy swell. The air was ionized by the passage of the UFO and had a curious odor, probably caused by ozone. After the jet had shot away towards the Isle of Man in its futile attempt to catch the UFO, the security guard saw this object climb up from under the ocean and spiral away into the clouds.

According to an MoD "suggestion," this F-111 was "probably" part of a military exercise and just happened to be in the area that night. But I find it very unlikely that any authorization would have been given for such a low-level military flight over population centers and through air traffic lanes at 2:45 a.m.—at least not unless there was an extreme necessity for the jet to be in that position.

This is one of the very few cases where the evidence suggests that the UFO involved was more than just a natural phenomenon. The signs of intelligence indicated by any craft that can hide under water to avoid a military confrontation hardly need spelling out. But intelligence does not necessarily equate to alien intelligence.

During the mid 1980s, reports of triangular UFOs continued to come in, and there was a major wave of sightings in the Hudson Valley of New York State during 1985. Other sightings occurred over California and Nevada where people described seeing dark shapes rush overhead at tremendous speed and hearing unexplained sonic booms. I spoke with one British pilot who was flying a business jet towards Los Angeles in the spring of 1992, and he had managed to take a photograph of a "blurred mass" as it shot by his aircraft at great speed while he flew over Nevada.

The possible cause of these many encounters was given a new twist with the revelation by the Pentagon that they did indeed have a top secret aircraft known as the Aurora that used "stealth" technology. This was designed in a beautiful aerodynamic fashion with smooth black surfaces. Its profile from below was undeniably triangular. Stealth was designed not only to fly fast and very quietly but also to limit its radar profile so that it could be almost invisible to detection.

Although it was admitted that Stealth was flying by about 1988, it took some years before the full story was unraveled. Indeed some aspects of it are still subject to top secrecy. However, according to aviation sources quoted by Jane's (the aircraft historians) and by aero engineers that I met when I visited the U.S. in 1992, Stealth has been airborne since 1977. There were several crashes during the early years and these were hushed up. I was told that the way any sightings would be mistaken for UFOs was actually used to great advantage and the aircraft were sometimes allowed to look more UFO-like to further that prospect. After all, why else would UFOs need lights? This implies that someone wanted them to be seen and to be seen as resembling alien spaceships. Otherwise, they would surely not have displayed themselves so well.

From my conversations and discussions with USAF pilots based at Lakenheath and Bentwaters air force bases, I was told that the first U.K. flights of Stealth jets were made in 1978 and were based at Alconbury. I think this makes it virtually certain that the "silent vulcan" was indeed the result of secret test flights of this American aircraft. Of course, technology does not stand still and remarkable progress has been made in new types of secret aircraft in the years since the prototype Aurora jets flew. (An astonishing book detailing the history of these projects and their relationship with UFO sightings is Tim Matthews' superbly researched *UFO Revelations*. It shows just how many and how long-lasting these projects have been.)

The base where Stealth aircraft were first developed in the U.S. is in an area rich with secret sites, such as Nellis Air Force Base, the adjacent Tonopah test range, and other facilities at the dried-up bed of Groom Lake. These are in the mountains to the north of Las Vegas in Nevada. However, some of the components for covert projects are flown in from the notorious Lockheed "skunk works" in California. That these locations so closely match the area where strange objects have been seen is surely no coincidence.

But, predictably, UFOlogists view the fantastic aircraft technology in these areas as having a very different origin. The base in the Nevada desert has the code name "Area 51" (or, to those who work there, "Dreamland," because of its extraordinary technology). During the early 1990s, some truly astonishing small craft were regularly seen and filmed flitting about the sky. At the same time, several people were coming forward with amazing claims that these were not just secret aircraft but alien spacecraft!

Stories ranged from the barely credible to the frankly ridiculous. "Insiders" and "scientists" who had worked there but who could offer no proof alleged that an alien craft had crashed in New Mexico in 1947. From the gradual understanding of its fantastic technology, centuries ahead of our own, new aviation developments were occurring thanks to what is termed "reverse engineering" of the alien capabilities. The U.S. was maintaining its global lead by jealously guarding this secret.

The remains were stored underground in Area 51 along with prototype UFOs built by the U.S. government. These were flying around the skies of Nevada and occasionally were to be seen on spy missions all over the world. Nobody minded flying these over foreign countries because, if they were witnessed, they would be assumed to have an alien origin. When they crashed (as they sometimes did), a massive clear-up operation was mounted to silence any witnesses and clean away the evidence.

If this was not fantastic enough, some "leaks" from Area 51 even alleged that the U.S. government was in league with the aliens, and it had extraterrestrials based in Nevada who were helping the U.S. to build and fly spaceships. This wonderful tale of Uncle Sam jingoism is just one of the absurd yarns to come out of this covert base in recent years.

To be honest, the activities of the Pentagon have not helped to quash these stories. Indeed, I suspect, they may even have embellished them further as a way of concealing the more mundane truth about what they are up to at Groom Lake from potentially influential sources.

Concern has been raised about the "black budget," whereby vast funds seem to have been siphoned into Area 51 under various pretexts. Indeed, the Pentagon only admitted it had a facility there at all in 1995, despite Soviet satellite photographs, released after the fall of communism, that had

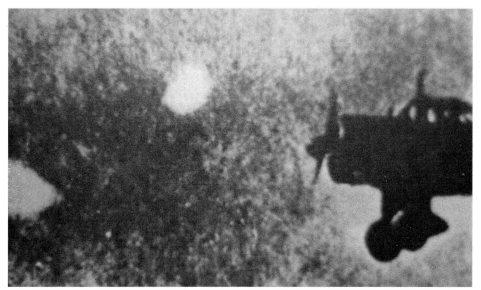

1. These luminous objects were seen in the midst of a formation of Tachikawa Ki 36 reconnaissance airplanes in flight, 1942.

2. One of the stills released by the Italian Air Force and filmed near Istrana Air Base in June 1979. They claim this is the "balloon" captured by the camera aboard Officer Cecconi's aircraft during his midair close encounter. This "black lozenge" is visually identical to many objects seen in close proximity to passenger aircraft over Britain and other parts of the world throughout the 1900s—some of which cannot have been balloons.

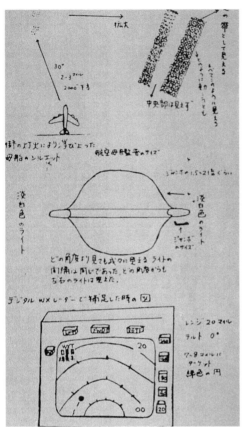

3. Sketches made by Japan Airlines' Captain Terauchi that depict what he saw above Alaska while piloting his Boeing 747 in November 1986.

4. A still from video footage obtained in September 1991 from U.S. space shuttle Discovery. The fast-moving dot is seen departing from the curvature of the earth and heading into space.

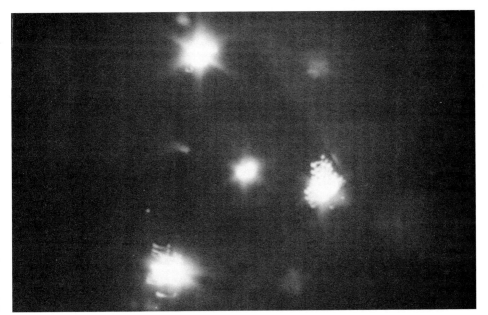

5. Is this the huge triangular object witnessed by many across Europe in the years since the Belgian wave in 1990? It was created by Belgian researcher Wim van Utrecht. He has doubts about the status of the flying triangle, following his study of the wave in his native land.

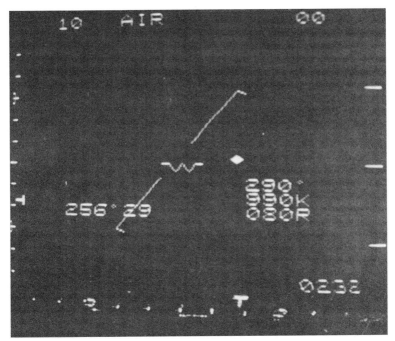

6. The on-board radar telemetry image released by the Belgian Air Force in April 1990. It depicts part of the attempted intercept between one of their jet fighters and a UFO that took place the previous month.

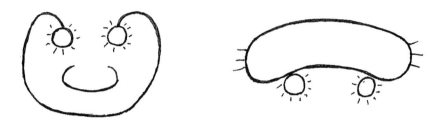

7. Two very different sketches of the same "object" seen by witnesses over Lincolnshire in 1975. The only common denominator is the two white lights, and this is all that was actually in the sky. Human perception created the "craft" that witnesses "saw" around these lights.

8. The UFO that never was. This classic UFO shape is seen easily by the eye but is not, in fact, there. The dark circular shapes fool the senses into believing they are behind a large white object. Optical illusions such as this operate during UFO sightings time and again.

Fireman in Lancashire

Housewife in Norfolk

Police officer in Hertfordshire

Chiles–Whitted, Eastern Airlines case

Still from movie film of object taken in
Lancashire showing all that was actually visible

9. Some of the drawings made by witnesses who saw the reentry of space debris from Cosmos 1068 on December 31, 1978. All that was actually present was a trail of blazing material and gas crossing the sky. Bright bolides and space junk often produce such witness misinterpretations. Note how similar they are to the sketch by the pilots Chiles and Whitted during the Eastern Airlines (1948) encounter.

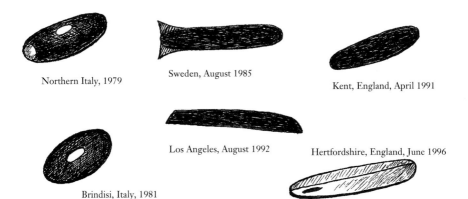

Northern Italy, 1979

Sweden, August 1985

Kent, England, April 1991

Brindisi, Italy, 1981

Los Angeles, August 1992

Hertfordshire, England, June 1996

10. Various sketches of "missile-like" objects seen in daylight
in close proximity to aircraft 1991–97.

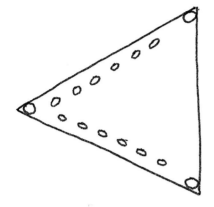

Witness sketch, Nottingham, May 1988.
Estimated height: 500 feet.
One large triangular craft with many lights.

What was really visible:

At height of 40,000 feet,
a large tanker aircraft and a
dozen small fighter planes,
all brightly lit, were flying
in "echelon" formation and
being refueled by "tube."

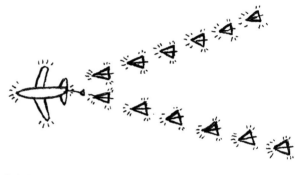

11. How reports of "football-field-sized UFOs" in Europe 1988–90 were explained.

12. *Above:* Sketch based on First Officer Mark Stuart's drawing of the UFO that flew past Flight BA 5061 over Derbyshire in January 1995. *Below:* Author's suggestion as to what might have been seen—the bright bolide.

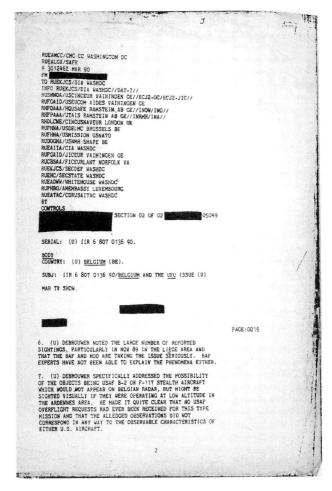

RUEAMCC/CMC CC WASHINGTON DC
RUEALGX/SAFE
R 301246Z MAR 90
FM ▓▓▓▓▓▓
TO RUEKJCS/DIA WASHDC
INFO RUEKJCS/DIA WASHDC//DAT-7//
RUSNNOA/USCINCEUR VAIHINGEN GE//ECJ2-OC/ECJ2-JIC//
RUFGAID/USEUCOM AIDES VAIHINGEN GE
RHFQAAA/HQUSAFE RAMSTEIN AB GE//INOW/INO//
RHFPAAA/UTAIS RAMSTEIN AB GE//INRMH/INA//
RHDLCNE/CINCUSNAVEUR LONDON UK
RUFHNA/USDELMC BRUSSELS BE
RUFHNA/USMISSION USNATO
RUDOGHA/USNMR SHAPE BE
RUEAIIA/CIA WASHDC
RUFGAID/JICEUR VAIHINGEN GE
RUCBSAA/FICEURLANT NORFOLK VA
RUEKJCS/SECDEF WASHDC
RUEHC/SECSTATE WASHDC
RUEADWW/WHITEHOUSE WASHDC
RUFHBG/AMEMBASSY LUXEMBOURG
RUEATAC/CDRUSAITAC WASHDC
BT
CONTROLS
                              SECTION 02 OF 02 ▓▓▓▓▓▓   05049

SERIAL: (U) IIR 6 807 0136 90.

BODY
COUNTRY: (U) BELGIUM (BE).

SUBJ: IIR 6 807 0136 90/BELGIUM AND THE UFO ISSUE (U)

MAR TV SHOW.

PAGE:0015

6. (U) DEBROUWER NOTED THE LARGE NUMBER OF REPORTED
SIGHTINGS, PARTICULARLY IN NOV 89 IN THE LIEGE AREA AND
THAT THE BAF AND MOD ARE TAKING THE ISSUE SERIOUSLY. BAF
EXPERTS HAVE NOT BEEN ABLE TO EXPLAIN THE PHENOMENA EITHER.

7. (U) DEBROUWER SPECIFICALLY ADDRESSED THE POSSIBILITY
OF THE OBJECTS BEING USAF B-2 OR F-117 STEALTH AIRCRAFT
WHICH WOULD NOT APPEAR ON BELGIAN RADAR, BUT MIGHT BE
SIGHTED VISUALLY IF THEY WERE OPERATING AT LOW ALTITUDE IN
THE ARDENNES AREA. HE MADE IT QUITE CLEAR THAT NO USAF
OVERFLIGHT REQUESTS HAD EVER BEEN RECEIVED FOR THIS TYPE
MISSION AND THAT THE ALLEDGED OBSERVATIONS DID NOT
CORRESPOND IN ANY WAY TO THE OBSERVABLE CHARACTERISTICS OF
EITHER U.S. AIRCRAFT.

2

13. Typical of material on UFOs available via a nation that operates a Freedom of Information policy. The U.K. has a 30-year rule that delays all data on UFOs via the Official Secrets Act (except for rare instances and errors, such as the MoD document shown on the next page). The U.S. releases hundreds of files each year. This one was made public almost immediately after the incident that it describes. The intelligence transmission from the USAF in Europe to Washington discusses the wave of sightings over Belgium in 1990 and the option of secret aircraft being the cause. Note the huge distribution list (top left). This shows how a country that, according to the Pentagon, stopped collating UFO data in 1969 nonetheless circulates evidence to the likes of NATO, Allied Command, the Defense Intelligence Agency (DIA) in Washington, and to various U.S. government posts in the U.K. No British data proposing any evaluation of this wave is set to be released until the year 2021, despite the aerial contacts being right on the U.K.'s doorstep.

22	JAVELIN	569	Self	WALLINGTON	N.F.P.1
23	JAVELIN	627	Self	WHITE	P.1
23	JAVELIN	628	Self	WHITE	N.F.P.1
23	JAVELIN	625	Self	WHITE	P.1 (N.F.)
27	JAVELIN	628	Self	WALLINGTON	P.1
27	JAVELIN	619	Self	WHITE	P.1.
29	JAVELIN	625	Self	WALLINGTON	P.1.
30	JAVELIN	626	Self	WALLINGTON	P.1
30	JAVELIN	627	Self	WALLINGTON	P.1. UFO!
30	JAVELIN	627	Self	WALLINGTON	P.1
31	JAVELIN	628	Self	WALLINGTON	P.1.
31	JAVELIN				
12	ANSON	951	Self	3 PASSENGERS	BIGGIN HILL, ROC FLYING
		8h	SUMMARY FOR	AUGUST 1956	
	O.C. F.1.	U.N.T	46 SQDN.	AIRCRAFT	JAVEL.
		DATE	31.8.56	TYPES	ANSON
O.C. UNIT.	SIGNATURE			

14. Part of the log retained by RAF pilot "Wilbur" Wright describing his midair encounter with a UFO. This took place over the Solent in August 1956 while he was flying Javelin number 627. There is no official MoD record of this incident, although the Public Record Office does list much confirmatory data about Wright and his squadron's activities for the period that contains this official "non-event." Had Wright not kept his own log to prove that it happened, then the MoD stance might remain unchallenged. How many other case files have similarly "disappeared"?

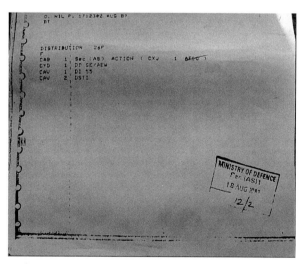

15. A copy of an MoD sighting report describing lights seen by police officers in 1987. It is significant for the distribution list in the lower left. This was released on only a few MoD files, and then by mistake, during the late 1980s. It shows that the only publicly admitted department (Air Staff 2(a)) is but one of several sources that receive incoming sightings. Others include the AEW (Airborne Early Warnings) radar unit, DSTI (Directorate of Scientific and Technical Intelligence—the covert scientific analysis team), and DI 55 (a Defense Intelligence Unit that visits witnesses, debriefs them, and secures hard evidence on UFOs).

shown it! They were even selling "Area 51 Guidebooks" at the Pentagon gift store while denying there was any such place!

The U.S. government has been strict in enforcing its plan to stop witnesses from viewing its tests. Not only do they arrest people on mountains for miles surrounding Area 51, but the government has also bought up so much land nearby that you can now hardly get close enough to see anything at all. Film has been confiscated that shows strange, zipping lights. People on Freedom Ridge (15 miles away) are often chased away.

This has provided a bit of a boom for local small towns, such as Rachel, Nevada, where they have a UFO theme motel called "The Little Ale-Inn" and other tourist attractions. Bus tours visit from Las Vegas. UFOlogists flock there regularly to go spaceship hunting. It is good fun, but no doubt ensures that few ask what is really going on in the Nevada desert.

I have asked. I met with aviation engineers in Nebraska, including some who had worked out there. While I cannot pretend that what they told me was any more accurate than these other tales of misinformation, it was certainly more rational. I was told that new generations of Stealth technology have been under constant development, including near-invisible remote-controlled helicopters and the new TR-3 spy plane. Secret aircraft of terrestrial origin but fantastic capabilities are being flown. Some have revolutionary propulsion systems, including almost silent nuclear motors, electromagnetic flight systems, and pulsed microwave "gliders." Others use computer technology that can change the color of paint on an aircraft to match the terrain over which it flies.

Although planes using these principles are flying, already many are so secret that the world will probably not see them at air shows for some years. If indeed Aurora was flying from the U.K. in 1978 and yet was not officially revealed for more than a decade, I do not have a problem believing these claims.

Of course, the U.S. will not be the only nation attempting to build new aviation technology. This is occurring in Britain, and test flights are frequently mounted in the belief that they will be mistaken for UFOs. Indeed, one test pilot from Nottinghamshire told me this when I gave a lecture to the officers' mess at an RAF base. There is a delight in certain quarters from seeing how many UFO sightings a particular test flight can generate: "It is a bit like having 'kills' on the side of your aircraft during wartime, only now we are merely shooting at the imagination of gullible folk who think we come from Mars."

Is this what was behind the infamous Belgian wave of 1989/1990? What we do know is that on the night of November 29, 1989, there were many sightings of a slow-moving, dark triangular shape above the Belgian/German border area, especially near the town of Eupen. Some of the witnesses were police officers. These sightings created immediate press headlines in Belgium and promises from the authorities that they would investigate. Because they had reports from official sources, they were taking them very seriously.

In fact, there had been similar sightings across the North Sea in England only weeks before. One in particular occurred at Alvanley in Cheshire and involved a senior Cheshire police officer who was off duty and driving in the countryside at night with his wife. Their account of a flying triangle on October 23, 1989, was very much like the manta rays of a decade earlier and the then imminent Belgian sightings.

However, other British sightings had a somewhat different interpretation. Witnesses in Staffordshire, Nottinghamshire, and Lincolnshire had on several occasions reported seeing a gigantic object "the size of a football field" moving slowly across the sky towards the east. It was said to be triangular and if any sound was reported (often none was) this was said to be merely a faint buzzing or droning. The similarities between these reports and the sightings over Belgium soon afterwards were marked. Witnesses there also often spoke of the "football field" size of the objects they saw.

Stafford MP Bill Cash took up the cause of his constituents but never really got much of an answer from the Ministry of Defense. However, UFOlogists had more success and eventually solved the British sightings. Whether these have any relevance to the Belgian wave that followed some months later is hard to know. The "football field" triangle heading across the East Midlands towards the North Sea was an illusion—but an illusion triggered by real events. They were part of a secret military exercise to practice midair refueling as a prelude to planned allied bombing raids against Libya and future attacks against Saddam Hussein.

These exercises are quite dangerous and must take place over the ocean, but the aircraft involved were lining up while still over land. The mission involved huge tanker aircraft, the size of jumbo jets, filled with aviation fuel. These fly in tight formation with fighter jets who then load up on fuel, using umbilical cords strung between them while they fly in close proximity to the tankers. Such a refueling option saves time on long-distance flights to the Middle East, avoiding having to land en route.

Of course, this operation is not without risk—hence, the ban on such exercises over land. The tankers are potentially flying bombs, and having dozens of smaller jets in close proximity at night requires great skill. The formation is dressed up with very powerful additional lighting to help in this endeavor.

From the ground, witnesses see a massive formation of lights shaped like a triangle and may hear the combined noise of all these aircraft. Because the spectacle is so strange, it is readily misperceived. Witnesses assume they are seeing the lights on one single object (of triangular shape) and naturally guess that this object must be flying at a fairly normal height for an aircraft. This means that it appears to them to be much lower and of quite enormous size (hence the football field reference). It also appears to be making a faint noise. In reality, they are seeing many smaller aircraft close together and very high up.

Undoubtedly, some of the British reports in 1988 and 1989 stem from these exercises, which were also possibly occurring over Belgium in the same way at that time. The U.S. Air Force was responsible and could have been heading towards the North Sea from its bases in Germany, merely crossing Belgian airspace in the process.

However, surely we might expect the Belgian authorities to have known about these exercises? Britain did. Then again, as loyal NATO allies, the MoD remained silent and let its own people think they were witness to UFO activity. The same reasoning could have applied in Brussels.

After sightings in Eupen on November 29, 1989, there were many other reports championed by the media. A good few of these were misperceptions trawled in as a result of thousands of people now watching the skies who might otherwise never have done so. They also had a friendly media ready to publish any new report. UFO waves are often artificially generated in this way.

From the witness descriptions of three balls of light moving around the sky, I have little doubt that some of these later sightings were of laser searchlights guided by computers to project a display from the underside of low clouds. In 1989, these were a relatively new technology, and most people in Belgium (or anywhere else outside the U.S.) had never seen them in operation. They certainly do look very odd if you have no idea what is causing the spheres of light to race across the sky. Given the optical power of these devices, they can be viewed up to 30 miles from the location from where the projection is occurring.

Interestingly, the Belgian government appears to have suspected that the Americans were to blame for some of the UFO activity being reported. This suggests that they did not know what was behind the sightings but had cause to wonder. Because of the triangular shape, they asked Washington whether there were any U.S. Stealth aircraft overflying Belgium. Records released by the U.S. Freedom of Information Act allegedly show their attempt to verify this and their denial to Brussels. The complete denial stated with assurance that "the F-117 Stealth fighter has never flown in the European theater."

This is either a brazen lie or else it evades the question on a technicality. What if the Americans code name any Stealth flying in Europe as, say, the F-117 E? Then, of course, they will have told the truth by saying no F-117 has ever flown. Or maybe the word "theater" should be read to mean that no flights have occurred during hostile actions and, thus, the statement does not cover peaceful operations.

That some Stealth aircraft have flown in Europe is a certainty. Indeed, only a few weeks later the lie was admitted by USAF Colonel Tom Tolin, who confirmed to a French journal, "F-117s are flying in Europe during night missions, sometimes piloted by U.K. RAF pilots, but we are not authorized to tell you where."

Even the former French Minister of Defense, Robert Galley, confirmed that he had proof of this. He had once sent an interceptor after a Stealth overflight despite a categorical assurance by Washington that they would not spy on a friendly nation. This Stealth was doing precisely that—

taking photographs of a uranium enrichment plant at Pierrelatte. The French government persuaded the U.S. to hand over the film footage secured, which had been sent to Ramstein Air Force Base in Germany.

Remarkably, on the night of March 30–31, 1990, the Belgian government took part in a skywatch exercise with the UFO group SOBEPS. While the UFOlogists coordinated reports of sightings on the ground, two F-16 fighters were on standby to intercept anything that was seen.

Police officers near Wavre reported some flickering lights and the interceptors quickly became airborne. Although the pilots saw nothing, they did pick up targets moving erratically at speed across their path. Both jets were equipped to film the high-tech radar screens on board. One of these cameras failed, but the other captured footage of the radar tracking.

At this point, mistakes were made. Stills from the radar were bought by a French newspaper and, as a result, the Belgian media forced their air force into staging a rapid press conference. This was chaired by Major-General de Brouwer and made headlines around the world. The case was still being assessed, but looked very strong at the time—so that is how it was reported.

However, according to UFOlogist Wim Van Utrecht, de Brouwer soon came to regret holding this conference. It was eventually revealed that the police officers had probably seen stars through unusual atmospheric conditions. The F-16 radar lock-ons had never correlated with these sightings, and the aircrew had seen nothing in the sky. It was later decided that the targets picked up by their radar were probably nothing more than one F-16 sensing the other jet as it was crossing its path.

What appeared a very important wave of sightings with a highly significant radar tracking has turned out in retrospect to be no such thing. Of course, something was seen on November 29, 1989, but it may have been a covert USAF aircraft. Maybe they did not fly any F-117s over Belgium that night. Perhaps by then something much better had been cooked up by Area 51. Was this on a practice run—possibly as part of the same NATO trials for the coming bombing missions to the Middle East that had provoked the midair-refueling "UFOs" seen widely over Britain?

The story of these flying triangles by no means concluded after the Belgian wave disappeared. Indeed, if anything, it has become far more obvious a part of the UFO legend since the mid 1990s. But we will look at that in a little while. For now, it is wise simply to bear in mind that when aircraft encounter strange objects in midair they can sometimes turn out to be real craft and not just lights in the sky. But those real craft could have decidedly terrestrial, not extraterrestrial, origins. Secret aircraft are really out there and, for good reasons, there are people who are happy for you not to know. They are happier still if you buy into the tall tales that these craft are from another world.

12 DANGER SIGNS

In the winter of 1990–91, I was paying particular attention to a large number of unusual fireballs that were being seen crossing the sky. Often, of course, they were being reported directly to UFO investigators because witnesses regarded them as an alien spaceship. I knew that they were not, but their bright colors (vivid blues and greens), long duration, and regular occurrence suggested they were an interesting phenomenon. They were more powerful than straightforward meteors and more like the green fireball mystery that has bugged UFOlogy for most of its existence.

Since I investigate sighting reports that are submitted to the Jodrell Bank radio telescope, I discussed the matter with staff there. They had already proved very helpful the year before by assisting our North-West UFO group, NARO, to solve a series of sightings at Heywood in Lancashire.

Odd lights were seen by an ambulance crew and by various police officers at the nearby station. All of these witnesses watched the colored glows over a nearby hill for some minutes, and there were even reports of strange effects on the ambulance station telephone. We quickly established that the "effect" was not connected (a radio station had called for a live report and, not having replaced the receiver at their end of the line, had temporarily rendered the ambulance phone inoperative). Jodrell Bank ran a computer program to test the levels of atmospheric ionization. Air traffic control staff at Manchester Airport helpfully provided me with data on possible mirage effects in the atmosphere, and an astronomer used his computer database to check whether any bright stars or planets were distorted by these factors. From this research, the UFOs proved to be a combination of weather effects, atmospheric forces, and misperception. The witnesses had indeed seen something interesting, but it had a scientific explanation—as, of course, so many UFO sightings do.

Sadly, the media could not wait for this detective work to proceed. They had to publish daft tales about alien saucers right away. The public is all too often misled by the inability of the media to treat UFOs as sober news. Plenty of UFO buffs are equally willing to rush to judgment and smile at a camera.

As a result of our research, it seemed possible that excess ionization in the upper levels of the atmosphere might be causing quite spectacular fireball effects as brilliant plasma jets were ejected by them.

One such colorful event occurred on November 5, 1990, and blazed a trail amidst the comparatively feeble rockets of Bonfire Night. Others followed on March 23, 1991 (a beautiful blue one), and on April 17, 1991, at Limerick in Ireland, about which I typed up this rather appropriate witness account: *There once was a funny green light that shone for two ticks in the night. It made the air glow, but nobody knows, if the answer we've got for it's right.*

Joking aside, it was clear that something of scientific value was occurring in the atmosphere above the British Isles and that a natural phenomenon was responsible. So I was not surprised to discover yet another multiple sighting of another fireball within this wave. The calls started to flood in directed from Jodrell Bank and referring to the events of around 7:20 p.m. on February 20, 1991. This is a flavor of the reports received as I spent the day talking with witnesses.

At Stoke on Trent, several office workers had seen a vivid white streak of fire that shot across the sky and exploded like fireworks.

One witness at Mow Cop, a Staffordshire hill, described a "big glow shooting across the sky."

But I particularly focused on the story from a highly articulate woman in an isolated farmhouse near Sandbach, Cheshire, who had seen a very brilliant fireball that moved on a slow and majestic downward arc, pulsating as it blended through different shades of green. She thought this was a crashing aircraft until she realized that nothing reappeared from the far side of her wall as its trajectory indicated that it should have done. It had simply vanished.

Although these sightings were all from one fairly small area, I did have other reports that day from further afield, including Oldham, Burnley, and Blackburn.

It was not difficult to conclude that these people had witnessed yet another of the spectacular fireballs, as the evidence all pointed that way. But early that morning, as I was still finding my way through this mass of incoming evidence, BBC radio called to ask if I would comment on the sightings. I did so, noting what I thought was the likely explanation and adding that it was early yet and much investigation would follow. By lunchtime, I was amazed to hear my tentative solution appearing on TV news bulletins, being reported secondhand as if I had definitively explained the whole matter!

After this unexpected TV revelation, my telephone starting ringing hot with irate callers demanding to know why I was trying to ridicule them. They had seen the UFO and were sure it was an alien craft. Patiently, I explained my thinking, indicating why I believed they had indeed seen something rare and (by irony) of true extraterrestrial origin, but pointing out also that there was no reason to assume it was a spaceship.

In addition to this unwelcome blitz, I picked up rumors that there might have been a sighting by an aircraft heading into Manchester Airport. No further details were added, but I decided to try to discover more about this aspect of the case. Following proper procedure, I asked for a copy of any relevant reports on that night's UFO activity from Owen Hartop, the man that was then in charge at the MoD's London UFO desk ("Air Staff

2A"). He was soon to relinquish his duties to the new man, Nick Pope, who has gone on to make a big name for himself by writing books alleging that UFOs really are alien craft. But Hartop was, as he always had been, very friendly and willing to cooperate.

Hartop wrote to tell me that Air Staff 2A had just two reports for that night. He copied both of them and noted the following: "I can confirm that we have no reason to link these sightings with a satellite reentry. I regret that I cannot be more positive in offering a definitive explanation for what was witnessed."

Translating this news, I realized that the only other likely solution for the case—that space junk had burnt up on reentering the earth's upper atmosphere—had evidently been eliminated after consulting the NORAD (North American Air Defense) computer records that predict and log such incidents. This meant that a bright bolide type of meteor was the most feasible answer, but the MoD appeared reluctant to accept that opinion.

One of the MoD reports I received told of a sighting in Manchester. Although the name of the witness and his full address were blocked out, as is common practice, there were clues within the file to leave me suspecting his identity. According to the MoD, this person was a well-known UFO buff. I had already wondered whether this very man had been the first caller to my ex-directory line in the wake of the lunchtime TV news report. For that caller, a Mr. McGregor, was in my opinion not who he said he was, and had been using a rather dubious Scottish accent in his efforts to berate me! The anonymous MoD report said that the man, who may or may not have been the same person who had called my home, had seen a pulsating "emerald green light" at 7:20 p.m. that night.

Intriguing as this news was, the second MoD sighting report was more important. For this was a detailed copy of the message channeled through from Manchester Airport. This indicated that the UFO had been witnessed from the air traffic control tower. By now, of course, the media fuss had long since disappeared. It was a dead case as far as they were concerned. The local press had published absurd stories, calling the sighting a "close encounter of the third kind" then, once the joke was over, they had forgotten about it.

However, the official account, which was sent by telex from the airport to the MoD at 7:30 a.m. on the morning after the sighting, told how control staff had seen an object with "a line of light inside a broad band, very bright, changing from green to yellow to white." This was very like one of the descriptions of the sighting; a witness I had spoken with felt that he saw more than just a light. Instead, he claimed that the object he saw at Burnley was a fluorescent green, wedge-shaped craft with a band along its side.

With the help of the MoD data, I composed a letter to the ATC at Manchester advising of my interest in the case and of the various options for some sort of atmospheric phenomenon that might lie behind what was seen. Thankfully my letter, which carefully avoided mention of alien UFOs or any other wild speculation, led to a call from a senior air traffic controller and the possibility of a better insight into the events at the airport that night.

The tower had logged the sighting at 7:19 p.m. and said that they saw it at a bearing of 200° to 220° (i.e., southwestwards). It was in the sky for 5 seconds and moved at speed, but not excessively quickly, at an elevation of between 15° and 25°. No fewer than four of the radar operators on duty saw the UFO, but they had not picked it up on their screens. Even so, they had never seen anything like it before, despite having over 60 years combined experience of viewing the skies from the wonderful perspective of air traffic control towers.

I spoke at length to the most senior officer involved, who had 35 years experience as an ATC. He noted that because the object was not tracked on radar, they at first paid little attention to the matter. They did call Cheshire police at Knutsford, but they had no knowledge of the events. What changed the view of the ATC was the experience of the two crew members aboard a Manx Airlines ATP turboprop aircraft. They were flying the short hop from the Isle of Man to Manchester and during the 30-minute flight had two separate encounters.

The first occurred at 7:07 p.m. as they crossed the Wirral in the early stages of their descent. Flying at 10,000 feet, they saw a brilliant blue ball of light that appeared in the south and traveled for a few seconds on a parallel course with the plane. They estimate they were above the town of Wallasey at the time. However, they chose not to report the incident by radio.

Twelve minutes later, the aircraft had landed and was on the runway about to taxi in. This gave the crew an expansive view of the sky all around. Suddenly, they saw an even more brilliant bluish-green light that was so intense it was picked out ahead of them even through the glow of the runway landing lights. This second sighting made up the minds of the Manx crew to report both incidents to the control tower.

The Manx Airlines pilot chose not to file an "air miss" report because in both incidents the object was clearly some distance away from the plane and was not considered a threat. He and his copilot did not wish to make their own report to the MoD but agreed to allow the fact that an aircraft had confirmed the sighting to be added to the ATC officers' report when it was submitted to London.

I spoke with the controller some months after they had sent their report to Air Staff 2A. He was surprised, and disappointed, that no MoD or CAA official had gotten back to them to even try to suggest an explanation. He is not alone in feeling disquiet when aircrew and support staff sightings are given such a casual brush-off by the authorities. I have heard the claim often.

The ATC said the initially favored story of the operators was that it was some kind of atmospheric aurora—but they were not looking north. He added that there was a definite sense of "electric arcing" to the light, which was akin to the sort of glow that might be emitted by a malfunctioning power station. This confirms my suspicion, and indeed the suspicion of some of the scientists who have investigated these mystery fireball cases ever since the events over Los Alamos in 1948, that some kind of atmospheric ionization must be taking place. The question still outstanding is, What causes this to occur in the first place?

I was still investigating the Manx Airlines case when news broke of a second event. This time the MoD had endeavored to keep it quiet, and succeeded for several weeks. However, a rather frustrated pilot had chosen to break the curfew. As he worked for the Italian airline Alitalia, not even the men from the ministry could stop him. As you have seen, by 1991 the Italian government had a much more liberal attitude about releasing news of official UFO encounters than was evident down Whitehall way.

With the cat out of the bag, the MoD was forced to comment and was incredibly open. They insisted that they had not attempted to cover anything up but had "decided not to talk about it." As for what had taken place, it was "one of those things" and "yet another UFO"—all said as if these sort of things happened every day. In fact, that was remarkably true at the time, but the British public was not told why.

It has taken some time to compile a full account of this case—and, of course, that same British public never got to see the true story, because by the time it was collated the brief media interest was over. I have the official report submitted to the MoD and numerous exchanges with the CAA and ministry on the matter. My colleague Clas Svahn has also interviewed the pilot in Rome. Here is what took place.

Alitalia Flight AZ 284 was 23 minutes from the end of its 2-hour journey from Milan to London Heathrow. The date was April 21, 1991, at approximately 8 p.m. In charge of the MD-80 jet with fifty-seven passengers—code sign Whiskey Charlie (I-DAWC)—was Captain Achille Zaghetti. His copilot, who preferred not to be identified, also saw the incident.

Whiskey Charlie was crossing the Channel and heading northwest on a bearing of 321°. It was about 10 miles off the coast and some 30 miles south of the Biggin Hill beacon. The aircraft was under control of London Heathrow ATC and descending at 2000 feet per minute from 26,000 feet while traveling at a speed of about 400 mph.

Another aircraft was dead ahead of them by about 15 miles, but at a much lower height. Even so, they were monitoring its progress, as their increase in speed during descent was causing the MD-80 to close this gap. Night was falling, although there was still some twilight at their height. Nevertheless, they could see only the flashing lights of the aircraft ahead—not its outline.

As they passed through 22,100 feet (later confirmed by the radar records), Zaghetti caught sight of what was to him an amazing and rather frightening object—but that will appear all too familiar now to readers of this book. Heading across their path from left to right was something "similar to a missile, light brown or fawn, about 3 meters in length but without any exhaust flame."

The object was on a near-collision course, moving to pass by at an estimated 1000 feet above them. The captain yelled, "Look out! Look out!" But by the time these words were properly digested by his copilot, the "missile" had flown by. There was no wake turbulence. The copilot had been looking ahead at the other aircraft and so had easily seen the UFO cross their path.

Zaghetti told Clas Svahn that he did not believe the object *was* a missile—just that it resembled one. As soon as it had vanished, he radioed to London ATC to ask whether they had anything on radar in close proximity to Whiskey Charlie. About a minute later, the radar operator confirmed that they did—moving away at about 10 miles behind the jet. This persuaded the pilot to file his report when they landed.

Next day, the ATC told him they had solved the matter. It was a helicopter on a routine flight. Zaghetti pointed out, as the CAA must surely have known, that helicopters cannot fly at 23,000 feet, and suggested that they use the film of the radar to track back to the origin of the UFO. At that point, the CAA and MoD went quiet, and Zaghetti never heard from them again.

The silence caused him to speak out about the matter when he got back home. He added that a year after the events nobody from the British MoD or civil aviation authorities had bothered to contact him further despite his report's being officially and very clearly logged as a "Near Collision—Air Traffic Incident Report." This was something he felt undeniably merited a serious inquiry. After all, lives had been at risk.

Despite his lack of support, Captain Zaghetti tried to come up with an explanation. He had considered the possibility of a rogue missile firing but felt his aircraft was too high to encounter a ground-launched missile. The normal ceiling for one of these is 10,000 feet. Zaghetti also believed that the authorities would not minimize the risk to other air traffic by covering up such an answer.

He had actually checked his instruments after the sighting to confirm the wind speed and direction. From this, he knew that the object could not have been a balloon, as it was clearly moving across the prevailing winds. This vital information put an end to the "toy balloon" theory that was beginning to gain attention for similar cases—even if a balloon could be shown to reach such phenomenal heights as this.

While the captain sat waiting forlornly for an answer back in Rome, not speaking to the press as he believed a serious "air-miss" investigation was underway in the U.K., the British authorities were behaving very strangely. They seemed keen to persuade the few interested media who had picked up on Zaghetti's story from Italy that this really was a UFO! Of course, you may be tempted to suspect this was a diversionary tactic to steer the media away from any thought that a real missile was involved.

There was an army proving ground at Lydd in Kent from which such a launch could have occurred. But checks revealed that it was not operational at the time. Subsequent questions in parliament from a local MP confirmed that this was the official position. There was no missile launch to blame.

Eventually, B.H. Dale of the Safety Data and Analysis Unit at the CAA admitted that, despite "extensive civil and military investigations," they had failed to identify the object seen by Whiskey Charlie or tracked by Heathrow radar (at a vanishing speed estimated by Zaghetti as around 200 mph). They had checked with NORAD and no space junk had entered the atmosphere at the time. They had eliminated weather balloons. As a result, by only July 25, 1991, they "closed the investigation and listed the sighting as an unidentified flying object." Note that there was no mention of the helicopter they tried to persuade Zaghetti he had seen 24 hours after the sighting. Was that a ruse designed to stop him from going public?

UFOlogist Paul Murphy waged a fascinating battle by letter with the Earl of Arran, who was under-secretary for the armed forces at the time. He wanted, quite rightly, to know how the MoD could be so dismissive of a case that ought to have triggered the air defense warning systems of the U.K. like any real "missile" would surely do. Just how reliable were these systems?

Arran responded that no UFO event ever recorded had been judged a "defense threat"—a pat answer often cited by the MoD. This is clearly not a response that would satisfy those pilots, such as Zaghetti, who have found themselves flying all too near to a solid object that was tracked on radar to prove its substance. There seems a very evident "threat" implicit here—whatever the object was.

Interestingly, Arran insisted that the air defenses did not react to the sighting and its attendant radar recording, because the system had built-in safeguards to ensure that "any response is appropriate to the circumstances." Once more the public was fobbed off without an explanation for an incredible midair encounter, even though, as this book has shown, the Alitalia case by no means stands alone.

Indeed, even as the powers that be washed their hands of this matter with unseemly haste, I was finding from my own investigations that it was far from unique even during that summer. The year 1991 was generating more midair encounters over Britain than ever. It was a truly disturbing series of events. This wave was causing all my doubts to evaporate and it was a matter that could not be ignored. Unfortunately, the British public was not in possession of this information and no doubt accepted the judgment of the CAA and MoD—thus presuming nothing significant was taking place. The public was being seriously misled.

The disgraceful lack of positive action by the authorities had an effect on Captain Zaghetti. Like many other pilots before him, he regretted speaking out and had expected better when he bravely chose to do so. He confirmed that it was standard practice when something was seen to ask the ATC to back up the sighting with news of a radar tracking. "We ask the radar first if he saw what we saw," Zaghetti told Clas Svahn in 1992. "If he says that he did not see anything, then we did not see anything either." How often have aircrews been forced into that lamentable position of a false denial because of the attitudes displayed by the investigating authorities whenever UFOs are discussed?

As this case was being scrutinized by the UFO community, news began to filter in about a second incident. When I first heard the rumors via my ATC contacts, I wrongly noted the airline involved. My BUFORA colleague Ken Phillips, who lived near their head office, began inquiries and got a curious reaction. It soon became clear that, while the case that I had heard about involved a different airline, the one we were erroneously pursuing had experienced a similar encounter at about the same time! We found this by accident and I began to wonder just how many more cases we were not being told about.

The first of this quite alarming summer series occurred 6 weeks after the Alitalia affair, on June 1, 1991. A Britannia Airways Boeing 737 was on a flight from Dublin to London Heathrow. It was 2:38 p.m. on a bright afternoon and the aircraft was descending through 8000 feet, heading eastwards towards the airport while flying some 30 miles west of Heathrow (i.e., not far from Reading in Berkshire).

Both pilots observed a craft that rushed past their right-hand side. It was a cylindrical object not unlike a missile and colored yellow/orange. There seemed to be a wrinkled appearance to the surface. The object was said to be about 10 feet in size. The close similarities with what Captain Zaghetti reported are more than obvious. Yet again a rogue missile was contemplated and ruled out. There are, thankfully, no launch sites beneath the flight path into one of the world's busiest airports!

The crew members were quizzed by the CAA about the possibility of a weather balloon but argued that the object was clearly moving towards them at speed, given the rapid rate with which they passed each other. As a result, the CAA concluded this was not likely to be the answer. However, the toy balloon theory was considered more viable in this case because of the relatively low height of the jet and "wrinkled" description. But that explanation does not work for the Alitalia case and these two events seem identical—so it would be unwise to feel the Heathrow case is solved. Unfortunately, radar did not record this object.

However, there was that other case from the airline that Ken Phillips and I were wrongly chasing. It occurred just 2 weeks later, on June 17, and quite astonishingly was over that old stomping ground of UFO activity—Rendlesham Forest!

In this instance, Dan Air Flight 4700 (call sign Echo Lima) was a Boeing 737 from London Gatwick to Hamburg in Germany. It was 6:30 p.m. on a clear evening and the jet was flying eastwards over the border between Essex and Suffolk, climbing through about 5000 feet, heading for 12,000 feet. A group of four passengers spotted the object off to the left of the aircraft (i.e., northwards in the Ipswich/Rendlesham area). The main spokesperson for this group was Walter Leiss, a German engineer. He filed an official report with the cockpit crew and, while it appears that they saw nothing, they were sufficiently persuaded to make their own radio report. They felt the description, by one passenger, of a "wingless projectile" very nearby, merited attention. They called through for assistance, but London radar confirmed that they had no other object on screen that could account for the sighting.

Leiss agreed to tell his story to BUFORA. In this, he explained how the witnesses observed an all too familiar object that was "slender, gray and, so it seemed, sort of cigar-shaped. Its flight path was parallel to our own, but diametrically opposed."

This latest "missile attack" flew just above the cloud layer and headed towards them at a steep angle. It passed directly under the jet and would have collided with Echo Lima but for the fact that it was about 1000 feet below them. Given the good weather and relatively long duration (more than a minute), the witnesses had a perfect opportunity to view the UFO. It was definitely not another aircraft. Indeed, it appeared to "oscillate" in a curious manner not unlike a yo-yo.

Once again the matter was simply logged—not as an air miss this time, because of the failure of the crew to observe anything. As before, neither firm conclusions were formed nor actions taken. Indeed, the Dan Air in-flight safety officer, Derek Harper, confirmed 14 months later that the airline had not received any correspondence giving any explanation as to this particular sighting. Note those words—the inference being that there are other Dan Air sightings we know nothing about.

Although these two cases in June were not as significant as the Alitalia affair, the same cannot be said for the fifth British encounter that I had uncovered since February 1991. This incident was perhaps the most disturbing of all, because passenger aircraft were clearly at risk in the judgment of ATC staff and one was actually scrambled out of the path of the UFO.

It happened on July 15, 1991, and again involved Britannia Airways and another Boeing 737. This was on a vacation charter flight from Crete to London Gatwick at 5:45 p.m. Again the weather was fine and sunny. The jet was crossing the Sussex coast and descending through 15,000 feet when the copilot spotted something ahead and at an estimated distance of only half a mile. He yelled to the pilot as the object rushed past their right-hand wing. It was in view for only a couple of seconds and did not cause any wake. They felt that it came within about 300 feet of the Boeing, although this was hard to estimate. They suggest that it was only a couple of feet long. Of course, if it were somewhat farther away, then its size would have been correspondingly larger—but it was definitely not a large device. Note that in most of the other midair encounters the size is often estimated as being no greater than 10 feet long.

Once again the description of this object was a "black lozenge" and the course it took was regarded as "near collision." The matter was the subject of an official air-miss report by the crew and on this the pilot rated the danger of an impact as "high." The aircraft was even checked over on landing in case there was any damage, but none was in evidence. This Britannia crew was not in any doubt as to how close they had come to leading their unsuspecting vacationers into disaster.

Immediately after the "lozenge" flew by the 737, London ATC was contacted. Gatwick confirmed that they did have an unidentified radar echo that was now behind the jet and streaking out into the Channel. Radar plotted its departure at a speed of 120 mph. The target was not any known aircraft because it failed to exhibit a "transponder" signal—the electronic code given to all aircraft to identify what they are. The blip was heading towards the path of a second inbound commercial aircraft. This was at a greater height, but the ATC decided to take no chances and called the pilot to divert his course. At this point, the UFO changed direction and disappeared out to sea, being lost from radar a few minutes later. The second aircraft saw nothing as it headed into Gatwick. Of course, having this radar confirmation was all the incentive that the crew of the Britannia 737 needed to file their air-miss report.

Investigation of this matter was hampered by tabloid journalists. They had heard of the story (the radio conversation was intercepted by air spotters). According to both the airline and the CAA, they seemed desperate to turn this into an "alien spaceship" drama and a saga of how the aircrew and passengers had squared up to little green men. All involved were disgusted by this attitude as they were sure that some kind of rational explanation would be found. They did try very hard to achieve just that.

All the usual suspects were considered. The most likely seemed a weather balloon. One of these was launched from nearby Crawley, but its course was plotted and it did not come close to being in the path of the 737 at 15,000 feet at the time. The Met Office also confirmed that the witness description did not match. In fact, this weather balloon was then heading east at 42 mph with the wind—whereas the UFO was heading south at three times this velocity. In my estimation, such speed rules out the possibility of any kind of balloon.

The great height was also a problem for the toy balloon theory then being avidly considered as the cause for these by now numerous "missile" encounters. But then, as you have seen, the same cause had been suspected for several years—dating back at least to the object photographed over northeastern Italy in June 1979.

One balloon photography expert, Adrian Bishop, was willing to suggest that one of the small silver balloons that you can buy at fairgrounds could appear as this object did against a bright sky. He alleged that they had been reported reaching 7000 feet—probably more. The Met Office felt that such balloons were unlikely to go above 6000 feet. Fairground balloons are only about a foot in diameter and you would have to be very close to one in order to get a view of it at all from a fast-moving aircraft. It is improbable that they could be detected on radar and they certainly cannot travel at over 100 mph. If driven by wind speeds this great, they would almost certainly be destroyed.

In any event, we have to see this Sussex case not in isolation but in comparison with the various others that appear to describe the same thing. Putting the data together, we can see that these objects are too big, have been recorded on radar at too great a speed, have clearly flown against prevailing winds, and have changed course. These seem to be overwhelming grounds for rejecting the toy balloon theory—although, you may be surprised to hear, this is what the CAA tried hard to prove with the Sussex case.

In the end, the CAA was unable to offer any definite conclusions and left the event as unexplained. The working group's evident uncertainty is betrayed by the wording of its report: "Members [of the team] were unsure what damage could have occurred had the object struck the aircraft [but] the general opinion was that there had been a possible risk of collision." However, Group Captain John Maitland of the investigating Joint Air Miss Division at RAF Uxbridge, home of the working group, admitted a year later that even without proof he "suspected" that the object was "probably some sort of small balloon."

If 1991 was a remarkable year for bringing home the sheer numbers of midair encounters, it was not to prove unique. The sightings have continued to escalate ever since and, if they are the result of rogue missile launches, then the world of commercial aviation is in serious trouble. If they are being caused by a global flotilla of toy balloons climbing much higher than anticipated and flying into the paths of jetliners, they are still disconcerting. For even if they pose no physical threat, there is the risk of creating panic that could cause an aircrew to make fatal errors of judgment. As such we need to clearly identify the source.

It would be impossible to discuss all of the recent midair cases, because there are so many of them; however, just to give an indication that this is not an isolated flurry of events confined only to the crowded skies over Britain, some more recent global examples are given below.

On July 8, 1992, a French military helicopter was flying from Le Luc to Aurillac at a height of 6000 feet. The weather was clear and sunny. As it passed over the town of Brignoles, the crew and troops on board suddenly observed a "long black lozenge" that was "not unlike a missile." This was heading towards them at speed and rushed underneath and out of view.

Just a month later, on August 5, 1992, United Airlines Flight 934, a Boeing 747 flying to London Heathrow, had just taken off from Los Angeles. It was 1:45 p.m. and Flight 934 was climbing through 23,000 feet heading northeastwards when the crew spotted something heading for them. It streaked underneath the jumbo at an estimated range of under 1000 feet. The United crew spoke of the object's being dark in color and like a sleek cigar or rocket without any sign of wings. The fuselage appeared rounded. Their official report seemed to suggest that this had to be some kind of covert military aircraft. But both the USAF and the Department of Defense emphatically denied that they would blunder into the path of a civil airliner. Then the U.S. government tried to suggest that it could have been a secret experiment by someone else—for example, the CIA and other "intelligence agencies" that have "strange projects."

On September 14, 1992, Australian Airlines Flight 405 was heading from Melbourne to Hobart, Tasmania. At 18,000 feet, on descent towards the island, a "black, cigar-shaped object" appeared dead ahead and came close to the jet as it passed by. The UFO was quickly masked by the hills to the west of the town of Derwent. The local weather center suggested to the investigation that a cloud formation might have been mistaken. That could work as a solution to the occasional sighting if there were not so many of these encounters that are so chillingly similar in nature.

Britain was not left out. In July 1993, a British Airways Boeing 767 was on a flight from Edinburgh to London and crossing the Pennine hills "somewhere near Manchester" at around 30,000 feet. They called Manchester Air Traffic Control to report a "long dark object" that flashed by them. Radar confirmed that it had a brief target on screen that disappeared within a couple of sweeps. Further details have been difficult to obtain because of the policy adopted by British Airways and the apparent tightening of controls by the ATC. Perhaps they do not wish it to be known just how often these incidents are taking place.

However, on the evening of January 6, 1995, the combined forces of both the CAA and British Airways failed to prevent news from filtering out about what has become the most celebrated of recent midair encounters. Within days of its occurrence, there were press reports. This was followed by a new wave of interest a year later when the CAA published their astonishingly frank air-miss report.

I have spent a good deal of time pursuing this case and its various possible solutions. Here is an account of what seems to have taken place.

British Airways Flight 5061 was a Boeing 737 from Milan to Manchester with sixty passengers aboard. It had headed north across Britain and was now being vectored to a landing on Runway 24. In order to achieve this, aircraft are often sent out over the Derbyshire peaks, and 5061 was heading north over the Whaley Bridge/New Mills area at 6:48 p.m. when the events took place.

The sky was very dark and there were thick, low clouds. This obscured the view of the aircraft from ground level. Flight 5061 had been cleared to descend to 4000 feet and was skimming in and out of the tops of the clouds as it approached this height. Suddenly, First Officer Mark Stuart spotted something out of the corner of his eye. He was actually monitoring the instruments, but the thing he saw was so bright it rapidly distracted him. Looking out of the cockpit, he saw something heading right for them. He let out an instinctive yell, ducked because it seemed to be about to smash into them, and began to move forward towards the controls. He had barely moved before the object had sped away to their right.

The first officer looked at the pilot, Captain Roger Wills, and said, "Did you see that?" Roger Wills agreed that he had. Both men had monitored its passage to their side and had it in view for at most 5 seconds, although a more realistic estimate is a couple of seconds only.

Obviously, they had much else on their minds as they prepared for landing, but they did call Manchester ATC to ask if they had recorded any "conflicting traffic." Manchester said that only the Boeing was on radar—a fact subsequently confirmed when the radar film was electronically reconstructed during the air-miss investigation filed on landing by the two shaken crew members.

After touchdown, Stuart suggested to Wills that both men sketch the object that they had seen. This was after a few minutes spent discussing the episode. They believed the drawings would be useful to the air miss team. Both drawings were fairly similar, but there were marked differences.

In general, the men thought they had seen a long, sleek, wedge-shaped craft with little evident sign of wings. It had been dark against a dark sky and so its shape should be regarded with some caution. Although they thought it had passed by within just a few feet, this seems highly improbable given the lack of any turbulence.

The first officer was convinced that he had seen a structured and quite solid craft. He has always described it as such and even claims there was a horizontal stripe down the middle. Captain Wills was less persuaded that he had seen anything structured, referring to and drawing a mass of brilliant lights.

Both men debated these differences, and Mark Stuart suggested to Roger Wills that he had seen the same craft, but that the lights had not been generated by the object; rather, the lights of the Boeing 737 had reflected from its metal surface. Of course, for that to be the case, the object would need to have passed by extremely close to the British Airways plane. The lack of a shock wave and resulting turbulence seems to refute that idea. Of course, perhaps the UFO was stationary and the crew saw it only at the very last moment, when it reflected their lights from its surface. This may explain why it did not appear on radar—as stationary targets tend to be eliminated by the computers. However, the view of the pilots was that the object appeared to be moving, and that the relative closing speed of the UFO and 737 was enormous.

Defying ridicule from colleagues and the desire of the airline not to get involved, they released the story but decided not to give media interviews. Over a year later, Mark Stuart did do so just once, but the captain declined. Whether the already stated position of British Airways on midair encounters was an issue in his decision is not clear.

The yearlong CAA Air Miss Study was, I am told by one of its members, "very thorough." But the final report is remarkable and was guaranteed to create worldwide interest anew, for it terms the sightings as "inaccessible" and indicates that no answer was found. However, it mentions the possibility of "extraterrestrial activity" and concludes—"fascinating though it may be [this] is not within the Air Miss group's remit and must be left to those whose interest lies in this field."

That comment was seemingly intended as idle speculation. It was not meant to imply that the CAA had decided that the British Airways jet had even a possible close encounter with aliens. But you can see why the media gleefully pounced on these rather ill-chosen words as if it had suggested precisely that option.

What we appeared to have here was a case in which two experienced pilots had seen an exotic craft close-up and in which the official investigation had almost sanctioned the alien possibility by referring to it in the report. To UFOlogists, it appeared to be a vindication of years of effort, and I have seen this case presented by them in numerous articles as a true classic. It will no doubt be cited as such for years to come.

However, we do need to remember that a UFO is a UFO and not necessarily a spaceship. While that distinction appears to have eluded the CAA during their yearlong study, we cannot ignore it here. Undoubtedly, these two pilots saw something unusual and spectacular. Of that I am certain—just as I am sure that they described it well and behaved correctly throughout. But in trying to assess what they saw, there are a number of important clues to be taken into account.

First, despite all of the publicity that has surrounded this case, none of the passengers have ever come forward to say that they saw something. This does not surprise me, because only the cockpit crew had a clear view to the front of the aircraft. But it does confirm that this was a sighting of very short duration, and that the size and proximity of the object might not have been quite as dramatic as Wills and Stuart understandably believe. I find it hard to imagine that all sixty passengers would have missed a large alien craft (well-lit or very reflective) that sped by within just a few feet of the right-hand wing. But they could have missed a light phenomenon that shot by within just 2 seconds well to the front of the 737.

I think it is likely that the object was at a much greater distance ahead of the aircraft than the crew assumed, and that it was probably moving across their path, not down the side. This is not to question their judgment or belittle their undoubted expertise. I say this after years of interviewing UFO witnesses and realizing just how difficult it is to make such estimations at night. Neither man had faced a situation like this before. No blame can possibly be attached. But I have talked to hundreds of witnesses who have gone through such circumstances, and I know that they frequently misreport distances and other factors to a considerable degree. Equally well, I suspect that the CAA lacked experience with UFO reports and was as guilty as most people of presuming that what the pilots saw was what was really there. But anyone who has ever investigated a UFO sighting at night knows that presumption is likely to be incorrect.

The lack of wake turbulence or radar tracking further suggests that the object the two men saw, if indeed it was moving, was probably located some distance from them. It could very easily have been a huge object miles high in the atmosphere (where no ground radar would have tracked it), as opposed to a smaller object much nearer to the 737 as they assumed.

We saw, when discussing the midair refueling encounters, that witnesses frequently make this error because their minds judge the most likely height of the object and then come up with a size to match. Here, I suspect, Wills and Stuart believed the object was very close and so interpreted what they saw as "aircraft sized." Or, indeed, being pilots, they may have presumed that the object had to be of "aircraft size" and their minds adjusted the distance to suit. Either way, it is perfectly possible that they were really looking at a huge object many miles away.

One person from Stockport did come forward after the publicity for the CAA report and said that he had seen a gigantic structured object from the ground that day. He achieved considerable attention, and a spectacular painting of what he saw was featured in the media. I have met this witness. While I respect his opinion, I am not convinced that what he reports is relevant to this case. This man was 20 miles from where the aircraft had its encounter. He claims that his sighting was made earlier that day in daylight. Certainly nobody on the ground could have seen what the crew of BA 5061 did, because of the weather conditions at that time.

Whatever this ground witness may have seen, it does not constitute reasonable confirmation for the later sighting by the pilots. I find it hard to imagine that any kind of massive triangular craft could have roamed the skies surrounding a major airport amidst one of its busiest traffic periods without being noticed until it almost collided with the incoming flight from Milan. These two sightings must be considered as quite distinct from one another and are markedly different in many respects.

The CAA report seemingly only considered what "craft" might have been in the area, because, of course, the pilots were adamant that they had encountered some kind of structured object. They explored and rejected various options, such as helicopters, hang gliders, and microlites. There was even a debate about a Stealth aircraft, but the military denied any such association. In any case, Roger Wills had seen a Stealth jet at close range and was adamant that that was not what had flown past them that night.

The possibility of a different kind of secret aircraft has been mooted. This is because of the wave of "flying triangles" that came to plague northwest England during 1995 and 1996. Tim Matthews, who became convinced that a secret aircraft was being built by the British aerospace plant at Warton near Preston, investigated the case. He received an "anonymous tip-off" from the base that they were indeed to blame. A remotely piloted drone had been built to test the new aircraft. This was being flown by "virtual reality" headsets back at Warton and had gone out of control and strayed into the path of the 737.

I am impressed by the work of Matthews and I believe that he has established that there really are intriguing secret aircraft being flown from Warton. But I find this idea hard to swallow. Certainly it is not unlikely that experimental aircraft would first be developed as unpiloted examples—in effect super-sophisticated model aircraft that can be flown within a 50-mile range of base. This is cost effective and safer for test pilots in the early stages of pioneer projects. Nevertheless, it seems very unlikely that anybody would be stupid enough to test such a device anywhere near the flight route into a busy airport, and it begs the question as to what happened to the drone after it flew past the 737. It seems hard to imagine that it simply crashed somewhere in Derbyshire a few minutes later and nobody noticed.

An ingenious theory was suggested by aviation writer Steuart Campbell, who proposed that Flight 5061 saw a mirage distortion of the lights of the M62 motorway some distance to the north of the jet. I have flown into Manchester several times at night, passing along the same route as 5061. I think it very improbable that this could occur—but it is not impossible.

However, Campbell has since offered support to my conclusion about this case. It is my belief that the aircraft had an encounter with a bolide. One of these would not appear on radar, or shake the 737, because of its great distance from the plane. But past reports clearly show that witnesses commonly describe the blazing trail of debris burning up in the atmosphere as being a cigar-shaped or wedge-like craft with a line of windows or lights along the middle.

The British Astronomical Association reported other sightings of a bright bolide over northern Europe on the very evening of the encounter by Flight 5061.

As I explained earlier in this book, there are also marked similarities between the 1948 encounter of a UFO and an Eastern Airlines DC-3, and this more recent episode involving the British Airways jet. This implies that the 1995 encounter was probably also with a bolide. (See pages 28–32.)

However, we will probably never know for sure. The aircrew may well not be willing to accept this solution, and they were there. I was not. I am merely suggesting the most likely answer to this case.

I have also been accused by UFOlogists of destroying my own argument that aircrews should be more willing to speak out, because I am ridiculing two pilots who have bravely come forth. But I am not ridiculing Roger Wills and Mark Stuart. If they did see a bolide, then it was a spectacular sky phenomenon. It is almost certain that these two men had never seen the likes of this object before. A bolide is far bigger, brighter, and more fantastic to behold than most lights in the sky. As for their "misperception," this is merely the natural way that our perception works. If Albert Einstein and Sir Isaac Newton had been flying the plane, they would still have seen the object in the way that Roger Wills and Mark Stuart did.

So I hope that I am not belittling these men, or indeed any witnesses. I greatly admire their decision to speak out and hope that it serves as a signal of how other aircrew members can behave with decorum in future. Just because a possible solution presents itself here does not mean that the sighting is invalid, or that all sightings will be resolved. But it is surely our responsibility to try to find answers to these cases. The day that we start treating UFO reports as immune to resolution is the day we cross the line from science into superstition. That is all too easy when dealing with UFO reports. We may disagree on an explanation, but the quest to turn UFOs into IFOs (identified flying objects) must go on.

Of course, the cause of some of these midair encounters remains presently unknown. Real disasters follow our inability to discover the truth—and that inability owes a good deal to the false perception that we have solved the UFO mystery by designating sightings as visits by alien starships.

What bothers me is that the public is still unaware of what happened, or what still happens, in these midair encounters and that no special working party seems to have been created by airlines and civil aviation authorities around the globe. Such a body should now be taking over the job of the UFOlogists, because they will continue to be committed to extraterrestrial possibilities when the truth may well be far more down-to-earth and yet no less dangerous. Maybe there is even a way for serious UFOlogists to assist in the process of trying to define what lies behind these midair contacts.

Dr. Richard Haines reported in October 1997 that these matters are still not being given due respect by the proper authorities and that this situation is potentially catastrophic. At the very least, we have to create a better climate where it is not considered ludicrous to report these matters. Airline and investigating teams also must not feel the need to hide the truth. Informed research into the probable causes should be mounted as quickly as possible, bringing together all those who may be able to contribute.

The traveling public deserves nothing else.

On the night of March 30–31, 1993, a remarkable phenomenon was witnessed over France, England, Wales, and Ireland. Dozens of people at 1:10 a.m. spotted two bright lights with trails of vapor pouring from their rear, crossing the sky in silent majesty.

UFOlogist Doug Cooper was called in to investigate by local police in Devon and Cornwall. He responded immediately in the middle of the night. By breakfast, he had tracked down and started to interview a dozen officers who had seen the phenomenon while on patrol in these counties and across in Gwent, South Wales. All were describing the same thing. This suggested that a solution might be found.

After he contacted Nick Pope, who was at that time the man running the UFO desk at the MoD department Air Staff 2A, it was revealed that Whitehall had also been swamped with reports of sightings the night before. These included one made by a meteorological officer at an RAF base on the English-Welsh border who had seen the UFO sweep across the sky and alerted another base in its path. A retired RAF pilot had also seen the two lights and been baffled by them.

As the investigation proceeded, it was officially reported that a Soviet military satellite, Cosmos 2238, had burnt up miles above the earth as it plunged into the atmosphere. Undoubtedly, much of what was reported that night was the result of this activity, we were told. But could it all be so readily dismissed?

Cooper and Pope had both found serious anomalies—sightings that did not match the reentry. In one case, fishermen by the River Parrott had seen a huge catamaran shape (like two Concordes stuck together) crossing the sky, but at completely the wrong time. A scout leader on the Quantock Hills in Somerset had seen something similar, hours *before* Cosmos burned up. Either these witnesses were wildly inaccurate with their stories or something else that mimicked the blazing satellite had also flown over that night.

Nick Pope later told me, when we lectured together in Gothenburg and discussed this case, that he felt the date was crucial. Any press story concerning these incidents would appear in newspapers on April 1st. Any reports would be mixed up with the legitimate sightings of the burning debris known to be due to be visible that night or would be written off as an April Fools' joke, because of the date. It was as if someone wanted this activity to slip through the net. I was able to find several other episodes where the same situation had occurred—big sightings at holiday times blamed on satellites, but when the media would not feature the case in quite the same way as at other times of the year. Christmas Day and New Year's Eve were two prime examples.

In late 1997 came news that there had been some very interesting midair encounters involved with that March 1993 object. Although data from the British MoD had not of course been released, I am pleased to say that this was not the case across the Irish Sea. I thank Ann Griffin and Pat Delaney for supplying copies of the official reports. These were submitted to their military and, they tell me, were made promptly available when they heard of the sightings and requested the evidence to help in the study of this case.

According to a report headed "Unidentified Airborne Sighting," signed by Commander H. O'Keeffe of the Headquarters, Air Corps Group, this is what occurred:

On the night of March 30–31, 1993, Commander O'Keeffe was captain of an air corps Dauphin helicopter with five other servicemen aboard. They left Baldonnel at 00.30 hours on March 31 and headed towards Finner Camp in Donegal. They were flying at 1500 feet at an air speed of 140 knots.

When 10 miles east of Mullingar, they had what O'Keeffe terms "a visual sighting." He describes this in detail. He reports:

> I and the copilot observed a light being turned on at a point above us in our 2 o'clock position at 10–15 miles. The observed light came on and went out in a period of 1–2 seconds. We continued to observe the position and noted two white lights at a fixed distance apart in the horizontal plane. These lights continued to close our position moving from our 2 o'clock towards our 8 o'clock. This track was in a northwest to southeast direction.

O'Keeffe explains that by now, in a 2-minute duration for the sighting, all on board the Dauphin were watching the UFO. He continued to track the object using "handheld NVGs" and, via these night vision glasses that enable the military to see in the dark, he could spot "what appeared to be condensation trails." The whole thing then passed over the top of them, and they all assumed it was an unusual form of aircraft.

However, there was a problem. They contacted Dublin Air Traffic Control, who insisted that no air traffic was on the course reported. Captain O'Keeffe urged them to call Shannon Radar to check for military targets, but Shannon had nothing on screen, presumably because the object was far higher than those aboard the Dauphin were assuming it to be.

During this conversation between helicopter and ground control, the captain of Iona Airways Flight 961 joined in. They were heading for Ireland from Europe and crossing the coast of southwest Wales at 20,000 feet. They confirmed the sighting of fast-moving lights heading north to south across their path.

On landing, the captain filed his report with Shannon, who by now had received several ground sightings from police and other witnesses at places such as Askeaton and Bantry.

There is no doubt that the air corps crew saw the same phenomenon that most of the witnesses in southwest England and south Wales reported at that same time. It has been officially explained by the authorities as the fiery doom of the Cosmos 2238. Yet, interestingly, NORAD (the U.S. space defense command that tracks satellites) told Shannon ATC when they called that night to investigate the possibility of such a burn-up that they had no record of this event. Later NORAD backed up the official story that these sightings were that satellite.

Perhaps this incident was a simple misperception of a blazing satellite. It could well have been, particularly because the wide spread of sightings over hundreds of square miles effectively proves that the object was at a great height. If so, then the case is instructive, because the carefully documented report by experienced military aircrew can be compared with other cases where blazing space debris (either satellites or bolides) is also the suspected culprit. That includes the British Airways affair in January 1995.

You can see from O'Keeffe's account how witnesses generally report the object quite well but seriously underestimate height and distance. The air corps report indicates that the consensus amongst the six personnel on board the Dauphin was that the UFO was between 500 and 3000 feet above them. In truth, if it was Cosmos 2238, it was up to 50 miles overhead—far too high to be tracked by Shannon radar.

Of course, if it was not Cosmos 2238, then the case poses even bigger questions as to what this aircrew saw and why the authorities were so determined to persuade the witnesses that it was space debris. The probability that something else was afoot was clearly suspected by all the UFOlogists who investigated the case. Doug Cooper came to believe it, according to the Irish group IUFOPRA in its published findings on the sightings. And Nick Pope, in his book *Open Skies, Closed Minds*, mentions the sightings that he got while at the MoD that night and says that some of them just did not fit the Cosmos explanation.

The pattern was certainly just as puzzling in Ireland as it was in England, where those anomalous sightings gave timings that did not match those of the other witnesses. In fact, in Ireland there is a quite stunning case that defies all understanding. It appears to be exactly the same thing as everyone else saw, but reported at completely the wrong time. Even on the wrong day.

This third incident did not occur in the air, but involved a naval support squadron captain who saw the object as he was driving through Newcastle, County Dublin. This sighting was, however, easily the most puzzling, because it refers to an event 3 days to the minute before the Cosmos incident—that is, 1:10 a.m. on March 28, 1993.

Captain D. Cotter reports that he stopped the car and got out as "two bright white lights (as in aircraft landing lights) were visible traveling at speed along the night sky." These lights were "in perfect line abreast formation" and estimated at 5000 feet in height. They were moving NNW to SSE and "a definite contrail [was] stretching behind both lights for a few hundred feet."

This by all logic has to be a description of exactly what all the other witnesses saw. The only question seems to be, Why has the witness gotten the date wrong by 3 whole days? There is no question as to when the Cosmos satellite reputedly burned up or, indeed, as to when the main body of sightings occurred in unison with it. If the date on this Irish military report is correct, then we have a major dilemma: a copycat UFO appearing days before the midair sightings. It seems very hard to imagine that Captain Cotter did get his date wrong. He signed his report on April 1, 1993. If it had occurred when all the other sightings did, then he signed the report the very next day. One presumes that, just hours after so memorable an event, a military officer could be sure that it did not occur the day before.

13 WHAT IS REALLY UP THERE?

This book is not designed to convey answers but to set the agenda for what needs to be explored with a more open-minded attitude. However, it is worth highlighting some of the possible areas within which we might seek an explanation. In fact, I strongly suspect that we will need more than one category of UFO to explain the various things that are behind these midair encounters. This is not to account for rogue missiles or toy balloons with unexpected properties, which could indeed explain some of our cases.

Starfire

I have little doubt that some of the aerial sightings in this book result from strange phenomena that are entering our atmosphere from space.

We have long been aware that the universe does not consist of vast emptiness between the stars. It is teeming with microscopic debris and various types of radiation and energy. From time to time, these can come into contact with the earth, with potentially destructive consequences.

When tiny particles enter the upper atmosphere, they burn through friction. The result is the typical "shooting star," or meteor. Tens of thousands of these are visible every year, and the earth's orbit passes through clouds of debris that can be predicted in advance, allowing over a hundred an hour to be seen on some clear nights. Mid-August is a particularly good period, and between August 12th and 15th each year UFOlogists are on the alert for sightings of very bright examples, which usually get misreported within this active meteor shower known as the Perseids.

Meteors are very brief in duration and are rarely more than just a flicker of light. But, of course, some of them can be much larger and run the gauntlet all the way to the earth's surface. Each year, a few meteors become meteorites and actually reach the ground. Usually they fall harmlessly, but the potential for damage is there. That they might strike an aircraft on the way down is certainly possible. The odds of it happening are extremely remote and so far as is known no accidents have resulted, although the possibility should be considered by aviation authorities. In fact, on December 14, 1997, the first proven deaths were attributed to a meteorite fall in Pitalito, Colombia. Four children were killed in a blazing homestead that was badly damaged by impact from a fireball. It fell in three pieces that crashed from the sky and punched holes through the metal roof, striking with the force of a huge bomb. The investigating authorities, given the forensic tests and eyewitness testimony, concluded that the tragedy was almost certainly the result of a disintegrating meteorite.

Some plane somewhere will eventually draw the short straw. After all, someone wins the lottery every week. This is especially true with "space junk"—our own manmade garbage yard in orbit composed of clapped-out satellites and booster rockets. What goes up eventually comes down, and many objects are resistant to destruction. Some have nuclear power sources. One day an aircraft will surely collide with falling debris.

It is more likely that the fiery death of a large chunk of rock or the metal casing from some military satellite will simply be witnessed by an aircrew as it falls. Some of these large meteors tend to be composed of heavy metals that do not burn up so readily as they crash through the atmosphere. This means that, like the artificial rockets and satellites that create space junk, they can exhibit colors and have very long tails of fire. Red, orange, and yellow meteors are common enough, and we should be aware of this possibility if an aircrew describes a short-lived encounter of this type.

Truly gigantic meteors are exceptionally rare, maybe one a decade, but are an amazing sight. Film taken in Colorado of one such "killer" object skimming the upper atmosphere shows the awesome majesty as this brilliant globe with a dagger-like tail sailed silently across the mountains. It was in view for almost a minute and was as bright as the sun despite the clear blue sky. Looking at the video, you would probably estimate that the meteor was close, but it was miles high in the atmosphere—thank goodness! Had it hit the earth, it would undoubtedly have wiped out any city that chanced to get in its way. The risk to aircraft in the path of such a huge object is clear.

Larger meteorites, or even asteroids, can be up to several miles across. A modest one strikes the earth every thousand years on average, while a huge one collides every few million years. The impact of a truly big example can be so destructive that it is worse than all the atom bombs ever built detonating together. One big example 65 million years ago probably churned up so much debris into the atmosphere that it blocked out the sun for months, changed the climate patterns of earth, and wiped out the dinosaurs.

Thankfully, most meteorite strikes are nowhere near as dangerous. But should an unusually bright one be witnessed as it blazes across the sky, it is almost certainly thanks to modern belief systems that it is misperceived as an alien craft.

Other debris can hit the earth in the same way. Comets, composed of ice and dust, sometimes intercept our path, and the spectacular effects of a comet hitting the planet Jupiter in 1994 were well seen from the TV. Had that comet struck the earth, life would almost certainly have been extinguished. But even a smaller one can be incredibly destructive. In June 1908, a fairly small comet exploded in midair over Tunguska, Siberia. It devastated hundreds of square miles of forest, killed thousands of animals, and burned humans long distances from the impact point. Even in London, its effects were clearly visible in the sky, with the reflecting ice crystals cast into the atmosphere making it as bright as day in the middle of the night. The shock wave from the blast circled the entire earth twice.

Comets entering our atmosphere are thought to be very rare, but one physicist, Dr. Louis Frank, has successfully challenged scientific wisdom on this point. He analyzed thousands of photographs taken from high orbital satellites and was fascinated by the tiny points of light that seemed to cross the sky at speed and then flare into brilliance on the edges of space. Their composition showed that they were not meteors. After some years of effort, he proved that they were micro-comets, smaller than snowballs. These were striking the earth with incredible frequency—thousands a day.

Most of these mini-comets simply burned up in the atmosphere to create brief optical effects. But he felt that "aggregates" of several of these ice balls could be created. These could bash their way through the atmosphere and produce a very strange and colorful display as they headed for earth. Some probably made it all the way to the ground. Indeed, there have been numerous cases of people suddenly finding lumps of ice crashing out of a blue sky and smashing their homes. The usual cause is presumed to be ice shearing off aircraft wings, but these ice bombs were recorded long before aircraft.

Of course, as Frank himself has realized, the amazing descent of one of these ice bombs through the atmosphere will produce quite startling visual images. The friction will cause various vapors to be given off, creating a vivid display. Because they are falling great distances, they could be visible for several minutes. This is without any possible electrical effects that may be caused by the friction of ice crystals rubbing against each other in flight. Some UFO reports may turn out to be this kind of natural phenomenon.

Indeed, it is likely that there are other things occurring within our atmosphere that we are only just beginning to discover through our exploration of space. The film taken (see page 104) during the space shuttle program, of drifting clouds of ionizing energy that float through the upper atmosphere, is one case in point. In a few years' time, we may well understand this as some kind of "space storm," and discover that it can float downwards to a point in the stratosphere where it becomes visible, especially to aircraft. Today, however, because there is no science to adequately explain such a mystery, we label it a UFO, as if that magic word will make the problem go away.

Some midair encounters, such as the JAL case over Alaska, may well prove to be this kind of phenomenon on the boundary between our upper atmosphere and outer space. And, of course, who knows what other as yet undiscovered wonders may give rise to UFO sightings in freak meteorological or atmospheric conditions? Perhaps the BOAC Stratocruiser case over Canada is an example of this type.

Energy Fields

As we have seen, there is considerable scientific research that points towards clouds of radiating energy that can suddenly form within the atmosphere. These may well appear visually when electrical chain reactions ionize the air, but on other occasions may not be seen at all.

One interesting case occurred in 1963 when a light aircraft, "Victor Juliet" (C-FLVJ), was flying over Niagara Falls in Ontario, Canada. It was taking a group of tourists over this spectacular area and was witnessed to strike something invisible in midair and then fall to the ground like a brick. The comparisons here with the more recent case of the rescue helicopter in the Polish mountains are apparent.

When it struck the ground, the impact killed all on board. It was discovered that half of the left wing of Victor Juliet had been sheared away. But the lengthy investigation revealed no trace of metal fatigue or any structural failure. The only logical reason why such catastrophic destruction had occurred was that it must have had a collision with a very solid force in midair. But whatever it collided with was invisible to the many tourists who saw the tragedy from the ground.

Extensive efforts were made to test winds and to check weather records. Today many tourist flights traverse the area at low height every day. If there were some kind of CAT or wind-shear effect that could chop off an aircraft wing as easily as it did to Victor Juliet, then this had to be discovered or it might well happen again. Nothing was found and the investigation could reach no firm conclusions as to how this aircraft crashed. To all intents and purposes, it had simply flown into an invisible object.

The research of Dr. Michael Persinger into his so-called "transients" may well offer a means of understanding such accidents. Persinger has established a solid body of evidence that proves that these free-floating fields of energy can indeed be created by the magnetic field of the earth itself.

Work has been carried out by Paul Devereux and the geologists Dr. Brian Brady at the U.S. Bureau of Mines in Colorado and Dr. Paul McCartney in the U.K. This has further demonstrated that the stresses and strains inside the rocks of the earth can cause changes in the electrical field above the surface and generate glowing balls of energy that ride the magnetic currents. These researchers have recreated "earthlights" in the laboratory by putting a lump of rock under pressure and filming what happens with a high-speed camera. On the much grander scale of mountains and landscapes, the brief flickers of light so produced would take the form of huge floating glows that would be reported as UFOs.

Indeed, Devereux and his team have established that there is a correlation between UFO events and fault lines under the earth's surface—the very places where rocks would be put under the necessary strain. Also, at these locations people have been seeing strange lights in the sky for thousands of years. Only in modern times are these earthlights interpreted as alien craft. But they have always been there.

The research of such people will probably convince science quite soon that there is indeed a natural phenomenon that is being created by dynamic forces within our own planet. This phenomenon may not be seen unless it triggers glowing energy forms as a side effect. When visible, it may merely be an interesting distraction for any passing aircraft. When invisible, as the cases from Canada and Poland suggest, it could be potentially catastrophic. For obvious reasons, we should not be writing amusing accounts of aliens, or seeking crashed starships, perhaps forlornly. We must quickly legitimize this work and invest scientific time and money in resolving how these things occur and, therefore, how to stop them.

Fireballs

Aviation experts are aware of certain electrical phenomena that our atmosphere can produce. St. Elmo's fire is one example. Here, charged particles emitted from wing tips act rather like lightning conductors. These can produce a spectacular blue glow. Generally, this sort of phenomenon is harmless, and modern aircraft have developed technology that helps the energy to dissipate without leading to this effect.

Such technological progress is a good example of how various practical methods can be devised to minimize any danger when a series of reports is accepted as describing a real event. After all, if we ignored the study of thunderstorms altogether and left them to the superstitions of the age, people would be needlessly killed. Nor would we have discovered a source of power that is being used all over the world. UFOs are in many respects today's equivalent of an ancient myth behind which lurks, almost unseen, scientific realities that could benefit mankind.

I believe that a number of the UFO sightings that trigger midair encounters may well point us towards unexplained wonders of an electrical nature within our atmosphere. By dismissing them as "alien contacts," we run away from trying to cope with the problems they create. If these phenomena can, in freak conditions, not merely provoke strange sightings but lead also to instrument failure or other unknown reasons for the demise of an aircraft, then it would be folly to ignore them. It is essential that we start a more systematic collection of the evidence free from the often cynical exploitation these sightings receive—both by the media and the UFO community.

One phenomenon that is becoming legitimate is ball lightning. Although we still know very little about its formation processes, it certainly does not occur only during thunderstorms but relies also upon factors connected with the ionization of the air. What makes ball lightning truly strange is that it can appear inside rooms—not only out in the open. Although the word "ball" defines one of its common shapes, it is often seen as like a cigar, tube, or lozenge. Its color varies from white to blue to orange to yellow. It can even be black. In size, it is usually only a few inches in diameter, but it can be up to several feet across.

Black cigars being encountered in midair should sound rather familiar by now, of course.

BL, as physicists call it, is rare, but not that rare. Several examples are studied every year. There are a few photographs but still no good footage of it. This is one reason why it has, until quite recently, been treated alongside UFOs as of dubious provenance. However, once the data was seriously probed by physicists and meteorologists, the existence of BL became accepted. Today's debate rages not over its existence but its cause. I hope that this same transformation can apply to other types of UFO that are creating midair encounters.

Ironically, it was a sighting of BL inside an aircraft that really persuaded science to take note. One ball formed inside the enclosed cabin of an Eastern Airlines plane that was flying over New York. It rolled a few inches off the ground the full length of the aisle and then popped out of existence. By chance, a physicist, Dr. Roger Jennison, was on board, and his reports soon convinced his peers that they were missing out on something potentially very interesting.

BL has remarkable properties. It has been known to plunge into a barrel of water and evaporate this in an instant. It has melted a metal fly-swatter, which one rather foolhardy witness used to shoo it away. It has created eddy currents that have burnt the fingers of witnesses underneath metal rings. It has caused fluorescent light tubes to glow as it floated nearby, even though they were switched off. BL has fused glass in a violent explosion. It can be very deadly stuff. Yet, in almost baffling contrast to such cases, it has passed right through the body of one woman standing in front of her cooker. Although it burned a hole in her oven glove, she was completely unscathed! Such benign treatment by this phenomenon has been reported before.

Some cases imply deadly power and others hardly any force at all. This is a paradox. All kinds of theories have been mooted—from nuclear breakdown to ionization. Some laboratories, notably in Japan, are hard at work trying to create artificial BL that is stable for more than a few moments. Professor Yoshi Hiko Ohtsuki at Waseda University has had some limited success. Billions of yen are being invested because the laboratories know that a potentially lucrative new power source is available should this hurdle be overcome.

I strongly suspect that UFO sightings are relevant to BL in two ways.

First, it is more than possible that some UFOs are extreme forms of BL. Because science is generally reluctant to look at the data, it never takes these cases into account. It is not surprising that it has failed to unravel the nature of this mystery if all the best cases are being reported elsewhere as UFOs. Science is trying to complete a jigsaw puzzle with half the pieces missing.

Equally, some of the phenomena that cause UFO encounters may be atmospheric processes that have a genesis similar to BL while not being identical to it. Science misses out because it never sees this evidence, despite its coming from impressive observers such as pilots. This data has real physical attributes like the ability to stop car engines or create chemical changes in the ground. Physicist Dr. Terence Meaden, for example, reported on one case where a strange electrical phenomenon stopped a car engine at Valognes in France on July 20, 1992. He regarded this case as a scientific anomaly, but UFOlogists would have recognized it instantly as identical to dozens in their data files. Science needs the full range of UFO sighting evidence if it hopes to fathom what is going on.

UFOlogists, on the whole, view such cases in a most inappropriate manner—as an alien invasion. Too little is done either by them or scientists to try to understand what may be a fascinating, perhaps even dangerous problem, and certainly one that offers a potentially invaluable source of energy. After all, we live in a world where we will soon need all the new energy sources that we can get.

This is one reason for the so-called cover-up regarding UFOs allegedly conducted by the authorities. I believe that long ago, all major nations realized that most UFO sightings are examples of mistaken identity and others stem from strange natural phenomena. Few, if any, have the remotest likelihood of resulting from an alien invasion. Yet, any government scientist worth his salt will have advised his respective administration that these reports offer insights into some untapped energy source. The race is on to harness this power and become a global leader in a hot technology that everyone will want during the 21st century.

In those circumstances, it would be a positive advantage if people only ever talked about UFOs in the context of aliens and little green men because this would ensure that scientists not under government control do not spend much time investigating these matters. If you want the political edge, then you must tackle these issues covertly and not share what you are discovering through the pages of *New Scientist*.

Covering up the presence of aliens on earth seems a feeble reason for any alleged government conspiracy. Why on earth would they bother? The best way to combat aliens is to pull together as a planet. But if commercial reasons are paramount in the UFO issue, secrecy makes sense. Governments may well utilize the amazing capacity of UFO buffs to shoot themselves in the foot by believing in a dozen impossible things before breakfast time. It would be easy to get its many vociferous proponents to discredit UFOlogy simply through overcommitment—and all without much effort by Whitehall or the Pentagon.

This smoke screen, I suspect, is actually covering up a desperate desire to unlock the science behind these phenomena before any other country succeeds in that task. Then you can sell your secrets to the world and build offensive and defensive weapons that nobody else possesses. Sadly, this is a realistic view of life in the next millennium, while hiding little green men in underground vaults seems a long way from that to me.

An interesting case occurred at Traunstein in Bavaria in June 1991. The witness was a schoolteacher. She was driving her car amidst a storm when suddenly, "I saw a bright green phosphorescent ball that dropped to the ground behind a minibus driving in front. It fell to the road and rolled towards me."

Knowing that a car acts as a Faraday cage that insulates the occupant from electrocution, the woman put her feet on the rubber mat and watched as the green ball drifted towards her. It was about 3 feet in diameter and had a spiky appearance. It seemed to be fluidic and composed of bright and dark spots. This object then struck the car with a thump. As it moved to her right, it finally disappeared over a field behind her, but not before she noticed how the front and sides of the car emitted a curious turquoise glow almost like it was radiating energy.

There is no doubt that this was a close encounter with BL. The case was thoroughly investigated by Dr. Alex Keul for the *Journal of Meteorology*. But it is easy to see how similar this "car encounter" is to the various midair encounters reported in this book. Even the color is almost identical to those notorious "green fireballs." One can envisage how such a ball would appear if it rushed towards a Boeing 737 and then shot away down the right-hand side of the cockpit.

There are a number of cases where either BL or some similar energy ball has evidently been attracted to the metal surface of a car. Of course, an aircraft in flight would form an equally attractive target if an electromagnetic effect were occurring. This makes it all the more important that we investigate these cases thoroughly.

Floaters

I hope that you will begin to see a pattern behind the following series of reports.

1)   At 3 p.m. on January 22, 1945, a British prisoner of war was paraded with many others in the courtyard at the Heydebreck camp in Upper Silesia, Poland. They were about to be led on a 4-month trek by the Germans to evade the liberating Soviet army. Suddenly an American bomber appeared overhead at an estimated height of 18,000 feet. There were gasps from the prisoners as what seemed like a fire erupted from one of the engines. But then they realized that it was a free-floating sphere of white light—maybe a foot in diameter. This was dancing around the aircraft, buzzing it, trailing in its wake, sticking to it like a fly annoying someone in the garden. Then, as if tired of the game, the ball broke off and sped away at an acute angle, vanishing into the sky. The bomber flew on as if unaware of what had happened.

2)   Thirty-three years later, on December 11, 1979, at 11:45 a.m., flying instructor Leslie Groves was with a young pupil on a routine trip aboard a

Cessna 150, call sign Whiskey Echo (G-AXWE). They had left Barton Airfield in Irlam, Lancashire, and were north of the M62 motorway heading northwest towards Bolton. Suddenly Groves, who was monitoring as the pupil flew the plane, saw a bright object appear out of a cloud over Winter Hill. They were at 4500 feet, and this object appeared to be moving below them. At first, Groves assumed it was another light aircraft, especially when it disappeared into the clouds. But when it reemerged rather closer to Whiskey Echo, it was obvious that the bright white ball of light was not a sunlight flare off an aircraft but was the entire object itself. The sun was rather dull due to cloud cover and there were no strong reflections off any aircraft or birds seen that day, but this "tennis ball" was dazzling white. It was seen to fly between them and the clouds at 2000 feet—thus putting the object at about 2500 feet. Groves ordered his pupil to put Whiskey Echo into a cloud bank, and the student pilot did see the object for himself, but only in the distance as it pulled away in a seemingly well-controlled swooping motion. The case was investigated by Ron Sargeant. He was an experienced flyer from Irlam who, therefore, knew this area well. Ron was convinced that something strange had been seen, after initial skepticism about a possible reflection off a seagull. Moments after the UFO disappeared, the weather deteriorated markedly and a frontal system moved in.

3)   In April 1980 at about 2 p.m., Kevin Owen was in his garden at Shipston-on-Stour in Warwickshire when a light aircraft passed overhead. He looked up and then noticed that a small "dot" was chasing the aircraft, like it was playing tag. Intrigued, he picked up his nearby telescope and watched the object through this. It appeared as a bright silvery ball of small diameter that was matching the aircraft for speed and direction. His calls brought out one of his brothers, who also took a quick look at the object through the telescope. Then both saw the ball change direction and leave the path of the aircraft at a tangent, just like a ball bouncing off a hard surface.

I had a very similar experience myself in May 1969. My diary recorded the details, although I was not involved in UFO research at the time. I was standing outside my house in Rusholme, Manchester, watching a BEA Viscount pass over at about 3500 feet. I was interested because I had a school holiday job at the airport taking the bookings for a pleasure flight company. In the wake of the Viscount, I also saw a small ball, and even had a telescope with ×30 magnification to watch it. The ball was a silvery sphere, perfectly smooth, and, I would estimate from the size of the aircraft, about a foot in diameter. It was matching the airspeed of the plane (probably between 150 and 200 mph) and was definitely in a very close proximity to its tail fin. It maintained this station for about 30 seconds, then circled under a wing and was last seen in that position moving upwards and disappearing at an angle. I considered all options. However, there was no doubt that this ball was immediately hugging the back of the Viscount. I eventually decided that I must have seen a small balloon caught in the slipstream of the aircraft. This satisfied me at the time, but I never really considered the practicality of a balloon being pulled intact at such a speed.

I have now seen many UFO reports like these—some from times and places when balloons were very unlikely. This has given me cause to suspect that I possibly witnessed an atmospheric phenomenon that has a penchant for appearing near aircraft—perhaps being attracted to the fuselage in flight.

There is even a piece of film footage taken from an aircraft flying alongside the prototype Concorde in 1971. This film was used as a promotion for that new marvel of the air. In the film, a small white ball only a few inches in diameter appears near the side of the aircraft, swoops around it, and finally darts away at speed, taking an acute angle. Camera experts have suggested that this motion and appearance is a result of the camera operator's use of the zoom lens, although I certainly do not get that impression myself. Even if no real object was flying near Concorde, this optical fluke is worth studying as it looks remarkably like the ball that I saw chasing a Viscount 2 years earlier. It also seems to be what many other people have seen near aircraft ever since.

These cases continue on a regular basis. One of the most recent occurred on August 6, 1995, at Trefnant in the Vale of Clwyd, Wales. Two men, one of whom was an engineer, were watching a commercial jetliner passing over at about 7000 feet. It was heading southwest into the evening sky and had just taken off from Liverpool Airport, bound for Ireland. Suddenly, the men observed a glowing silver-white object that looked like a half moon and that was about one quarter the size of the aircraft tail fin. This rushed towards the jet, believed to be a Boeing 737, circled its fuselage in a complete loop, then sped away at a sharp angle. The small glowing thing then made an almost instant reversal of its course and shot away at great speed.

However, possibly the most impressive evidence of this type that I have encountered is a case that was investigated at the time by Peter Johnston. He sent me the full data, including witness interview tapes, and I was able to speak with one witness. It is a very significant encounter.

Unfortunately, I have to be a little cautious about revealing details, for reasons that are very proper. However, I can say that the incident took place in daylight at 4 p.m. on April 19, 1984, from the control tower of a civil airport in eastern England. I will use pseudonyms for the three ATC operators who were all witnesses. While I know their real identities and the location of the tower, they decided not to file an official report with the CAA. As they were unsure if this was a breach of the regulations, they prefer not to be identified.

Dave was a senior controller and had been at the airport for 15 years. As the shift was about to end, he went to the control tower to supervise this process. His deputy controller, Bernard, was in charge, and had himself been an air traffic operator for almost 10 years. A third controller, Rose, had even more service experience at various airport and radar sites.

It was a brilliant day with no clouds at all below 5000 feet. Because of the excellent visibility and the winding down of operations, the radar was temporarily off-line. Just one Cessna light plane was currently on approach.

Dave heard the conversation between Bernard and the aircraft, in which it reported turning onto "base leg"—meaning that it was lining up for approach. Idly gazing out towards the runway to look for this aircraft, Dave spotted a bright white glow that he assumed to be sunlight reflecting off the incoming Cessna. It was only when the pilot called again to confirm the runway he was turning onto (I will call it "A") that Dave realized the object was coming in on a different runway (which I will call "B"). I need to use these inappropriate terms because the real numbers of these runways might help identify the airport. Runway B crossed the path of A, and they were not used simultaneously because of the risk of collision.

Mildly concerned, Dave called to Bernard, "You have something coming in on Runway B." He was about to mention the possible traffic conflict when Bernard insisted that there was only one aircraft inbound and it was clearly lining up for Runway A. Rose, meanwhile, was working on the instruments and did not look up. Dave decided not to push the matter, thinking he might be mistaken. But as he watched the bright light making its approach to B, he knew that something was definitely wrong.

By now the brilliant light was so low that it seemed set to land on Runway B. Dave snatched the binoculars for a better view. He could see that the object was not sunlight shining off any aircraft; it was a brilliant ball of white light that itself was churning out light. He describes the effect as "like a mass of silvery paper all crinkled up." Considering the strong daylight, the amount of light emitted was staggering. This description is very like that offered in other cases. Without doubt, now this object was a cause for concern. It had virtually landed on the runway and was displaying controlled flight. Dave instinctively called out.

Bernard and Rose looked up, shocked, and saw what Dave was worried about. However, the ball, estimated as just a few feet in diameter, had already struck the runway. It hit too steeply to be a normal touchdown. Yet, rather than crash or explode, it instantly rebounded into the air at a very steep angle, just like a dot on a computer screen during a game of video tennis.

The ATC estimated that this ball was now climbing at an angle of 80° to the horizontal—that is, almost vertically. No aircraft could perform like this. Yet there was no sound at all. As it climbed, it was accelerating to a phenomenal speed and was several thousand feet up in less than a minute.

Bernard, suddenly remembering the Cessna, returned to the radio to talk this down onto Runway A, his voice exhibiting as little strain as he could muster. A minute later, the plane landed and never mentioned having seen anything. The ATC decided not to enlighten the pilot.

Dave contacted the nearest military air base to ask if they had anything flying. They did not. They had also closed their radar only minutes before the object appeared. As the RAF man was getting rather suspicious of these questions, Dave ended the conversation.

Bernard was very shaken, and both he and Rose asked that the matter not be reported to the CAA. Dave was mindful of the possibility of a "traffic conflict" and felt they really ought to do the correct thing. However, Bernard was so upset that they pored over the rule book and concluded that this stated that sightings *made to them* should be submitted to the Air Ministry, but it did not say what to do if ATC operators saw a UFO themselves! Bernard agreed this interpretation stretched the regulations somewhat.

I think that some of these encounters may well show the flip side of a situation we have often confronted in this book. The ball of light is clearly a real phenomenon. From the pilots' perspective, we know that it can sometimes be witnessed from midair, leading even to avoiding action being taken. But the observations from the ground give even more cause for concern, for these suggest that the objects might come into close proximity with aircraft many times when they are not witnessed at all by the aircrew.

It does appear as if the phenomenon is attracted towards the metal surface of the aircraft—thus suggesting that it is some kind of natural phenomenon. It also appears to emit a tremendous amount of light energy—thus possibly other forms of energy as well. One fears for the consequences should one of these objects "discharge" into the electrical or computer systems of a large airliner or even a light plane. Thankfully, the evidence appears to suggest that their interaction with aircraft is largely benign.

To my mind, the numerous cases, of which the few that I have presented are but a small fraction of hundreds on record, are so consistent that they must represent the same phenomenon. Of course, perhaps balloons are being caught in the slipstream of aircraft and the answer is as simple as that. But can they be towed along at over 100 mph, bounce off runways at steep angles, circle aircraft in mid-flight, and accelerate from a standing start to unprecedented velocities? I doubt it. Just as I doubt that many balloons were floating over German war camps or other remote spots where these sightings have occurred.

It is far more probable that this is a genuine atmospheric anomaly that is sufficiently "attracted" to our aircraft to be considered a threat. As Dave so rightly surmised, it often brings about a "traffic conflict" situation, and we simply cannot afford to take chances by ignoring this fact.

The Halo Effect

On August 27, 1979, at 2:40 p.m., a Cessna 150, call sign November X-ray (G-BBNX), took off from Blackbushe Airport in Surrey. Aboard were flying instructor Laurie Adlington and his student from Sandhurst military college, Lieutenant James Plastow. At 2000 feet, as Plastow was preparing to take his pilot's test, Adlington suddenly grabbed the controls and threw the Cessna into a steep bank and descent. The officer then saw an object rush past the front of the aircraft—coming within a few yards of them. The object was maybe a foot across and doughnut-shaped, shining a bright silver color. Adlington told investigator Omar Fowler it looked like a blob of mercury. The instructor twisted and turned the aircraft, hoping to keep up with the UFO, and indeed it appeared to fly around November X-ray as if inspecting them. He put through a radio call to Blackbushe saying the thing was "playing" with the Cessna. It was definitely under powered control as it swooped beneath them and then climbed up to 3000 feet. The Cessna flew after it, and Plastow in particular got a very close view at one point. He says it was made up of a series of metallic honeycombs and was rotating at about one revolution a minute. The surface was reflective, and there was even a suspicion of a small aerial sticking out. Next day, Simon Spence, another pilot from the airfield, had a distant view of the object heading towards Farnborough.

In my opinion, this is a classic description of what we would probably now term an RPV, or Remotely Piloted Vehicle. In effect, these are ultra-sophisticated, remote-controlled, small-sized planes. There is a huge industry in these covert devices. They are used, for example, to take aerial photographs in war zones without putting pilots' lives at risk. Inevitably, the latest developments are kept secret and it seems unlikely that they would often be flown in commercial lanes of traffic for fear of causing an accident or being spotted by unwelcome eyes. But the way this object headed towards Farnborough, home of experimental aviation design work, is possibly significant.

There are certainly cases on record where midair encounters can be explained in this way. All manner of strange aerial technology is flying about and one can only imagine how things have moved on since this 1979 encounter. We know about only a fraction of the things that are flying in our skies, because the powers that be choose not to share the secrets of their technology. RPVs and other remotely controlled "drones" that are used as test beds for new aircraft design are undoubtedly behind some of the strangest UFO sightings. They may well, from time to time, stray into the paths of civilian aircraft.

In February 1998, on a research trip to East Anglia, I met an engineer who told me of an instance where a drone had provoked a UFO sighting. Checking my records, I found that a medical research scientist had reported this April 1984 incident to me and sketched what she had observed. She had seen a massive gridlike object hovering above the road near the USAF base at Lakenheath in rural Suffolk. My contact advised that this was a drone that had gone out of control for several minutes and flown over an area where it was not supposed to go until eventually it was recaptured. The MoD did not admit the matter for some years, as the drone was then a military secret, and the MoD was very happy that witnesses at the time had assumed that they had seen a UFO.

We have already seen how, from around 1978, Stealth aircraft were probably mistaken for UFOs in the U.K. and no doubt elsewhere, and how our obsession with UFOs as alien spacecraft provides a smoke screen behind which new technology can be flown without its true origin being recognized.

This same factor is clearly at work today and is well seen by the so-called Halo project (Halo being an acronym for High Agility, Low Observability). UFOlogist Tim Matthews has gathered impressive proof that this is indeed under development at the British Aerospace plant at Warton in Lancashire and that a remotely controlled drone version—and possibly even prototypes of the plane itself—have been flying since at least 1995. Although much development work has centered on the Lancashire plant, Halo has flown from a number of other bases, including RAF West Freugh in southwest Scotland, according to his many sources. It is very likely that Halo derivatives have now begun flying all over the world.

There are three main founts of information about these sightings. If they do concern the Halo project, then this is officially not yet off the drawing board. But we should recall that the U.S. Stealth fighter suppos-edly did not exist for some years, according to the Pentagon, even while it was in service all over the world! The three sources are as follows: data leaked to Tim from the development site at Warton and his own surveil-lance of what has been going on there; various aviation experts who, in some instances, have even gone to the extent of developing their own high-tech tracking of flights; and the numerous reports of triangular-shaped UFOs that have been seen in northwest England and latterly further afield. Such sightings occur at the same times as the other sources listed here say that Halo has been flying. All of these things fit together remarkably well. If you plot the UFO sightings on a map, for example, they clearly center on Warton, and that cannot be a coincidence.

According to Matthews, this cutting-edge project is not just a mundane aircraft. It incorporates a variety of novel propulsion techniques, one of which may involve the emission of energy pulses that as a side effect can interfere with electrical systems. This may result either from the drive sys-tem fitted to the craft or from some of the electronic countermeasures being fitted to it in order to try to defeat radar detection and other defen-sive capabilities. Halo is also believed to be a Stealth plane that can hover.

Tim believes that the object flown from Warton, at least in early tests, was fairly modest in size and not a full-scale aircraft. It was deliberately flown most often at night and from the Ribble Estuary south of Blackpool because, within moments of take-off, it was over the sea, minimizing sight-ings from the ground. However, as a protective measure, the device is well-illuminated to enhance its UFO-like appearance. Halo is also a strikingly unusual aircraft with a near-silent mode of flight. It has a quite appreciable capacity to turn at speed. So the scientists who were testing the device knew perfectly well that it would be reported as a UFO if it was spotted—with all the dubious connotations that provides. This was a useful advantage.

Since the news about a potential trigger for the northwest triangle sightings has been recognized by the UFO community, incidents have tailed off and a new wave of triangular UFOs has begun to appear in other locations. These include the area surrounding Rendlesham Forest in East Anglia and the east coast near RAF Donna Nook. Have project test flights moved to less populated areas, away from where the local media have come to know about Halo?

In January 1996, there were several sightings of a triangular object over the coast of Blackpool in Lancashire through Morecambe Bay. Some video, depicting a triangle of lights, was taken near Morecambe. At this time, there were several unexplained power outages in localized areas of the coast. I experienced one of these myself at around 1 a.m. that month, when I was living in Fleetwood. Although I saw nothing, I did later receive local reports of the mystery triangle.

At 6:45 a.m. on September 17, 1996, the triangle passed right over my house while I was fast asleep. I spoke to one witness on the beach just a few hundred yards away at Rossall, who saw it glinting silver in the rising sun as it spiraled to a great height and headed west over the Irish Sea. I saw a number of similar things myself during the 2 years I lived on the coast, but never at low height. These aircraft had already climbed to 40,000 feet and were performing twisting motions in the sky. For this reason, I could not be sure they were not Hawks or Eurofighters, which are the official projects being developed at Warton. Both these and Tornadoes did fly over my house, sometimes at low height, but they were always easily recognized. The triangular object over Rossall Beach was something that this local man had never seen before.

On August 29, 1996, twenty witnesses saw a "black triangle performing amazing aerobatics" near Kendal in Cumbria at sunset. A low-frequency humming noise was heard, and there were several instances of local radios and watches being affected. Houselights flickered when it passed overhead, as if some kind of electromagnetic pulse were being emitted. Radio and TV sets switched channels suddenly. Interestingly, witnesses referred to a change in an otherwise very calm night while the triangle flew past. They said the air became heavy and charged with static electricity as if a thunderstorm were brewing.

It may be relevant that electrical effects were also reported by citizens living in villages near Louth in Lincolnshire as triangular lights flew overhead. Static interference, TV sets jumping suddenly from one channel to another, and electronic clocks and watches showing "impossible" times were noted. These villages were in the few miles surrounding RAF Donna Nook, where in April 1997 a tourist actually took a video of a flying black triangle. Even the Donna Nook base commander saw the strange lights during the earlier wave, and was so puzzled by what was passing overhead that he submitted a report to the MoD!

Another impressive report came to Tim Matthews in September 1996 from a retired RAF officer who saw the triangle flying out to sea from

Ulverston in Cumbria. He was stunned by its capabilities and particularly its silence. He knew that it was no ordinary aviation project.

An intriguing photograph was also taken from the Rivington Pike area near Chorley, Lancashire, in January 1996. The photographer, Brian White, was taking landscape shots and neither saw nor heard anything odd. However, one of his developed photographs depicts what appears to be a white and very smooth triangle hugging the contours of the land. Tim Matthews argues that Halo is alleged to use computer-controlled camouflage to change its fuselage color in mid-flight. But, while it is obviously possible that the cameraman filmed Halo by chance in this mode, I have reservations about the picture. In the past, I have investigated a number of cases where a photographer saw nothing, but a UFO appeared when the film was processed. Often these turn out to be birds that have flown across the field of view unseen and were frozen into what can be amazingly UFO-like poses by the fast shutter speed of the camera.

More dramatic still, video instrument telemetry of something taking off from Warton and heading out into the Irish Sea up to 50,000 feet was captured on several occasions during 1995 and 1996. This was by a group of aviation experts fascinated by Matthews' work. The data was shown to a former Warton scientist who had helped develop the Eurofighter, as well as to several ATC staff. These experts were all stunned by the 9G turns of the object being detected moving at high speed. Although they had done simulations of such feats at Warton, this was not considered possible in actual flight even by the supposedly futuristic Eurofighter. Whatever was flying covertly late at night was doing things that no manned aircraft could yet replicate, as the G forces involved in its sharp twists and turns would have killed any human aboard.

Many of the ongoing triangle sightings occurred from the sandy area around Banks and Meols Cop to the north of Southport. This is located due south of Warton directly across the Ribble Estuary and would be the perfect place to see any covert flight activity that was heading out to sea. Reports tell of cars stopping and staring in awe at the triangle as it hovers and then "gathers its lights into one" and streaks skyward. Other reports from the area tell of seeing a small black triangle being shepherded by Tornado jets, which clearly were coming from the direction of Warton.

One of the best cases occurred on February 24, 1996. At 2:45 a.m., three residents of a house at Banks were shaken from their beds by a vibration that was pulsing through their house with a noise that wormed its way into their skulls "like a drill." As they pulled up the blinds in the bedroom to look outside, the whole building appeared to be shaking apart. Hovering over fields towards the estuary was a large dark triangle. It had a white, red, and green light in each apex point and a glow emerging from the underside. It hovered for 3 or 4 minutes, and then accelerated at a phenomenal speed westwards into the Irish Sea.

Warton denied any tests, saying they did not fly at that time of night without good cause. Air Staff 2A at the MoD in London insisted that there were no military exercises, and they had no explanation for this sighting. You may notice that it was 17 years *to the minute* after the major encounter in 1979 where a UFO flew over a nearby caravan park. Was this coincidence or a crafty flight plan to boost the UFO evaluation?

One location where flying triangles have often been seen during recent years centers on the village of Daresbury, near Warrington. This is the birthplace of the Reverend Charles Dodgson, alias Lewis Carroll, and has thus been dubbed "Wonderland" by UFOlogists after his world-famous children's stories. Witnesses in the rural area between here and Preston Brook have seen the strange craft above the M56 motorway, which has also been the location of several alleged close encounters.

The most recent as I write took place on January 9, 1998. Two men driving to the Midlands on a delivery run in the early hours encountered two bright lights as they headed towards the M6 junction. Thinking them to be an aircraft heading towards Manchester Airport, an event they had witnessed often, they ignored the matter until it became obvious that the craft was hovering low over the road ahead. As such, they slowed down and drove directly underneath where they observed what they told me was a "huge triangular craft...it had white lights on the corner and a red light in the middle. On the underside were what looked like jets or rotors—some kind of structure. It was silent and it just sat there."

This classic description has been offered many times by witnesses, although few get as close as these two brothers did to this extraordinary triangular craft. Neither witness was aware of the significance of where they were located and assumed that "flying saucers" were shaped like discs, not triangles, because that is what space-age folklore contends. As one put it when Jodrell Bank put him in touch with me only 6 hours after the sighting: "Until this morning, I had no time for those who said they had seen such things. I just did not believe them. But now what can I say?"

On December 15, 1996, Gemstone 904, a two-engine prop aircraft on a mail run from Belfast to Coventry, became the latest to meet the mystery head on. At sometime between 2 and 3 a.m., in a conversation recorded by air enthusiast Jim Sneddon, they reported passing at 11,000 feet and heading into the Manchester control zone. They had crossed the Isle of Man and were over the Irish Sea heading towards the west coast of England between Southport and Liverpool. Suddenly, they observed something in the sky ahead of them, which would be in the vicinity of Warton. The ATC advised that they had nothing on radar to match the object seen (unfortunately no description by the crew was recorded).

"There's absolutely nothing showing on radar. You are the only traffic I have on that airway," ATC told the pilot. We do know the object was ahead at their 2 o'clock position and was a constant mass of light without any obvious aircraft navigation beacons. The ATC identified an aircraft at 37,000 feet—but 50 miles from Gemstone 904. The crew saw this, but it appears that the unidentified object they were observing was lower and nearer to them. As a result, ground control contacted the more sophisticated radar at Manchester, but they too had nothing that matched the target ahead of the inbound flight.

On October 9, 1997, there was a sighting of the triangle from a royal navy vessel, HMS *Shetland*, then stationed off the Lancashire coast some miles out into the Irish Sea, apparently connected with security for the Conservative Party Conference in Blackpool. Not only was the object seen streaking past the ship, but it was also witnessed by several people on the Fylde Coast.

To my mind, all of this wide-ranging evidence, when put together, strongly demonstrates that something really has been flying around the Lancashire coast in recent years and that it is an aircraft of remarkable capabilities. Given that the Halo project is real—whether or not we accept the claim that no tests have yet flown—we have to consider terrestrial air traffic a far more likely explanation for these interlocking stories than extraterrestrial activity.

I doubt very much that this is the only example where our own earthly and rather secret technology is responsible for the sighting of strange objects—seen both from the ground and in midair. It is yet another possible source of these dangerous midair conflicts and a further complication in our work. I hope that others will join Tim Matthews in his crusade to uncover the truth.

14 AND STILL THEY FLY

Midair encounters are happening today and the numbers appear to be increasing. This is a phenomenon that I can demonstrate. With the help of Scottish aviation enthusiast Jim Sneddon, something of an experiment has been taking place since 1995. He has been continuously monitoring the air band frequencies over northern Britain and logging every instance where pilots let slip that they have seen a UFO.

How often do you think this would have happened in a 2-year period—given that we are talking about the airspace over just one-third of one small country? Two or three times? Maybe four or five? The truth is disturbing. Over twenty cases of midair contacts have been recorded. Here are just a few of them:

On July 28, 1995, two aircraft had a close encounter between 11:45 p.m. and 12:15 a.m. Midland 8802 was a cargo Boeing 737 on a flight from London to Edinburgh. Foxtrot Alpha was a Piper Aztec on a mail run that had just left Glasgow heading south.

Foxtrot Alpha, then climbing through 5000 feet, reported how "a flash" shot across its path and "it just missed me." Within moments, Midland 8802 confirmed the incident and said that it "resembled a strobe light going all the way around the aircraft." He reported his position as 40 miles south of Edinburgh. ATC asked for further details. They were told that the object was like a blinding glow that emerged from a cloud; it flew towards the aircraft and "faded back into clouds again."

Various options were discussed with ground control. The possibility of a distress flare was taken seriously as this would require emergency action, but the pilots felt that the object was too high. Scottish radar eventually suggested a firework from a factory at Sanquhar and reported that police were being sent to investigate. There was no evidence found that this was the case, and the pilot of Foxtrot Alpha was having none of it—saying, rather sarcastically, "good firework."

There is a possibility that this was a fireball meteor, but there were no other known reports.

Moving to September 12, 1995, a British Airways Boeing 757 approaching Aberdeen on a flight from London had a visual encounter with a steady red light that paced the aircraft for several miles around 9 p.m. Predictably, nothing further about this was revealed by the airline.

More impressive was a case recorded on January 23, 1996—amid the wave of reports of flying triangles over Lancashire that led to power failures (see Chapter 13). At about 8 p.m., U.K. Air 645, an F-27 turboprop, was at 12,000 feet on a flight from Aberdeen to Humberside Airport while Knightair 819 (a Bandeirante) was at 8500 feet heading towards Leeds/Bradford—also from Aberdeen. They were traveling on the same airway with the U.K. Air plane a few miles ahead.

U.K. 645 reported the sighting of an unidentified aircraft that looked "strange." As they were discussing this with the ATC, Knightair 819 came into the area and reported, "We seem to have something parallel in our 3 o'clock range, beneath us, and probably I estimate 7 or 8 miles away."

After Scottish radar confirmed they had nothing on screen that matched this position—evidently agreeing with what U.K. 645 was seeing—the banter began. The ATC called it "bogey night" while the U.K. Air captain chipped in with "martians."

However, the ATC took the matter seriously and consulted with the military, noting that they had nothing operating in that area. By now the lights, which had been flying alongside both aircraft for some distance, had vanished. ATC said that they had tried both their primary and secondary radar, but there was nothing visible other than the aircraft. The military had told Scottish control that their radar showed nothing either.

Nevertheless, the ATC was unwilling to let the matter drop and reported a few minutes later with a rather interesting comment: "We will keep an eye on it anyway. The military are looking at it with their air defense radars, and we are looking out on these. If we see anything we will let you know." The phrasing of this comment does infer military radar might now have had a target.

Five minutes later, as the aircraft was passed onto Newcastle control, Scottish ATC reported, "U.K. 645, I am getting a primary return at your 12 o'clock, but it's static [stationary]." The F-27 said they could see nothing and radar suggested the possibility of a spurious weather return.

Whether the military air defense radar did indeed see something and/or took any action we may not know until the year 2027, after the expiration of the 30-year rule that prevents release of MoD files.

Another interesting case was recorded around 2 a.m. on February 1, 1997. Two aircraft were involved—Gilair 274P and Gojet 604. Gilair, which had the main encounter, was on a flight from Belfast to Newcastle. It reported that an object was in its 1 o'clock position and, "Ah, it's getting closer and closer, been getting closer in the last 60 seconds. Do you have anything on radar?"

ATC did not, but asked for a description of the object, which Gil 274 said was a "red flamy object" that a few moments later was said to have "gone steady."

After a few seconds, Scottish radar announced, "Gil 274P, ah, I have primary object [on radar] actually in your 12 o'clock—range about 7 miles. It's more or less stationary." ATC suggested this could be a spurious echo, but the Gilair pilot came on to say, "It could be the same one—yes, between maybe ½-12 to 1 o'clock position—stationary—but it got bigger in the last 60 seconds—it's been steady for the last few minutes."

Unwilling to take any chances, the ATC decided to route Gilair 274P around the target. "Just go left about 30° to avoid this. It's been steady there [on radar] for the last 2–3 minutes."

In support, Gojet 604 now came onto the radio. Unfortunately, the pilot's voice could not be heard, but, from the ATC response, it is clear he saw something in the same position. Radar cleared him to 25,000 feet and reported that the nearest thing that could be "ahead of him" was 20 miles to the west-northwest. Clearly, this did not satisfy the second aircraft, as the ATC replied, "OK then, fine, that's one for *The X Files*." Moments later, Gil 274P was told that they were well clear of the radar target and they could resume their normal course towards a landing at Newcastle. One wonders from this case just how often, when your aircraft takes a barely noticed, slight detour in flight, it is being routed around something in the air!

Perhaps the most interesting recent encounter of all was at 9 p.m. on April 16, 1997, when Zap 6 Alpha, an ATR 42 on a mail run from Inverness to Edinburgh, reported something northwest of Perth.

Zap 6 Alpha explained to Edinburgh ATC that it had been flying at 8000 feet, and an object had appeared "spot level with us—7 miles straight in front. Then we lost sight of it and the next we know Scottish radar told us that it was now behind us at 6 o'clock at 4 miles."

ATC asked for more detail of what had been seen and was told that it was "just white lights." But they were clearly impressed by the way in which Scottish radar had the target on screen and how, the moment they lost sight of it visually, it had moved around at great speed on screen to appear now on the tail of the mail plane. As yet no air-miss report on this event has been published by the CAA, but it may emerge in the near future.

However, as the conversation continued, it became clear why Edinburgh ATC was so interested in this event. The controller told the Zap pilot, "Your replies check with what I put in a report form about 3 months ago [i.e., January 1997]. It was almost like cabin lights at about 8000 feet, and they [the CAA] were not able to trace anything unfortunately." Evidently, he had filed an air miss then involving another plane.

Zap 6 Alpha agreed: "Yes, sounds like the same thing we had. It was definitely above the cloud by about 2000 feet and, like I said, I kept an eye on it and, next minute, Scottish told us it was now behind us."

This incredible series of events gives the lie to the supposed rarity of midair encounters. From these examples, it seems obvious that things are happening with alarming frequency. It is well-known to both ATC and aircrews. They joke about the matter. Indeed, one pilot was quite candid in his account on April 29, 1997. U.K. Air 607, a Fokker 50 on a flight from Norwich to Aberdeen, reported "strange traffic" over the North Sea off the coast near Newcastle upon Tyne. After ATC eliminated all known aircraft, the pilot mused quite matter-of-factly, "Must have been a Stealth fighter or a UFO in that case."

This wealth of data came from just one man monitoring traffic as often as he could in one small area by hooking up his air band receiver to a tape recorder and making a record of what happened during the night. For this is the time when the majority of these encounters take place.

It seems a certainty that this location is not unusual. If twenty cases occurred there within 2 years, then there were probably many more over the more densely-trafficked flight lanes around London and southeast England, for example—not to mention the flight chaos above a bigger nation such as the U.S.

Extrapolating from this one region onto a global basis suggests that between 1995 and 1997 there were probably at least one thousand midair encounters—and possibly far more than that. And yet the official records show no more than a small percentage of these. In fact, for the rest of Britain during those months, they record just one case—apparently the one that slipped through the net!

In this incident, on June 7, 1996, an Aer Lingus BAe 146 was on a passenger flight from Dublin to Stansted in Essex. It was 6 p.m. on a fine day, and they were descending through 9000 feet above Stevenage in Hertfordshire. The events that followed will sound all too familiar.

The pilot suddenly observed an unusual-looking aircraft coming towards them at speed. His call alerted the copilot, who noted that the object appeared to be trying to avoid a cloud bank. The object streaked past the 146 within a few hundred yards and an estimated distance of just 100 feet below.

Both men believed that they had seen some kind of small, very fast military fighter. Indeed, the copilot went so far as to say it looked like a Hawk jet and the pilot was sure he saw colored stripes along the side. The problem was that the 1-year investigation involving the CAA and the military failed to find any jet fighters, Hawk or otherwise, that were over the area at the time.

Once again radar was not much help. It tracked no object rushing past the Aer Lingus aircraft. The air miss working group (now renamed the airprox, or air proximity, working group) stated that they were "most disappointed" that they could not explain what had almost struck this commercial flight. However, they were fully confident that the pilots had seen something strange and noted how these men agreed "in some detail" as to what that something was. The decision by the CAA to term the report "inaccessible" should not be perceived as an expression of doubt as to the pilots' credibility. Rather, it meant they had no idea what was going on.

The group was very sure that the aircrew did not see another aircraft and that it was an "unknown object" that came so close to striking the 146. As far as the CAA was concerned, "the whole incident is a bit of a mystery and we will probably never know what happened."

Once again, a plane full of passengers almost collides with an object in broad daylight. Nothing appears on radar. The authorities are adamant that they accept the testimony of the aircrew but are equally adamant that they did not encounter any other known aircraft. It was, by every definition, an unidentified flying object, as we would have to agree. The only question is whether, as the U.K. Air pilot said while flying off the coast near Newcastle, this object "was a Stealth fighter or a UFO."

The cases continue throughout the rest of the world during the same period that we are monitoring—reported from time to time but surely masking many others that never see the light of day.

On August 28, 1996, the city of Pretoria in South Africa found itself facing an early morning flap when people for several miles around called to report a huge pulsing white light in the sky. Sergeant Johan Bekker of the police station at Adriaan Vlok in Centurion saw the object himself at 4 a.m. but had a hard task persuading his superiors that he was being serious, because the alien movie *Independence Day* was playing at movie theaters at the time. Soon, however, the sightings were flooding in and a massive police hunt was mobilized. This involved one hundred officers. Patrol cars chased the object towards the northeast but could not catch it. However, Sergeant Nico Stander managed to take some video footage of the object from his patrol car as it flew away towards Cullinan.

Eventually, at 5:25 a.m., Superintendent Fred Viljoen of the Air Division agreed to take off in a police helicopter. With him was copilot Sergeant Pieter Strampe. Three other officers were on board. Viljoen was at first very skeptical, but as soon as he saw the UFO, he knew that it was something strange.

They climbed to 10,000 feet, and he reports that "a bright light was above Mamelodi—70° above the horizon. I followed the white disk in the direction of Cullinan. It moved at high speed. We could not keep up with it and eventually had to give up when lack of fuel became a problem."

However, Viljoen did contact the military at Waterkloof Air Force Base. They explained that they had something unusual in the sky in the area where the object was. Rumors persist that the air force scrambled a Mirage fighter to investigate, but Lieutenant-Colonel Laverne Machine refused to say whether this was true. She insisted that they did have a UFO file, but it was "just speculation" that a Mirage was scrambled. When asked to rule out the possibility that one was sent up she replied, "I cannot confirm or deny that." Presumably that means that one was—otherwise it would have been quite easy to say no!

Of course, there are also some rather disturbing questions still outstanding about the terrible crash of TWA 800 on July 17, 1996. The Boeing 747 had just taken off from New York and exploded in flight at 8:19 p.m. at the start of a run to Paris. All 230 people on board were killed.

Even as the wreckage was being hauled from the ocean off Long Island, the FBI had marched in—leading to the belief that a terrorist bomb was considered responsible. There were good reasons for this suspicion. The aircraft had been used to transport troops during the Gulf War. The last sound recorded from the aircraft was of what appeared to be a massive explosion. And eyewitnesses who saw the disaster were all clear that the plane erupted into a fireball in midair.

But terrorist involvement was soon ruled out—although the intelligence agencies remained involved with the accident investigation for several months and it was not until November 18, 1997, that the inquiry into a possible terrorist act was officially closed. The U.S. government, in doing this, took the most unusual step of creating computer graphics to show the plane exploding and debris falling off into the sea, in order to try to silence the many eyewitnesses who insisted that they had seen a fiery object strike the plane. They had not seen this—the Pentagon insisted. The blazing trail was witnessed after the explosion, and it was burning wreckage falling off. Many witnesses disagree, saying they saw a "missile" collide with the jumbo.

There are other puzzles. The very first reports of the crash, within 3 hours of the event, described how "the unexplained streak" that "flew towards the aircraft" was picked up by radar as a fast-moving target heading on a collision course with the 747. These stories then ended, at about the time the FBI arrived on the scene, and officially there never was any radar evidence. Again, it is suggested that radar operators mistook the aircraft in two pieces falling towards the ocean after it had been blown apart. But I would have thought that experienced ATC could tell the difference between something heading towards a jet on a collision course and two parts of the newly destroyed aircraft separating from one another and falling to the ground after the fact. At least those of us who fly pretty regularly had better hope that they can!

A few weeks into the investigation, it was revealed that local woman Linda Kabot had by chance filmed the sky out over Long Island at some point within the hour surrounding the crash of the TWA plane. Her photograph had on it what seemed to be a dark, tube-like object. I suspect this was a processing mark.

Then, on November 16, two aircraft departing from New York witnessed a tube-like streak of light crossing their path. Pakistan Airlines Flight 712 called ATC to report the matter and was backed up by a TWA flight just behind. The authorities were sufficiently concerned to close the air route and divert aircraft outbound from New York for some hours until satisfied that radar had not recorded anything unusual to coincide with the sightings.

The next bombshell was dropped by a former advisor to President John F. Kennedy, Pierre Salinger, who told aviation chiefs in November that a document had been leaked to him "proving" that the aircraft had been accidentally blasted out of the sky after colliding with a "top secret" missile. He followed this up in March 1997 by releasing frames from what he said was film of the radar to the French magazine *Paris Match*. These appear to show exactly what those quickly silenced reports immediately after the crash had described—an unidentified radar blip on a direct collision course with the 747. Its speed, Salinger claimed, was 1500 mph. The U.S. government has flatly repudiated this evidence but, intriguingly, the film was immediately confiscated by an FBI raid, after which a statement was issued implying that

Salinger was misinterpreting the blips of other aircraft milling about on the radar film.

TWA itself even suggested as late as January 1997 that the aircraft might have been struck by some kind of object. By then the official position was hotly opposed to that view. The airline mooted the possibility of a meteor or space junk. But astronomers dismissed the chance of this as "remote."

According to the Federal Aviation Authority, the most likely explanation is that fuel in a near-empty tank expanded due to the hot weather and a spark turned this into a natural bomb. Aviation experts feel that the risks of leaving one of the fuel tanks empty to save money on relatively short flights could result in further freak catastrophes such as this. But they are still considering all of the evidence.

However, none of this will satisfy the dozen or so eyewitnesses who insist they saw something hit the Boeing, or the few others who say that a green glow was visible near the aircraft before the explosion. Throughout this book, we have come upon numerous cases (such as the Alitalia encounter over Kent in 1991) where the idea that an accidental missile launch almost destroyed a civilian airliner was taken seriously. This has always turned out to be very improbable. Yet here TWA 800 did indeed explode. The question remains as to whether it was a freak natural disaster or whether we should look seriously at the rather worrying evidence that a missile-like object was seen heading towards the aircraft. For, as we saw in many other cases, missile-like objects are not necessarily what they appear to be.

Could this have been the most tragic case yet of a midair encounter between a passenger jetliner and this truly terrifying wave of cylindrical UFOs (whatever one of those is)? Is that what the authorities seem so determined to cover up?

Sadly, we may never know. But if important evidence is being suppressed and the accident inquiry is being led along a false trail for political ends, those who lose loved ones would surely see this as utterly unacceptable.

Intriguingly, there was a not dissimilar event, although thankfully with less tragic consequences, on October 26, 1996. At 4:10 p.m. that afternoon, witnesses in and around the Isle of Lewis off the north of Scotland reported an explosion in midair.

Norman Macdonald, a joiner at Port of Ness, told how he was inside a shop when he heard the bang. Going outside with several customers, he saw several bright flashes of light and heard two more big bangs in the darkening sky. Out over the water was a cloud of smoke and debris falling into the water in two large chunks. The smoke was spiraling as it fell, which seems a curious feature that suggests that whatever exploded in midair might have been rotating as it flew.

Other witnesses tell of an object like a high-flying aircraft leaving a trail of white smoke that vanished amidst an explosion. They also describe how the sea underneath the phenomenon was burning for some minutes afterwards. The shock wave from the explosion hit the island like a quarry blast. People in the village of Cross say the sea nearby was quite literally on fire.

The calls started to flow in to the coast guard at Stornoway at 5:03 p.m. and the assessment of the consistent accounts led them to anticipate that an aircraft had exploded in midair. As a result, an air-sea rescue operation was put in motion. The lifeboat was already on its way because of sightings from Stornoway by that time. An RAF Nimrod was requested to assist. By midnight, nothing had been found, and it was now clear that no aircraft were missing. However, so convincing was the evidence that the search was resumed at dawn.

Eventually some £200,000 was spent on a fruitless investigation. When this was wound down on the following morning, the RAF was quoted as saying, "It has been a fairly massive search, but a complete blank has been drawn. We remain puzzled by what could have caused this." Simon Riley of the Stornoway coast guard guessed that a meteor burn-up might have been responsible. They had investigated the possibility of space junk entering the atmosphere, but this was eliminated as no such events had been recorded by the space authorities.

The MoD was interested in this case from very early on. A reason later emerged. RAF Kinloss had reported "three UFOs" heading north across Scotland that same afternoon, and they also had a report from a passenger on a transatlantic flight that had crossed Lewis about 4 weeks previously. They had seen a very similar midair explosion at 30,000 feet. This must have alerted Whitehall.

MoD involvement began by checking out radar sites, such as the high-powered facility at Fylingdales in Yorkshire, which is geared to track incoming ballistic missiles. They had no record of this object. However, the eyewitness stories now gave a clear insight into what had happened. An object had been seen crossing the sky. It erupted into a cloud of gas and fire, then split into two halves—both of which fell vertically into the water. They were about the size of a helicopter. The impact sounds of these smashing into the sea were heard, and burning fuel or wreckage floated on the surface for several minutes.

This information was consistent with only one thing—some kind of aircraft had exploded and smashed into the sea. The problem was that it was not a British aircraft, and allies, such as the U.S., were all denying they had lost any Stealth planes.

By what is said to be coincidence, there chanced to be a major military exercise scheduled for the sea around Lewis. This began soon after the civilian search ended on the Sunday morning. Dozens of ships, submarines, and aircraft were involved.

Jim Sneddon tuned into the communication links during the search. At the close of the civil operation, he heard reference to a Lynx helicopter's finding an object floating on the water. Later, in response to questions about this, the MoD said it was a misidentified cardboard box! A few hours later, Jim heard a military aircraft being directed to new sea coordinates as if implying that something had been found there. Then the search switched to a covert frequency and was no longer traceable.

To this day we do not know what fell into the sea off Lewis. But some fascinating clues have been gathered together. Two weeks after the incident, scientists from the highly secret Sandia labs in New Mexico joined the investigation team. Sandia is a high-tech weapons facility and has been in the thick of the UFO mystery for many years. It was involved in the green fireball overflights in 1948. The decision to call these people in strongly suggests that someone believed that an object of a secret technological nature was involved in this crash.

Yet, after 6 weeks of study, the Sandia research team quietly announced to the local media that there was no aircraft involved. A meteorite had probably fallen into the sea. Not so, insist the Scottish National Party. Their spokeswoman Margaret Ewing claims that they had received reports from fishermen of a naval frigate hauling the wreckage of what looked like some large metal object from the sea off Lewis. This had been shortly after the explosion and during the fortuitously timed sea exercise. Then, in April 1997, came the discovery of a strange, goo-like residue on Tangusdale Beach at Barra. This was unidentifiable but could have been some sort of fuel. Given the prevailing currents and short distances involved, this could easily have come from any object that fell into the sea off Lewis.

As with so many of these mysteries of the air, we are left to weigh the evidence and choose.

However, very soon each case becomes replaced by the next great riddle, and we are able to appreciate that this truly is an ongoing saga.

A recent case involves a Swissair Boeing 747 that had departed from Philadelphia bound for Zurich on August 9, 1997. While flying at 23,000 feet and climbing towards Boston, the pilot and copilot reported that a strange object passed them by at high speed and "dangerously close"— they estimate just 50 yards. You will not be astonished by the descriptions from the two pilots. "It was long, dark, and wingless"—yet another black cylinder or missile.

As I said, this is the latest in what is now a long line of such near misses at the time that I write this closing chapter. But one thing is as certain as any statement in this book.

By the time you come to read these words, there will surely have been others just like it. Midair encounters continue to occur within the British skies, and the public is still largely ignorant of what is happening. Another case occurred on December 9, 1997, and should cause few surprises.

It took place at 2:15 p.m. when the aircraft, a British Midland Boeing 737, was flying at 33,000 feet above total cloud cover. At that height, visibility was clear with blue sky and sunshine, but no witnesses on the ground could have seen what followed because of the clouds at a lower level.

The jet was on a flight from London Heathrow to Belfast and was heading northwest on the standard airline above the Wirral peninsula approximately over Wallasey at the time. As you may realize, this is the same location as several other midair encounters at the point where the Irish Sea begins. It is also where the supposedly secret Halo project aircraft is test flown from its base at Warton—just 30 miles north along the coast.

We do not know if the crew spotted the UFO. Given that it was at an acute angle towards their rear (off the right-hand wing and approximately over Lancashire), it may not have been obvious to them. Unfortunately, the radio communication was not overheard either so we do not know if air traffic control had tracked the object. The report of the sighting comes from a passenger who was sitting above the wing and chanced to be looking in the right direction. He was an engineer and familiar with aircraft technology, but this object completely baffled him.

The description of the object will sound all too familiar. It was said to be a "black thin vehicle shaped like a cylinder or tube with a bright white tip...the width-to-length ratio was about 20:1." In other words, it was once again the precise same UFO-type that has intercepted so many recent commercial flights. This UFO passed the aircraft at some distance, but seemed to be moving in the same direction and at matching speed, thus remaining visible for several minutes. Then it accelerated into a cloud bank and vanished.

It will be 1999 before the publication of any incident report that might have been filed by the aircrew or the air traffic control—assuming, of course, that either witnessed anything, then chose to file a report. Very often, as you have seen, aviation sources do not opt to report, and encounters such as this one go unrecorded. The true number that may be happening could prove very disconcerting.

This book has been filled with stories of strange aerial encounters. As I hope I have established, many of these are undoubtedly real, and there are very likely several different causes. Some may be unusual atmospheric phenomena. Others may result from our secret technology straying into the path of civil aircraft. I would not even entirely rule out the option favored by the vociferous UFO lobby—that there are rare intrusions into our airspace by the vehicles of an alien intelligence. Most often we do not need any such fanciful theory, but there are a few intriguing cases where the evidence of these theorists is at least open to debate.

Whatever the truth, we need to explore these matters much more rationally and objectively than we have done to date. We need to interest scientists across a broad base. It is because of their inevitable, and understandable, distrust of the "alien contact" stories that I feel we must draw back from such speculation. Instead, UFOlogists need to concentrate more on the hard evidence, the physical effects, and the things that they can prove. Establishing that something is really up there is one thing. Leaping to the conclusion that the earth is consequently in the grip of little green men is going several steps too far for now—and is the real reason why so little progress has been made.

You do not win friends and influence people when dealing with a subject as contentious as UFOs if you have already solved the mystery in fantastic terms before you have even started to collate the evidence. Too many people are selectively accumulating the bits of testimony that fit in with their own fanciful notions about UFOs and quietly burying under the mat the awkward parts that do not. No wonder few self-respecting scientists will take UFOs seriously.

However, as I hope that I have shown, the cases in this book form an area of UFO research where lives are, quite literally, at stake. So we need give and take on both sides.

Science, including CAA investigators and aircraft engineers, must be more tolerant of the data and appreciate that, even with the vagaries of witness perception, the evidence is strong that something really is happening. UFOlogists must learn to curb their overexcitement and take one step forward—not two steps back—by establishing what it is possible to prove as opposed to what it is most exciting to dream about.

The media have a role in all of this as well. For they are the shapers of public opinion. Too often they treat UFOs as light relief and promote the wild ideas of the absurd minority without thought of the consequences. Those consequences include deterring sober witnesses, such as aircrew members, from reporting important evidence in the future. They also include playing into the hands of those who wish the UFO subject to remain a source of amusement to protect their own covert activities.

This is not a game. It is a serious issue. The eventual truth may not shatter any views about the universe or prove that we share the cosmos with alien cavalry riding in to the rescue of a beleaguered earth. But it just might unravel a new type of energy, or reveal clues about some kind of dangerous natural phenomenon that can put our air safety at risk. I suspect that the authorities in most major nations are well aware of that fact.

Why else maintain an ongoing monitor on UFO activity despite claiming (truthfully, I believe) that they have never uncovered any hard evidence that aliens have landed?

Why else pay for scientific staff to study UFO data, as official government files prove conclusively to be the case in the U.S., U.K., and France (and no doubt elsewhere)?

Why else waste money in these cost-conscious times on something that all public pronouncements appear to suggest is just nonsense?

Three major nations throwing money away pointlessly chasing phantoms that they insist do not exist—that would be a cause for a public outcry if it were true. The real truth is, of course, that they know perfectly well that there is something behind these lights in the sky. It may have nothing to do with aliens but a very great deal to do with day-to-day life on this tiny blue planet floating around a small yellow star.

It is time that the rest of us woke up to this reality. For UFOs will not simply go away. They have been around as long as mankind has been on this planet, and if we are not very careful, they will still be here long after we are dust.

These sightings will continue because something is really causing them to occur. We can sit here and ignore them as long as we like and giggle at press stories about alien contact and dubious photographs paraded by the tabloid press. But the risk of disaster in midair will persist however much we pretend there is nothing to be concerned about. Eventually, we will have to square up to that responsibility.

All that we can do right now is make a start to change our approach towards the study of this mystery. That step is difficult because it pulls against the popular view and is not where all the money and the glamour seem to lie. Seeking aliens and pretending to be Fox Mulder living life amidst an "X File" is fun and wonderfully ego-boosting, but it is also quite simply self-deceptive.

We need to change the way society views the UFO phenomenon and that will be far from easy. To move on from here will require a maturity of thought and a cold shower of sobering reality. But it is a step we simply have to take before more lives are lost.

Over the years I, like many others, have flown dozens of times on flights all over the world. You may wonder whether I have ever had a midair encounter of my own during these trips. Although I have never actually seen a UFO heading towards the plane on which I flew, I may have been involved in such an episode.

On January 27, 1995, I had flown from Blackpool Airport to Belfast by Jersey European Airways. I had gone to Ireland to take part in the nation's top TV talk show, screened live to several million people, during which I had talked about UFOs. I found myself gradually winning over an initially very skeptical audience in the process.

My return flight on the 28th should have been routine, but the small aircraft developed a problem soon after take-off. The weather conditions were rapidly deteriorating, and it was decided that we could not risk flying on under the circumstances. So we landed at Ronaldsway Airport on the Isle of Man, and the twenty or so passengers faced a lengthy delay as the airline sent for a replacement plane.

After we waited for many hours the aircraft arrived, but by now the high winds and freezing rain were so bad that it was considered too dangerous to take off. Another wait ensued, before the aircrew agreed to make the attempt to cross the Irish Sea. Those on board were warned that it might not prove possible to land at Blackpool as conditions were very poor on the west coast of England.

It was not much fun being buffeted incessantly on that short journey, but I had to admire the skill of the pilot who got us safely across. However, as feared, and despite making a pass at the airport and circling Blackpool Tower, the weather was so bad that it was not deemed safe to land at what is a fairly small airport. As such, we were told that we would fly on to Leeds where the facilities were better and from where we would be returned home by bus.

The extended flight was completed without incident, although it was a very tough landing in the dark as winds and rain bashed against the small turboprop aircraft, causing it to rock from side to side. To be honest, none of us was looking out of the window as we came in. We were all more concerned about getting down in one piece; we burst into spontaneous applause as the crew managed a perfect landing.

Eventually I reached home about 12 hours late following what should have been a flight of less than an hour. But seeing the gigantic waves that crashed over the sea walls in Blackpool and hearing of how the near hurricane-force winds had sent signposts flying along the promenade like missiles, I was simply relieved that the airline had achieved the seemingly impossible and gotten us home that day.

I would have given the matter no more thought except that a few days later I received a report sent through to me from Jodrell Bank. The witness, a Mrs. Graham from Bradford, explained that on that Saturday she had noticed an unusual amount of air traffic heading into her local airport. (Other flights may have been diverted there.) Despite the bad weather, she still had to take her dog for his usual walk at around 6:30 p.m.

Looking upwards, Mrs. Graham was intrigued to see a small plane being buffeted by the wind and fighting its way towards touchdown. At this point, the witness notes:

> I suddenly saw a bright white light heading towards the aircraft. At first, I thought it was another inbound aircraft, and there would be a collision. Then I realized that the light was too small, only a few inches in diameter, and it was "escorting" the aircraft just a few feet away from it. It was almost as if it were guiding the plane towards a safe landing, hugging close by as both flew along in the same direction. The light traveled with the aircraft a short way towards Yeadon Airport and then flew off at a sharp angle, disappearing into the night. I went back home with the dog and was mesmerized by what I had just seen.

Given the time and date of this sighting, it is very possible that this was the aircraft in which I was then sitting. Although Mrs. Graham could not possibly have known this fact, we landed about the same time as she spotted this object, and I saw no other aircraft come in immediately before or after we did.

If so, then it is certainly intriguing that a ground witness saw one of these small UFOs flying alongside the plane involved in what is easily the most frightening journey that I have ever taken. Perhaps this was all a coincidence. Maybe, someone, somewhere, was looking out for me and the other people on board the plane that night. Or more probably this is evidence of just how many of these midair encounters are really taking place—usually when nobody on board is any the wiser.

I am not sure which prospect is the more daunting.

REFERENCES

The notes below will help readers to discover further information on topics discussed in this book. When not stated, the investigations were conducted first-hand and usually involve taped interviews and/or written statements. I would like to thank the following people for their great help in working on this book—by making notes available, conducting interviews with witnesses for me, and through many other aspects of selfless research:

David Alpin, V.J. Ballester Olmos, Keith Basterfield, Steuart Campbell, Bill Chalker, Jerome Clark, David Clarke, John Cordy, Paul Devereux, Eileen Fletcher, Omar Fowler, Margaret Fry, Paul Fuller, Clive Gammon, Barry Greenwood, Dr. Richard Haines, Owen Hartop, Lord Peter Hill-Norton, Peter Hough, Dr. J. Allen Hynek, Amil Jamal, Kent Jeffrey, Peter Johnston, Dr. Alex Keul, Dr. Bruce Maccabee, Tim Matthews, Dr. Terence Meaden, Justin Mullins, Ralph Noyes, Dr. Yoshi-Hiko Ohtsuki, Dr. Thornton Page, Ken Phillips, Nick Pope, Nick Redfern, Roy Sandbach, Ron Sargeant, Jim Sneddon, Clas Svahn, Philip Taylor, Peter Warrington, Nigel Watson

Addresses of magazines and organizations cited here are given on their first reference below.

1:
For more on IFOs, I recommend:
Randles, Jenny, *UFO Study* (Robert Hale, 1982)
Hendry, Allan, *The UFO Handbook* (NEL, 1982)

For more on optical illusions and perception, see:
Vernon, Dr. M.D., *The Psychology of Perception* (Penguin, 1971)
Rattray-Taylor, G., *The Natural History of the Mind* (Secker & Warburg, 1979)
Randles, Jenny, *Sixth Sense* (Robert Hale, 1987)

To follow the Cosmos 1068 story in more depth, see:
Randles, Jenny, *UFO Reality* (Robert Hale, 1983)

For more on the history of UFOs pre-1947, see:
Keel, John, "Mystery Aircraft of the 1930s" (*FSR*, vol. 16, nos. 3 and 4; *FSR Publications*, Snodland, Kent ME6 5HJ)

Research by David Clarke, Granville Oldroyd, and Nigel Watson is available from The Fund for UFO Research, Box 277, Mount Rainier, MD 20712, U.S.A.

Clark, Jerome, *The UFO Encyclopedia Project* (vol. 2; Omnigraphics, 1991)
Harbinson, William, *Projekt UFO* (Boxtree, 1995)
Hough, Peter & Randles, Jenny, *The Complete Book of UFOs* (Sterling Publishing Co., Inc., 1996)

Project Hessdalen reports are available from SUFOI, Postbox 6, DK 2820, Gentofte, Denmark.

For a look at how the alien contact belief has developed, see:
Hough, Peter & Randles, Jenny, *Looking for the Aliens* (Cassell, 1992)
Randles, Jenny, *Alien Contact: The First Fifty Years* (Sterling Publishing Co., Inc., 1997)

2:
For more coverage of the Mantell case, refer to the following sources:
Steiger, Brad (ed.), *Project Blue Book* (Bantam, 1978)
Dodd, Tony, "The Fatal Flight of Captain Thomas Mantell," *UFO Magazine* (July/Aug 1996), P.O. Box 60, Leeds LS15 9XD, U.K.

For an interview regarding the Skyhook balloon experiment, see *Just Cause*, P.O. Box 176, Stoneham, MA 02180, U.S.A.

3:
You can follow the debate on the Chiles-Whitted case via the Blue Book files in *Project Blue Book* (see above) and:
Hynek, Dr. J. Allen, *The Hynek UFO Report* (Corgi, 1978)

For a look at the Roswell case, check out:
X Factor Roswell Special (video plus magazine written by Jenny Randles; Marshall Cavendish, 1997)

Kent Jeffrey publishes his detailed assessment in the *MUFON Journal* (July 1997), 103 Oldtowne Rd, Seguin, TX 78159-4099, U.S.A.

To follow the work of Dr. Richard Haines, see his paper in the 1983 annual symposium published by *MUFON* and his book, *UFO Phenomena and the Behavioral Scientist* (Scarecrow, 1979).

4.
British records can be investigated via the PRO (Public Record Office), Ruskin Avenue, Kew, Surrey, U.K. The U.S. files are obtainable through the Freedom of Information Act or through Brad Steiger's *Project Blue Book* (see above) which has copies of many of the key cases. Also, for an inside view, an objective book is *The Hynek UFO Report* by Dr. J. Allen Hynek (see above also).

For the details behind the Washington, D.C. crisis the following books are important:
Ruppelt, Edward, *The Report into UFOs* (Ace, 1956)
Saunders, Dr. David & Harkins, Roger, *UFOs? Yes!* (World, 1968)
Condon, Dr. Edward (ed.), *Scientific Study of UFOs* (Bantam, 1969)

For more details on the background to government studies, see:
Greenwood, Barry & Fawcett, Larry, *Clear Intent* (Prentice-Hall, 1984)

Noyes, Ralph, *A Secret Property* (Quartet, 1985)
Warrington, Peter & Randles, Jenny, *Science and the UFOs* (Blackwell, 1986)
Pope, Nick, *Open Skies, Closed Minds* (Simon & Schuster, 1996)
Randles, Jenny, *The Truth Behind the Men in Black: Government Agents—Or Visitors from Beyond* (St. Martin's, 1997)
Redfern, Nick, *A Covert Agenda* (Simon & Schuster, 1997)

5:
For reports on the Salandin case, see:
FSR (vol. 30, no. 2; address as above)

For reports on the Lakenheath case (U.S. version), see:
FSR (vol. 16, no. 2)
See also Dr. Edward Condon's report in *Scientific Study of UFOs* (above), which has a full appraisal of this evidence.

6:
Reports on Project Twinkle can be found in *The Complete Book of UFOs* and Edward Ruppelt's memoirs, *The Report into UFOs* (see above for both).

For interviews with aircrew members, see the *Strange But True?* special episode entitled "Pilot Sightings" (LWT, first transmitted in the U.K. in October 1995).

More data on the BOAC case can be found in the Condon report (see above) and *Northern UFO News* (no. 118; 1987), 1 Hallsteads Close, Dove Holes, Buxton, Derbyshire SK17 8BS, U.K.

For green fireballs and Suffolk and New Mexico waves, see:
Randles, Jenny, *The UFO Conspiracy* (Barnes & Noble, Inc., 1987)
Randles, Jenny, *UFO Crash Landing: Friend or Foe?* (Cassell, 1998)

7:
Fulton, HH, "New Zealand Aircraft Radar-Visual Case," *FSR* (vol. 16, no. 1; 1970)

Australian UFO activity is expertly covered in:
Basterfield, Keith, *UFOs: A Report on Australian Encounters* (Reed, 1997)
Chalker, Bill, *The Oz Files* (Duffy & Snellgrove, 1997)
Further information may be found in Bill Chalker's report, published in Jerome Clark's *The UFO Encyclopedia Project* (see above).

8:
For reports on the Portuguese case, see:
Fowler, Omar, "UFO seen from Trident near Lisbon," *FSR* (vol. 22, no. 4; 1976)
Tap, J. (BUFORA) 1977 (BUFORA, 16 South Way, Burgess Hill, Sussex, RH15 9ST, U.K.)
Randles, Jenny & Warrington, Peter, *UFOs: A British Viewpoint* (Robert Hale, 1979)

For a report on the Spanish encounters, see:
FSR (vol 25, no. 5, and vol. 26, no. 6)
The interview with V.J. Ballester Olmos is published in *New UFOlogist* (vol. 4; 1996), 293 Devonshire Rd, Blackpool, Lancs. FY2 0TW, U.K.

For research into early missile encounters, see:
AFU (Box 11027, 6011 Norrköping, Sweden)

9:
The Urals encounter is reported by Dr. Richard Haines in *IUR* (CUFOS; Nov.–Dec. 1991), 2457 West Peterson Ave., Chicago, IL 60659, U.S.A.

For more on the Huffman, Texas, episode, see:
Butler, Brenda, Street, Dot & Randles, Jenny, *Sky Crash* (Grafton, 1986)

The report on the landing at Trans-en-Provence was published (in French) by GEPAN, at the Space Center in Toulouse, though a full summary can be found in *The Complete Book of UFOs* by Peter Hough and Jenny Randles (see above). History and data from GEPAN can be located in *Science and the UFOs* by Peter Warrington and Jenny Randles (see above also).

For investigations into the Brazilian and Alaskan encounters, see:
MUFON Journal (Sept. and Nov. 1986, Jan.–Mar. 1987 and Nov. 1987)
See also the assessment by Philip Klass in *The Skeptics, UFO Newsletter*, 404 N St. SW, Washington, D.C. 20024, U.S.A.

BUFORA has published a Vehicle Interference Report catalogue that lists hundreds of such cases.

For the New Zealand encounters, see:
Startup, Bill & Guard, Bob, *The Kaikoura UFOs* (Hodder & Stoughton, 1981)
Fogarty, Quentin, *Let's Hope They're Friendly* (Angus & Robertson, 1983)

10:
For further information on vortex phenomena, see:
Mullins, Justin, "Trails of Destruction," *New Scientist* (no. 2056; Nov. 16, 1996)
For detailed studies of the Valentich case, see:
Haines, Dr. Richard, *The Melbourne Incident* (Palo Alto, 1987)
Hough, Peter & Randles, Jenny, *Death by Supernatural Causes?* (Grafton, 1988)

11:
For Arnold's story, see:
Arnold, Kenneth & Palmer, Ray, *The Coming of the Saucers* (Amherst, 1952)

The investigation into the "gliding aircraft" mystery is reported in *The Pennine UFO Mystery* by Jenny Randles (Grafton, 1983). Refer also to *The Truth Behind the Men in Black* (see above) by the same author.

For an investigation into the 1979 "jet chase," see:
Randles, Jenny, *UFO Retrievals* (Cassell, 1995)

For information on the history of secret military aircraft technology and UFO sightings, see:
Matthews, Tim, *UFO Revelations* (Cassell, 1998)

To delve into the Belgian wave of UFO sightings you should begin by looking at reports in *New UFOlogist* (vol. 6; 1997). Very different perspectives are given in *The Belgian Triangles* by Wim Van Utrecht (SVLT, 1991; SVLT, Kronenburgstraat 110, B-2000 Antwerp, Belgium) and *A Deadly Concealment* by Derek Sheffield (Cassell, 1996).

12:
Many of the cases in this chapter were reported in *Northern UFO News* issues from 1991 to 1997.

The French case is featured (in French) in *Ovni Presence*, Casa Postale 102, CH-1000 Lausanne 7, St. Paul, Switzerland.

The Irish Air Corps data is researched by IUFOPRA, P.O. Box 3070, Whitehall, Dublin, Ireland.

13:
For more on meteors as UFOs, refer to *UFO Study* by Jenny Randles (see above) and *UFOs and How to See Them* (Sterling Publishing Co., Inc., 1992) by the same author.

The Tunguska event is reported in full in *UFO Retrievals* (see above).

More data on ice bombs can be found in:
Frank, Dr. Louis, *The Big Splash* (Avon, 1991)
Randles, Jenny, *The Paranormal Sourcebook* (Piatkus, 1997)

For investigations into the natural UFOs of transients and earthlights, see:
Persinger, Dr. M. & Lafreniere, G., *Space-time Transients and Anomalous Events* (Prentice-Hall, 1977)
Tributsch, Dr. Helmut, *When the Snakes Awake* (MIT, 1982)
Clark, David & Roberts, Andy, *Phantoms of the Sky* (Robert Hale, 1988)
Devereux, Paul, *Earthlights Revelation* (Blandford, 1989)

For the state of research into ball lightning, see:
The Journal of Meteorology (54 Frome Rd, Bradford-on-Avon, Wilts. BA15 1LD, U.K.)
Fuller, Paul & Randles, Jenny, *Crop Circles: A Mystery Solved?* (Robert Hale, 1994)

The latest developments on the search for secret aircraft behind UFO reports feature in:
UFO News (P.O. Box 73, Lancaster LA1 1GZ, U.K.)

14:
Reports on ongoing cases can be found in many of the sources referenced above—notably *Northern UFO News, FSR, MUFON Journal, UFO Times* (BUFORA), and *IUR (International UFO Reporter)*.

If you wish to make a report on any sighting, you can do so in complete confidence, if desired. Members of the British UFO Research Association (including myself) are governed by a code of practice that prohibits the release of witnesses' names and addresses without prior permission. Should you have any information that you wish to share, please write to the author c/o:

1 Hallsteads Close, Dove Holes, Buxton, High Peak, Derbys. SK17 8BS, U.K.

INDEX